Instructor's Resource

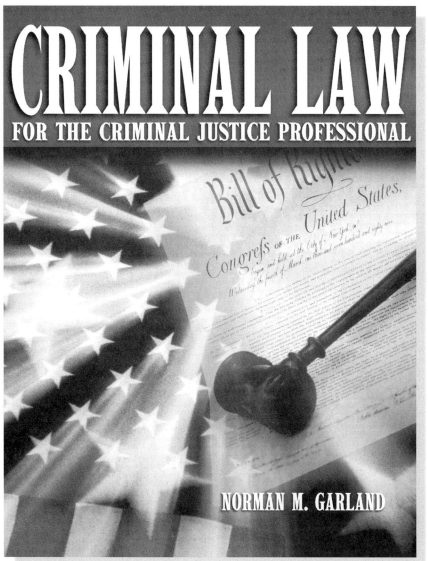

CRIMINAL LAW
FOR THE CRIMINAL JUSTICE PROFESSIONAL

NORMAN M. GARLAND

**Glencoe
McGraw-Hill**

New York, New York   Columbus, Ohio   Woodland Hills, California   Peoria, Illinois

Glencoe/McGraw-Hill

A Division of The McGraw·Hill Companies

Send all inquiries to:

Glencoe/McGraw-Hill
21600 Oxnard Street, Suite 500
Woodland Hills, California 91367

ISBN 0-02-800909-6 (Instructor's Resource Manual)
ISBN 0-02-800908-8 (Student Edition)

1 2 3 4 5 6 7 8 9 10   045   07 06 05 04 03 02 01

Contents

www.cl.glencoe.com

Criminal Law Syllabus
Ten-Week Schedule

Instructor: _____   Office: _____

Phone: _____   Hours: _____

E-mail: _____

Course Web site: _____
Instructor and student Web site: **www.cl.glencoe.com**

REQUIRED TEXTBOOK	*Criminal Law for the Criminal Justice Professional*, First edition, by Norman M. Garland; Glencoe/McGraw-Hill, 2003.
COURSE DESCRIPTION	This course introduces you to the essentials of criminal law and the most significant legal issues in today's American criminal justice system. You will learn the legal definitions of crimes and criminals, and the complex ways in which the police, courts, and corrections work together to apply the criminal law. Information on careers relating to criminal law will help you learn about the meaning of criminal law to those who work in the field, and will provide you with useful information that can aid you in career choices.
COURSE PURPOSE	This course teaches basic, practical information that provides a foundation for understanding the criminal legal system. After an introduction to the history and role of criminal law in American society, you will learn the difference between criminal and civil law and then move on to in-depth discussions of different types of crimes. In each chapter, you will be given an understanding of elements of each crime, the liability for those who commit such crimes, and how courts have applied the law against such criminals. The material in the textbook is based heavily upon real court cases, so that you can readily apply the situations and examples to your future criminal justice career. This course is required for all criminal justice majors, and any non-major will find it useful and informative.
COURSE OBJECTIVES	▪ Understand the history and purposes of criminal law ▪ Know the basic structure and operation of the criminal justice system ▪ Know the constitutional limitations on the criminal law ▪ Classify crimes and name the basic elements of criminal responsibility ▪ Identify and distinguish among the parties to a crime ▪ Define all types of incomplete crimes ▪ Know the major defenses to crimes ▪ Understand the different types of criminal homicide and their elements

- Understand other major crimes against persons and their elements
- Know and distinguish between crimes against habitation and crimes against property
- Identify and comprehend the various types of white-collar crime
- Know the major types of public order offenses
- Understand and define drug- and alcohol-related crimes
- Identify and comprehend the various types of crimes against the administration of justice
- Know the components, criminal activities, and differences among organized crime groups, gangs, and terrorists

COURSE REQUIREMENTS	

- ATTENDANCE: You are expected to attend each class and be on time. No more than three absences for a 15-week course (or two absences for a 10-week course) will be excused. Anyone more than ten minutes tardy will be considered absent for that day. Much of your progress depends on your prompt arrival and full participation, so come prepared!

- REVIEW AND APPLICATIONS: You will provide written answers to review and application questions and exercises from the end of each chapter. Remember to base your answers upon your understanding of what you have learned in the chapter. Many of these questions are open-ended and are meant to stimulate discussion, so be sure to express yourself fully when completing these assignments.

- CLASS PARTICIPATION AND IN-CLASS EXERCISES: You are expected to participate in class discussions by asking questions, offering answers, and debating issues. Although you do not have to be verbally involved in every discussion, you must be attentive to the discussion as it occurs. You are also expected to be involved in any in-class exercises.

- TESTING: You will take two tests and one final examination. Test will contain a mixture of multiple-choice, true/false, and essay questions.

EVALUATION

Your performance in this class will be evaluated based upon attendance, your answers to review and application exercises, class participation, your term project, and testing.

GRADING

During the term, you will have the opportunity to accumulate 500 points:

Two tests, 100 points each	200 points
Final examination	150 points
Class exercises and participation	75 points
Attendance	75 points
Total	**500 points**

NOTE TO INSTRUCTOR: This suggested grading system can be adjusted to suit the individual instructor's needs and expectations.

A Final Word about Learning Criminal Law

Without exaggeration, this course is extremely important for anyone living in the United States. All private citizens should have at least a basic understanding of the criminal law system to help them understand their rights as citizens. If you are planning a criminal justice career, you will find that this course provides necessary information for learning about the meaning and application of the criminal law, understanding why the system operates in the way it does, and deciding which criminal justice career would be best for you.

There are two important things to keep in mind while you take this course:

- You are responsible for your learning and for helping yourself and your classmates. The instructor cannot fill passive students with knowledge or with a single right answer. There are several right answers to many criminal justice issues, especially controversial ones such as the death penalty, three-strikes laws, and the role of rehabilitation.

- Learning in this course is based upon cooperation and experience. You are expected to participate in class discussions and exercises, and to apply the concepts to your own experiences.

NOTE TO PROFESSOR: Classroom discussions are scheduled to take place in the week following the reading assignment.

Ten-Week Schedule

First Day

Topics: Course introduction

Objectives: Learn the general scope of this class and how you will cover the material over the coming weeks. Learn about testing, class participation, and in-class exercises, all of which will affect your grade.

Homework: Chapter 1, Nature, Origins, and Purposes of Criminal Law; Chapter 2, The Structure and Operation of the Criminal Justice System

Week 1

Topics: Understanding Criminal Law and Its Context in the Criminal Justice System

Objectives: State basic definitions of law, common law, legality, and the MPC. Identify the principal purpose of the criminal law. Explain what distinguishes the criminal law from other law. Define punishment in the criminal justice system. Describe the fundamental structure of the American criminal justice system. Name the two basic police functions, and state what is required for a law enforcement officer to arrest a suspect. State when a defendant is entitled to an attorney at trial.

Homework: Chapter 3, Constitutional Limitations on the Criminal Law

Week 2

Topics: Criminal Law and the U.S. Constitution

Objectives: Identify who determines whether a legislative enactment violates a constitutional prohibition. List those areas of the constitution that limit criminal law enactments. List the provisions of the Bill of Rights that limit the government's ability to prohibit and punish crimes. State three categories of unprotected speech and three areas of personal privacy protected by the U.S. Constitution as it affects crimes.

Homework: Chapter 4, Classification of Crimes and Basic Elements of Criminal Responsibility; Chapter 5, Parties to a Crime

Week 3

Topics: Parts to a Crime and Defenses

Objectives: Differentiate criminal, tort, and moral responsibility. Explain the difference between felonies, misdemeanors, and petty offenses. Describe the requirement of a physical act (*actus reus*) and guilty mind (*mens rea*). Distinguish between specific intent and general intent crimes. Understand the difference between an accessory and a principal. Explain how causation affects accomplice liability. Understand the *mens rea* of accomplice liability. Explain the difference between accessorial and conspiratorial liability.

Homework: Chapter 6, Incomplete Crimes; Chapter 7, Defenses to Crimes

Week 4

Topics: Attempted (or Inchoate) Offenses, and Defenses to Criminal Behavior

Objectives: Explain the elements of the crime of attempt. Name the two principal defenses to attempt. Define the crime of conspiracy, as well as its *actus reus* and *mens rea*. List the three elements of self-defense. Describe when deadly force may be used in self-defense, and name two situations in which a first aggressor can claim self-defense. Describe the circumstances in which a person can use force to defend property and in which a police officer may use deadly force. List five tests for determining insanity.

Homework: Chapter 8, Criminal Homicide

Week 5

Topics: Defining and Understanding Types of Criminal Homicide

Objectives: Distinguish between homicide and criminal homicide. Understand when life begins and ends for criminal homicide. List the essential elements of murder. Describe the differences in voluntary manslaughter, involuntary manslaughter, and murder. Explain the felony murder rule. Distinguish between first-degree and second-degree murder. Describe the Model Penal Code's definition of murder.

Homework: Chapter 9, Crimes Against Persons: Other Offenses

Week 6

Topics: Other Violent Crimes Defined and Explained

Objectives: State the elements of battery, assault, and mayhem. State the elements of rape, and understand the difference between rape and statutory rape. Describe Megan's law. Define child abuse. Distinguish between the elements of false imprisonment and kidnapping.

Homework: Chapter 10, Crimes Against Habitation; Chapter 11, Crimes Against Property

Week 7

Topics: Property Crimes Explained and Defined

Objectives: Understand the difference between common and modern law arson. Explain the difference between specific intent and general intent arson. List the three elements of burglary. State the difference between burglary and breaking and entering. Name the elements of the crime of possession of burglar's tools. List the elements of larceny, and explain the difference between larceny from a person and robbery. List the elements of embezzlement. State the difference between embezzlement and larceny. List the essential elements of robbery. Differentiate among extortion, blackmail, and bribery. State the essential elements of forgery.

Homework: Chapter 12, White-Collar Crimes

Week 8

Topics: Understanding and Prosecuting White-Collar Crime

Objectives: Define white-collar crime. List the elements of tax evasion. List the elements for a civil action for false advertising. List the elements of mail fraud. List the elements of securities fraud. List the elements of an FDCA action. List the main federal antitrust acts and the elements of an antitrust action. Explain a monopoly.

Homework: Chapter 13, Crimes Against Public Order, Safety, and Morality; Chapter 14, Drug- and Alcohol-Related Crimes

Week 9

Topics: Defining and Explaining Crimes Against Public Morality

Objectives: Define the crimes that encompass breaching the peace, including nuisance crimes, traffic offenses, weapons offenses, obscenity offenses, sodomy, and illegal gambling. Understand the crime of prostitution and the parties involved. Identify the five major categories of controlled substances. Define the drug offenses of possession, possession with the intent to deliver, delivery, drug conspiracy, drug loitering, and possession of drug paraphernalia. State the elements of driving under the influence.

Homework: Chapter 15, Crimes Against the Administration of Justice; Chapter 16, Organized Crime, Gangs, and Terrorism

Week 10

Topics: Understanding and Prosecuting Crimes that Obstruct Justice and Organized Crime

Objectives: Understand the offense of "obstruction of justice" and recognize the scope of crimes it covers. Define the crimes of bribery, perjury, resisting arrest, compounding a felony, misprision of a felony, and escape. Understand the different types of contempt. Understand the historical development and typical activities of organized crime. Understand RICO and various other laws aimed at targeting organized crime. Understand the structure and activities of modern street gangs, and laws that target them. Understand terrorism, and describe the various laws that target terrorism.

Homework: Review entire book

Fifteen-Week Schedule

Instructor: _____   Office: _____

Phone: _____   Hours: _____

E-mail: _____

Course Web site: _____
Instructor and student Web site: **www.cl.glencoe.com**

Required Textbook   *Criminal Law for the Criminal Justice Professional*, First edition, by Norman M. Garland; Glencoe/McGraw-Hill, 2003.

> NOTE TO PROFESSOR: The requirements, purpose, objectives, evaluation and grading specifications for this 15-week schedule are identical to those linked on page iv for the 10-week schedule. Classroom discussions are scheduled to take place in the week following the reading assignment.

Course Outline: Fifteen-Week Schedule

First Day and Week 1

Topics: Course introduction

Objectives: Learn the general scope of this class and how you will cover the material over the coming weeks. Learn about testing, class participation, and in-class exercises, all of which will affect your grade. Begin discussion about basic concepts of criminal justice.

Homework: Chapter 1, Nature, Origins, and Purposes of Criminal Law

Week 2

Topics: Basic concepts of criminal law

Objectives: State basic definitions of law, common law, and legality. Explain what distinguishes the criminal law from other law. Explain what the MPC is. Identify the principal purpose of the criminal law. Define punishment in the criminal justice system.

Homework: Chapter 2, The Structure and Operation of the Criminal Justice System

Week 3

Topics: How the Criminal Justice System Works

Objectives: Describe the fundamental structure of the American criminal justice system. Name the two basic police functions. State what is required for a law enforcement officer to arrest a suspect. Describe the two alternative methods for charging serious crimes. State when a defendant is entitled to an attorney at trial.

Homework: Chapter 3, Constitutional Limitations on the Criminal Law; Chapter 4, Classification of Crimes and Basic Elements of Criminal Responsibility

Week 4

Topics: Defining Criminal Law and Understanding Its Constitutional Basis

Objectives: List those areas of the constitution that limit criminal law enactments. List the provisions of the Bill of Rights that limit the government's ability to prohibit and punish crimes. Differentiate criminal, tort, and moral responsibility. Explain the difference between felonies, misdemeanors, and petty offenses. Describe the requirement of a physical act (*actus reus*) and *mens rea* (guilty mind). Distinguish between specific intent and general intent crimes

Homework: Chapter 5, Parties to a Crime

Week 5

Topics: Defining and Distinguishing Among Parties to a Crime

Objectives: Understand the difference between an accessory and a principal. Explain how causation affects accomplice liability. Understand the *mens rea* of accomplice liability. Learn how justifications and excuses affect accomplice liability. Explain the difference between accessorial and conspiratorial liability.

Homework: Chapter 6, Incomplete Crimes

Week 6

Topics: Understanding the inchoate offense.

Objectives: Explain the purpose of defining attempt as a crime. State the elements of an attempt. Name the two principal defenses to attempt. Define the crime of conspiracy, as well as its *actus reus* and *mens rea*.

Homework: Chapter 7, Defenses to Crimes

Week 7

Topics: Defenses: Justifications and Excuses

Objectives: List the three elements of self-defense. Describe when deadly force may be used in self-defense, and name two situations in which a first aggressor can claim self-defense. Describe the circumstances in which a person can use force to defend property and in which a police officer may use deadly force. List five tests for determining insanity.

Homework: Chapter 8, Criminal Homicide

Week 8

Topics: Understanding Types of Criminal Homicide

Objectives: Distinguish between homicide and criminal homicide. Understand when life begins and ends for criminal homicide. List the essential elements of murder. Describe the differences in voluntary manslaughter, involuntary manslaughter, and murder. Explain the felony murder rule. Distinguish between first-degree and second-degree murder. Describe the Model Penal Code's definition of murder.

Homework: Chapter 9, Crimes Against Persons: Other Offenses

Week 9

Topics:	Other Violent Crimes Defined and Explained
Objectives:	State the elements of battery, assault, and mayhem. State the elements of rape, and understand the difference between rape and statutory rape. Describe Megan's law. Define child abuse. Distinguish between the elements of false imprisonment and kidnapping.
Homework:	Chapter 10, Crimes Against Habitation

Week 10

Topics:	Defining and Understanding Arson and Burglary
Objectives:	Understand the difference between common and modern law arson. Explain the difference between specific intent and general intent arson. List the three elements of burglary. Understand the intent required for burglary. State the difference between burglary and breaking and entering. Name the elements of the crime of possession of burglar's tools.
Homework:	Chapter 11, Crimes Against Property

Week 11

Topics:	Types of Theft
Objectives:	List the elements of larceny, and explain the difference between larceny from a person and robbery. List the elements of embezzlement. State the difference between embezzlement and larceny. List the essential elements of robbery. Differentiate among extortion, blackmail, and bribery. State the essential elements of forgery.
Homework:	Chapter 12, White-Collar Crimes

Week 12

Topics:	Understanding and Prosecuting White-Collar Crime
Objectives:	Define white-collar crime. List the elements of tax evasion. List the elements for a civil action for false advertising. List the elements of mail fraud. List the elements of securities fraud. List the elements of an FDCA action. List the main federal antitrust acts and the elements of an antitrust action. Explain a monopoly.
Homework:	Chapter 13, Crimes Against Public Order, Safety, and Morality; Chapter 14, Drug- and Alcohol-Related Crimes

Week 13

Topics: Defining and Explaining Crimes Against Public Morality

Objectives: Define the crimes that encompass breaching the peace, including nuisance crimes, traffic offenses, weapons offenses, obscenity offenses, sodomy, and illegal gambling. Understand the crime of prostitution and the parties involved. Identify the five major categories of controlled substances. Define the drug offenses of possession, possession with the intent to deliver, delivery, drug conspiracy, drug loitering, and possession of drug paraphernalia. State the elements of driving under the influence.

Homework: Chapter 15, Crimes Against the Administration of Justice

Week 14

Topics: Crimes that Obstruct Justice

Objectives: Understand the offense of "obstruction of justice" and recognize the scope of crimes it covers. Define the crimes of bribery, perjury, resisting arrest, compounding a felony, misprision of a felony, and escape. Recognize when constructive contempt takes place and how it differs from direct contempt.

Homework: Chapter 16, Organized Crime, Gangs, and Terrorism

Week 15

Topics: Understanding and Prosecuting Organized Crime

Objectives: Understand the historical development of organized crime. List some typical organized crime activities. Understand RICO and various other laws aimed at targeting organized crime. Understand the structure and activities of modern street gangs, and laws that target them. Understand the types of criminal activity that constitute terrorism. Describe the various laws that target terrorism.

Homework: Review entire book

SCANS Correlation of the Criminal Law for the Criminal Justice Professional Program

The Secretary's Commission on Achieving Necessary Skills (SCANS) was formed to encourage the development of a high-performance economy characterized by skilled workers. To help achieve this goal, the Commission recommended that educational institutions teach basic competencies needed for successful job performance. Central to this task are the SCANS definitions of the skills and personal qualities needed for solid job performance within designated curriculum and/or employment areas.

COMPETENCIES AND FOUNDATIONS	COMPONENTS
Resources: Identifies, organizes, plans, and allocates resources	All 16 chapters of the Student Text *Tutorial Simulations:* The Use of Common Law Precedents (Chapter 1); *Ex post facto* laws, Inmate Rights and the Eighth Amendment (Chapter 3); The Six Stages of a Crime, Tests to Determine *Actus Reus* (Chapter 6); Degrees of Burglary Charges (Chapter 10); The Crime of Larceny, The Elements of Robbery (Chapter 11) **www.cl.glencoe.com**
Interpersonal Skills: Works with others	*Text:* Chapter 3, Chapters 5–16 *Tutorial Simulations:* Possible Innocence in Accessory Cases (Chapter 5); Investigating Arson (Chapter 10); **www.cl.glencoe.com**
Information: Acquires and uses information	All 16 chapters of the Student Text All 16 chapters of the Study Guide All videos in the Criminal Justice Video Library *Tutorial Simulations:* **www.cl.glencoe.com**
Systems: Understands complex interrelationships	*Text:* Chapters 1, 2, 3, 4, 5, 12, and 16 *Tutorial Simulations:* Civil Versus Criminal Liability (Chapter 1); Courts and the Fourteenth Amendment (Chapter 2); *Mens Rea* and Juveniles (Chapter 4); Self-Defense in the Home, Defenses Based on Excuse (Chapter 7);

	Types of Child Abuse (Chapter 9);
	Prison Escape (Chapter 15)
	www.cl.glencoe.com
Technology: Works with a variety of technologies	*Text:* Chapters 8, 9, 10, 11, 12, and 16
	Tutorial Simulations: Obscenity and the Internet (Chapter 13)
	www.cl.glencoe.com
Basic Skills: Reading, writing, math, speaking, listening	All 16 chapters of the Student Text
	All 16 chapters of the Study Guide
	All simulations in the Tutorial With Simulation Applications CD-Rom
	www.cl.glencoe.com
Thinking Skills: Reasoning, thinking creatively, making decisions, solving problems	All 16 chapters of the Student Text
	Critical Thinking Exercises in all 16 chapters of the Student Text
	Tutorial Simulations: Charging Offenses as Felonies or Misdemeanors (Chapter 4);
	Accomplice Liability (Chapter 5);
	Malice Aforethought, First- and Second-Degree Murder Charges (Chapter 8);
	Differences Between Assault and Battery (Chapter 9);
	Drug Sentencing, DUI Offenses and Sentencing (Chapter 14);
	Arrest Issues in Organized Crime, Prosecuting Options for Organized Criminals (Chapter 16)
	www.cl.glencoe.com
Personal Qualities: Responsibility, self-esteem, sociability, integrity	*Text:* Chapter 3, Chapters 5–16
	Critical Thinking Exercises in all 16 chapters of the Student Text
	Tutorial Simulations: Constitutional Issues in Arrests (Chapter 2);
	Broker Fraud, White-Collar Crimes and Government Officials (Chapter 12);
	Types of Public Safety Offenses (Chapter 13);
	Witness Tampering (Chapter 15)
	www.cl.glencoe.com

Nature, Origins, and Purposes of Criminal Law

Chapter Resources

For the Instructor
Instructor's Resource Manual, pp. 1–10
Additional Activities, p. 7
PowerPoint Presentation and ExamView Pro Testbank
    CD-ROM for Chapter 1
cl.glencoe.com Web site

For the Student
Student Edition, Chapter 1, pp. 2–25
Review and Applications, p. 20
Tutorial with Simulation Applications
    CD-ROM for Chapter 1
cl.glencoe.com Web site

KEY TERMS

law	civil law	legality	utilitarian theory
common law	tort	Model Penal Code (MPC)	three-strikes laws
statutory law	*actus reus*	punishment	zero tolerance
criminal law	*mens rea*	retributive theory	

Lecture Outline

1.1. THE NATURE AND ORIGINS OF LAW
    Emergence of Written Laws
    Civil Law Versus Criminal Law

1.2 CRIMINAL LAW IN THE UNITED STATES
    Purpose of the Criminal Law
    Statutory Criminal Law
    The Principle of Legality
    Contemporary Applications of
        Common Law
    The Model Penal Code
    The Growth of Federal Criminal Law

1.3 PUNISHMENT IN THE CRIMINAL
    JUSTICE SYSTEM
    Definition of Punishment
    Retributive Rationale for Punishment
    Utilitarian Justification for Punishment
    Modern Views on Punishment

In-Chapter Questions

NOTE TO INSTRUCTOR: These answers serve as general guidelines to help you discuss these issues in class. These questions can be assigned to students, but many of their answers will be subjective.

Photo caption page 6

What is the common law, both historically and as it applies to modern law?

Historically, the common law is the historical cases from England that influenced America's first lawmakers. Today, it means either historical or modern law that is derived from court cases. Laws that are created or changed in response to U.S. Supreme Court cases are one example.

Criminal Law Online page 7

How does this site provide useful information to law students and professionals?

Law.com offers a variety of news covering different areas of the law and different types of cases. This is helpful because it gives law students and professionals a good understanding of current events and changes in the legal field.

1.1 Self Check page 8

Why does the complexity of the definitions of law vary so much?

It varies because of its different usage in different situations. When a person is speaking casually about laws and crimes, it is usually with less complexity than is seen by legislatures enacting laws and defining crimes that will affect their entire jurisdiction. Also, there are different types of laws: criminal and civil laws, which can be tried in courts, and moral laws, which cannot.

 ### *Keeler v. Superior Court* page 11

Could the defendant have been charged with another crime in this case? If so, what?

He certainly could have been charged with two counts of battery (or perhaps aggravated battery, depending on the circumstances). Today in California, he would not only be charged with feticide but also with domestic violence charges.

 ### Crime Prevention Officer page 15

What qualities do you think a person should possess to be a good crime prevention officer?

Helpful qualities may include thoroughness, persistence, good communication skills, and perceptiveness.

1.2 Self Check page 15

1. Explain the historical significance of the common law.

   The common law has provided the foundation of modern American and English criminal law. Even though most modern laws are statutorily derived, they generally have at least some common law background and influence.

2. Why is statutory law taking the place of common law in many situations?

   Statutory law allows lawmakers to create laws to address current crime issues and public outcry against such issues, rather than being forced to wait and depend upon judicial opinion. A more important reason for the decline of judicially created criminal law definitions is the principle of legality, a core concept of the American system of criminal justice that holds that no one can be punished for an act that was not defined as criminal before the person did the act. The three corollaries to the principle of legality are:

   - Criminal statutes should be understandable to reasonable law-abiding people.

   - Criminal statutes should be crafted so as not to delegate basic policy matters to policemen, judges, and juries for resolution on an ad hoc and subjective basis.

   - Judicial interpretation of ambiguous statutes should "be biased in favor of the accused."

Photo caption page 17

Do you agree that capital punishment of certain offenders does the greatest good for the largest number of people?

Student answers will vary on this controversial topic. Some will feel that certain serious offenders should be executed, for it will benefit society. Others will feel that capital punishment is overall harmful to society, and that it should be abolished.

Criminal Law Online page 19

Check out one section under Criminal Law, then write about what you have learned.

This exercise will lead students to a helpful legal Web site that is written in plain English. Students will probably report that this site was helpful and that it helped them gain a broader perspective on the section they chose.

1.3 Self Check page 19

1. Which do you prefer, retributive theory or utilitarian theory? Why?

   Answers will vary, but students' answers should indicate a clear understanding of each philosophy. Be sure that they do not confuse the retributive theory with vengeance, as the two are somewhat different.

2. Do you think that retributive theory is better for some crimes than utilitarian theory? For which crimes, and why?

Some students will feel that the retributive theory is better for more serious crimes, especially those committed by chronic offenders. This could include murder, rape, and sexual offenses against children, because these are very serious crimes and offenders who commit such crimes are a serious danger to the community. On the other hand, those who support the utilitarian theory may feel that such offenders will get the harsh punishments they deserve under this philosophy, since it serves the greatest good.

Review and Applications

NOTE TO INSTRUCTOR: These answers cover, and usually condense, material directly from the textbook. The answers sometimes include examples from outside sources that you can share with the class for further illustration.

Questions For Review

1. Name the various sources from which laws derive.
Today, in the United States, laws are derived from:
- the federal, state, or local enactments of legislative bodies.
- the known decisions of the courts of the federal and state governments (also called common law or case law).
- rules and regulations proclaimed by administrative bodies.
- proclamations by executives of the federal, state, or local government.

2. What is the difference between common law and statutory law?
Common law, also called case law, is law that is created by judicial opinion as the result of actual cases. It is the foundation of criminal law in England and many of its former colonies, including the United States, and still influences many modern legal principles. However, statutory law, which is law created by state and federal legislatures, is used much more frequently for the creation and codification of laws. All U.S. federal law is statutorily derived.

3. What is the difference between criminal law and civil law?
Criminal law is different from other types of law, and from civil law in particular, because it involves crimes. Modern crimes are violations of public rights and duties that create social harms that affect the entire community–and must be punished by the community in turn.

Civil law deals with matters that are considered to be private concerns between individuals. It includes laws dealing with personal injury, contracts, and property, as well as administrative law. A violation of civil law is called a tort, rather than a crime.

4. What is the history of the common law?
When William of Normandy conquered England in 1066, he established the eyre, which was a court with judges who traveled throughout the kingdom once every seven years to hear cases as representatives of the king. The decisions of these judges formed a large part of England's common law. The enforcement of common law simply consisted of the use of force against those who violated the King's peace, which could result in both punishment and the imposition of monetary sanctions.

When the 13 colonies were established in America, they adopted England's common law. As the colonies developed and the United States was formed, the law of the United States developed separately from the English common law tradition. Eventually, statutory law replaced common law, also known as judge-created law. American statutory law was, and is, created through the state and federal legislatures. Today, virtually all of American criminal law is statutory law.

5. How did Jeremy Bentham influence criminal law in England and the United States?

Jeremy Bentham was a utilitarian legal philosopher who spearheaded a movement for criminal law reform in England and the United States. He reorganized the law of crimes according to the amount of social harm they caused. As a result, the law of crimes in most American states has been recast into more or less coherent penal codes.

6. What is the Model Penal Code, and why was it created?

The Model Penal Code (MPC) is a comprehensive recodification of the principles of criminal responsibility that was based upon existing sources of the criminal law including codes, judicial opinions, and scholarly commentary. It was created by the American Law Institute (ALI), an organization of lawyers, judges, and legal scholars, chiefly due to general dissatisfaction with the criminal law. An overwhelming majority of the states have adopted revised criminal codes as a result of the MPC. The MPC stands as a model in the reform of principles of American criminal responsibility.

7. What document restricts federal law, and how?

The U.S. Constitution restricts federal power with respect to the authority of the federal government to define and prosecute crimes.

The Constitution explicitly enumerates certain federal crimes, and all other federal criminal jurisdiction emanates from the "necessary and proper" clause of article I, § 8 of the Constitution, which grants the power to Congress to pass legislation necessary to implement any enumerated federal power.

8. Define *actus reus* and *mens rea*, and explain why they are needed for criminal charges.

An *actus reus* is a willed and voluntary unlawful act. *Mens rea* is the guilty state of mind, or intent. This element does not require intent to violate the law, but rather the intent to commit the act that the law prohibits.

Both of these elements must be concurrently present at the time a crime occurs–that is, in order to be criminally liable, the defendant must commit the criminal act with the intent to do so. *Actus reus, mens rea,* and the concurrence

of these two elements are three of the five basic elements of criminal liability.

9. How are retributive justification and utilitarian justification different? Similar?

These justifications, or theories, are different because retributive justification focuses on punishment and utilitarian justification focuses on what is best for society; therefore, the former is more focused on the individual offender's "just deserts" and the latter is more focused on the needs of the community. Retributive justification, therefore, appears to be more personal, and utilitarian justification appears to be more impersonal.

They are similar because they both permit severe punishment, even the death penalty, when it appears appropriate from the perspective of their justification. They are also similar because both philosophies can find benefits in the philosophy of vengeance.

Students should be able to come up with many more examples of their similarities and differences.

10. How is punishment relative, and why?

Punishment is relative in that it is impossible to predict how strongly it will affect different individuals. This is because different sanctions affect people in different ways. For instance, a $100 fine will affect a wealthy person much less seriously than it will affect a poor person. A three-year prison sentence will affect someone who fears and hates prison much more than it will affect someone who does not fear prison and sees such a sentence as a badge of his toughness.

Problem-Solving Exercises

1. PRE-TRIAL DETENTION
   Answers could include the following:
   a. It can, because it constitutes a loss of liberty.
   b. This creates a situation in which the poor must experience the disruptions caused by incarceration without having the benefit of due process to determine if they are actually guilty. In addition, you can point out to students that suspects who are detained prior to trial come to trial in jail garb, which can create an impression of guilt in the jury's eyes.

2. PROTECTION AGAINST CYBERCRIME

Answers could include the following:

a. You can point to the problems with the crime in other jurisdictions, their methods of handling it, and the harm that it caused before being addressed by lawmakers. You can also discuss the backlash that may occur if lawmakers wait for a public outcry before acting.

b. You can work with the police to provide information via press conferences, radio and television interviews, and the police department's Web site to provide educational information about this problem.

3. SENTENCING GUIDELINES

Answers could include the following:

a. Due to ongoing problems with prison overcrowding and the current trend to provide treatment instead of incarceration for nonviolent drug offenders, it may be wise to segue into this new sentencing approach. Some students will feel that this change should occur quickly, some gradually, and others will feel that it should not happen at all. All will have different reasons, most of them related to their core beliefs regarding the criminality of drug use.

b. Students will be divided on this, since they may not feel that treatment-based alternatives are the best answer, either.

Workplace Applications

NOTE TO INSTRUCTOR: Many experiential activities in this Instructor's Resource Manual (there are others listed under "Additional Workplace Applications," at the end) and the following ones require the students to contact local criminal justice practitioners for information. When assigning any phone-related activities, be sure to emphasize to students the importance of telephone etiquette. Many criminal justice personnel are very busy, but will be happy to talk about their jobs with polite and articulate students.

Ask the students to introduce themselves by name, then explain that they are criminal justice students at College (or University

conducting research for a class assignment. Students may be surprised at the friendliness of the criminal justice personnel whom they interview, and some may even complain that they "talked their ear off." In any event, try to emphasize politeness for all phone interviews.

The same general etiquette applies to any e-mail inquiries. Students should greet the interviewee by his or her title and last name (i.e., "Dear Detective Smith," "Dear Lieutenant Voorhees"), spell-check each e-mail, and close the e-mail by thanking them for their time.

If students find themselves contacting the same person or department more than a few times over the course of the semester, they should be encouraged to send handwritten thank-you notes to each person in acknowledgment of the time spent on them.

1. PRISON BUDGET

Answers could include the following:

a. This would be a good time to discuss funding for more effective prevention programs, such as those that emphasize education and mentoring for young at-risk juveniles. It would also be a good time to emphasize drug treatment, rather than incarceration, for nonviolent offenders convicted of possession. Students will likely think of many other creative ideas for funding.

b. Colleges should still be a high priority, but so should prisons. The question is how to reduce the need for so much prison spending.

2. FIND OUT ABOUT LAW SCHOOL

Answers can include the following:

a. Courses are available that focus on criminal law, and a law student could focus on these to further his or her understanding. Internships or part-time work at a prosecutor's office or at a criminal defense lawyer's office would provide excellent experience. You can point out to students that such work can start while they are still undergraduates, so that they can build up their resume earlier than others.

b. After passing the bar, one could work at a prosecutor's office or as a public defender at an entry level, or could gain employment with a law firm specializing in criminal defense. With a few years' experience, a lawyer specializing in criminal law can move up in a county or state prosecutor's office or move on to work with a U.S. Attorney's office or some other legal position at the federal level. You can mention that experienced criminal attorneys may also become judges.

3. SENTENCING GUIDELINES

Answers could include the following:

a. Since this law unconstitutionally impinges on the liberty of these women and any others who are tried with these charges, the law should be struck from the books.

b. Although political factors are a reality in any courtroom workgroup, allowing the prosecutor to sway you would be a mistake for several reasons. For one, the prosecutor should not have such influence over a judge, even in less subjective matters. Secondly, this is a particularly outdated and absurd offense, so to convict people with it would undermine the integrity of your court. Finally, such a move could cause political backlash and serve to turn the women into political martyrs.

Internet Applications

1. OBTAIN LEGAL INFORMATION

Nolo.com covers most important areas of criminal law. Students may wish to see more detail and more specific issues. These appear to be missing because Nolo.com is a general-information site that covers a broad topic for a wide audience. Answers regarding crime topics will vary, depending on students' expectations.

2. INFORMATION FOR LAW STUDENTS

This site provides extensive resources on cases decided by the U.S. Supreme Court, U.S. Circuit Courts, U.S. Courts of Appeals, and state courts. It could help law students understand the use of common law by providing information on landmark cases that relied on common law for their decisions.

Ethics Issues

1. FIREWORKS BAN

Answers can include the following:

a. No, because the law is not yet in effect. You can remind them that they need to close down by July 1, but cannot arrest anyone and should not even threaten to do so because they have not created any problems.

b. At that time, you may arrest the person running the fireworks booth and, if you choose, any employees.

2. FORENSIC EVIDENCE

Answers can include the following:

a. This is a tough call because you do not want public opinion to sway against you. However, it is necessary to keep the other three cases open so that the other killer may be found. You should admit the truth now and explain that it is necessary to clear these matters before the case reaches trial so that the killer in your custody does not get released on a technicality.

b. This will allow the actual killer of the other three children to go free because he or she cannot be tried for crimes for which someone else has already been convicted. To make things worse, if you ever did locate this killer, the one in your custody could possibly be set free because of this technical error.

NOTE TO INSTRUCTOR: These additional activities are exclusive to this IRM. They are designed to meet the special needs of your students. If you or your students cannot access a Web site referred to here, go to *cl.glencoe.com* for the latest updated links.

As noted earlier, many of the additional workplace applications in this Instructor's Resource Manual require students to make contact with criminal justice professional and with the public by interviewing them about various criminal justice topics. This can be an extremely beneficial type of exercise, but it can cause initial discomfort for students who are used to more passive styles of learning.

As the instructor, you will want to note when students are not giving complete or detailed answers regarding interviews. Some students do not enjoy conducting interviews, and some try to avoid the effort involved, but most enjoy it once they get started. Make sure that students are handling the interviews accurately, completely, and truthfully.

Advanced Web Research

1. INTERNET

CRIME RISK

Have students visit "Crime Tracker: Rate Your Risk" at *http://www.kwvt.come/crime/risk_frame.html*. Ask them to take the three tests, which take about ten minutes each. Once they have completed the tests, have them answer the following questions:

- What were your scores? Do you agree with these scores? Why or why not?

- What, if anything, will you do to lower your crime risk?

This exercise will introduce students to a simple but effective way of determining one's crime risks. Although these tests are not guarantees that you will or will not be affected by crime, they provide many helpful hints and seem to cover many important factors.

2. INTERNET

CRIMINAL LAW

Nolo.com is an excellent source of free legal information. Ask students to visit them at *http://www.nolo.com*, and then click on "Criminal Law" in the left-hand menu. Have students read two items from Nolo.com's "Legal Encyclopedia" as well as "Today's Question." Ask students to summarize the information they have read, including the exact names and addresses of the pages that they read. Next, ask students what they have learned.

NOTE TO INSTRUCTOR: You should encourage students to explore this site thoroughly, as it will make legal matters seem more accessible and interesting to them. As an extra-credit assignment, you could assign extra readings from this site.

3. INTERNET

CRIME STATISTICS

Have students visit Crime.com at *http://www.crime.com*. Under "Information" at the bottom, have them click on "Crime Stats," and use the options at the bottom to learn about their state, county, and even zip code. Next, ask them the following questions:

- What is the total crime rating of your state, county, and zip code?

- How does this fit with your perception of these places?

- What other crime figures caught your attention?

- Do you agree or disagree with the rating system?

This exercise introduces them to one of several national crime rating systems found on the Internet. They should be able to report a total crime percentage for whatever region they examined, and accurately report any other crime figures that they noticed (they will usually point out ones that seemed unusually high or low, or contrary to their expectations).

Students' answers about whether they agree with this rating system will vary, and some may be in denial about the severity of the crime problem in their area.

Extended Workplace Applications

1. Review

Give students the following scenario: You are a municipal (local) police officer. You learn that a weekly high-stakes poker game is held in the home of a prominent doctor. The game is reportedly friendly, and is well attended by other law-abiding citizens of the community. Your community is plagued with drug traffickers and the numbers racquet is strong, so your chief has encouraged all officers to stamp out vice where they find it.

Next, ask students to review the situation by answering the following questions:

- Does this game appear to be related to other vice activity in your community? Why or why not?

- What action, if any, should you take with regard to the poker game? Why?

- How does the character of the offenders affect your judgment in this case? Why?

This game does not appear to be related to vice activity because there is no "house," no high stakes, and no indication of other types of gambling or vice.

Most students will state that they would not do anything, but that they might if circumstances changed, such as if criminals got involved or the stakes raised significantly.

This will probably affect the judgment of most people since they do not appear to have prior records and do not seem to have a criminal goal in mind. This may change over time, however, and appearances can be deceiving.

2. Evaluate

NOTE TO INSTRUCTOR: This exercise refers to the concept of jury nullification, which is discussed in the FYI box on page 4 in Chapter 1. You may want to ensure that the class fully understands this concept before assigning this exercise.

Give students the following scenario: The defendant in a criminal case has been charged with possession for having one marijuana cigarette in his pocket. The city attorney prosecuted the case, in an effort to establish a policy of zero tolerance for drugs in the community. The defense attorney is delivering the closing argument to the jury and begins to argue for jury nullification, claiming that, although the law technically prohibits the defendant's conduct, the jury should "recognize the realities of life" and acquit. Next, ask students to evaluate this scenario by answering the following questions:

- Should the defense attorney be prohibited from making this argument? Why or why not?

- How should the judge handle this situation? What about the jury?

Students should be able to answer yes, the defense attorney is not allowed to encourage jury nullification because this is illegal.

The judge should reprimand the defense attorney, who should know that this is an illegal action, and attempt to control the damage done by explaining to the jury why it is illegal for the defense attorney to say what he did.

3. Analyze

Give students the following scenario: You are a college student who has been busted for possession of marijuana. Since the laws of your state focus on rehabilitation for nonviolent drug offenders, you are sentenced to 30 days at a rehab center. Although the place is understaffed and you receive little actual treatment, you are treated well and can attend classes during your time there. While there, you meet someone else who is serving his third sentence for drug possession. He states that before the new laws were passed, nonviolent drug possession charges could result in harsh sentences. He tells you that he spent three years in a state prison, where he was beaten and sexually assaulted by tougher inmates.

Next, ask students to analyze the situation by answering the following questions:

- Which approach do you think is more appropriate for nonviolent drug offenders? Why?

- Do you think that either approach, as it works in the example listed here, is effective in combating recidivism? Explain.

- What needs to be changed for either strategy to work better than it has?

This fictitious story illustrates the problems found in the punitive and rehabilitative approaches to nonviolent drug offenders. Although most students will agree that the rehab approach is much better, especially for a first-time offender, they will also likely agree that it is not working at its optimum level.

Neither approach seems likely to stop recidivism. Obviously, the three-time offender has recidivated, and the hands-off approach to the first-time offender is not appropriate for helping him with his drug use.

For the rehabilitative strategy to be more effective, the facility apparently needs more staff to spend time with the patients and provide them with more structure and guidance. For the punitive approach, nonviolent offenders must be segregated from violent offenders who can endanger their well-being.

4. Role Play

Give students the following scenario: You are a local judge who is hearing a case regarding a defendant who showed up on a crowded public street in his swim trunks and started dancing in a way that blocked the sidewalk and forced people to walk into the street to avoid him. One of these people was hit by a bicyclist and suffered minor injuries. The man was arrested and charged with being a public nuisance. He contends that he has broken no laws. You review the public nuisance ordinance and find that it is rather vague and could apply to a variety of legal activities; you actually consider them unconstitutional because they could be used to hinder the liberty of innocent people. However, the man's behavior was obnoxious, and people had to walk around him to avoid being hit or kicked as he danced.

- Do you prosecute the man under this ordinance, even though it is not written as clearly as you would like, or do you let him go because the ordinance is vague?

Although this person is obviously a nuisance, the law should be changed to be clearer. This person caused people to walk around him to avoid injury, which in turn caused another injury. However, he could contest this vague ordinance in an appeals court and probably win. Students will be undecided as to how to handle this. Many will convict him anyway and hope that he does not appeal, then make an effort to modernize the nuisance ordinance. Others will feel that this is unconstitutional and will acquit him, then change the ordinance to ensure that this does not happen again.

The Structure and Operation of the Criminal Justice System

Chapter Resources

For the Instructor
Instructor's Resource Manual, pp. 11–20
Additional Activities, p. 17
PowerPoint Presentation and ExamView Pro Testbank
  CD-ROM for Chapter 2
cl.glencoe.com Web site

For the Student
Student Edition, Chapter 2, pp. 26–51
Review and Applications, p. 46
Tutorial with Simulation Applications
  CD-ROM for Chapter 2
cl.glencoe.com Web site

KEY TERMS

jurisdiction	recognizance	preliminary hearing	information
federalism	bail	grand jury	arraignment and plea
probable cause	bond	indictment	*habeas corpus*

Lecture Outline

2.1 STRUCTURE OF THE CRIMINAL JUSTICE SYSTEM
Law Enforcement
Prosecution and Defense
Courts
Corrections

2.2 OPERATION OF THE CRIMINAL JUSTICE SYSTEM
Arrest
Pre-Trial Procedures and Issues
Trial of the Case
Post-Conviction Procedures and Issues

In-Chapter Questions

 Public Defender page 31
What qualities do you think an effective public defender should have?

Many students will feel that a public defender should have the ability to make quick decisions, organize and manage a large caseload effectively, negotiate good plea bargains for all clients when possible, and have strong written and verbal communication skills.

Photo caption page 35

Why is cross-examination an important part of the legal process?

Cross-examination is necessary to gather additional information, check the veracity (truth) of someone's testimony, and also to confront and correct misleading statements.

Criminal Law Online page 36

What is the main focus of this Web site? What resources does it offer? How did it help you?

This site offers an online encyclopedic resource for all basic and intermediate legal concepts. Students can look up a variety of legal topics, and many will report that they bookmarked this site and found it extremely helpful.

2.1 Self Check page 37

1. Explain the differences between state and federal courts.

   State courts have jurisdiction to consider cases charging defendants with violation of state criminal laws, and federal courts have jurisdiction to consider cases charging defendants with violation of federal criminal laws.

2. What roles do jails and prisons play in the criminal justice process? How do jails and prisons differ?

   Jails are used to maintain custody of persons arrested pending prosecution and of those sentenced to short periods of confinement, usually up to but not more than one year. Prison facilities house inmates sentenced to over one year of incarceration, and are administered by a separate correctional agency of the state or federal government.

Photo caption page 44

What types of post-conviction relief are available for inmates?

Inmates can appeal their sentences based on alleged substantive, procedural, or evidentiary errors that were committed by the trial court. In addition, they can also take the legal action of *habeas corpus*.

Criminal Law Online page 44

Write a half-page report on whether you agree that these people have been denied justice. Explain your views objectively.

Students will have mixed feelings about this site because the cases are complicated and not all of the people featured here seem completely innocent. However, some have also been harshly mistreated by the justice system. Students should make their cases objectively and back them up with the available facts.

2.2 Self Check page 45

1. What are the only three bases for dismissing a trial? These three bases are:
   - The crime charged is not a violation of the jurisdiction's law.
   - The facts asserted in the indictment or information, even if true, do not constitute the crime charged.
   - No reasonable jury could find the facts alleged on the basis of the evidence presented at the preliminary hearing.

2. Explain the various grounds on which convicted criminals appeal their charges.

   Two grounds for appeal involve procedural and evidentiary errors alleged to have been committed by the trial court. The four substantive grounds are:
   - The charge on which the accused was convicted is not a crime, either because the legislature did not proscribe the conduct or because the proscription is unconstitutional.
   - The evidence was insufficient to support a finding of fact on all the elements of the crime beyond a reasonable doubt.
   - Not all of the necessary elements of the crime were alleged.
   - The jury was improperly instructed.

   If a defendant has exhausted all appellate remedies, he or she can file a petition of *habeas corpus*.

Review and Applications

Questions For Review

1. Name some of the ways in which law enforcement agents learn about criminal acts.

   Generally, law enforcement agencies learn about criminal activity through crime prevention, such as patrol, and crime detection. Prevention is carried out by low-ranking officers assigned to cruise an area and watch for criminal activity. Detection is usually performed by specialized squads consisting of older, more experienced, and higher-ranking officers.

2. Explain the difference between release upon recognizance and bail. What is a bond?

Recognizance is a promise to appear in court; therefore, release upon recognizance means that the court is taking the defendant's word that he or she will show up in court. Bail is set for people who are not granted release upon recognizance, either because of the severity of the crime(s) charged against them or because they are considered a moderate flight risk. (Serious flight risks do not even get to post bail, and must remain in jail until they are sentenced or acquitted.) Bail is a deposit of cash, other property, or a bond, guaranteeing that the accused will appear in court. A bond is a written promise to pay one's bail. It is posted by a financially responsible person, usually a professional bondsman.

3. What is a grand jury, how does it work, and which jurisdictions use it?

A grand jury is a large panel of private citizens that act as a special type of jury that charges suspects with felonies.

They are chosen through strict court procedures to review criminal investigations and, in some instances, to conduct criminal investigations. Grand juries decide whether to charge crimes in the cases presented to them or investigated by them. When a grand jury charges a person with a crime, it does so by issuing an indictment.

Today, the federal system and many states use grand juries and indictments. Other jurisdictions use an information, which is written by a prosecutor.

4. What happens at an arraignment? What happens in response to the pleas of guilty or not guilty?

After formal charges have been filed, the defendant appears at the arraignment (or arraignment and plea) to respond formally to the charges by pleading guilty or not guilty.

If the defendant pleads guilty, then the case will be set for sentencing, which is generally accomplished through plea bargaining. If the defendant pleads not guilty, the case will be set for trial.

5. What is the burden of proof in a criminal trial?

The burden of proof is "beyond a reasonable doubt." This means that the defendant is presumed innocent until found guilty and the evidence against him or her must be adequate to convince any reasonable person that the defendant committed the crime "beyond a reasonable doubt."

In contrast, a police officer needs only probable cause to arrest someone, and you can share with students that only a preponderance of evidence is required to prove liability in a civil lawsuit.

6. What are the basic elements of the criminal trial? Include the different motions and actions of the prosecution and defense.

In jury trials, the actual trial process begins with jury selection. Next come:

- The opening statements by the prosecution (and sometimes the defense)
- The presentation of evidence by the prosecution
- The defense's motion for acquittal
- (Usually) The presentation of evidence by the defense, rebuttals, closing statements
- The judge's instructions to the jury
- The verdict
- Sentencing or acquittal

In the event that the jury cannot reach a verdict on a charge, the judge will declare a mistrial and the prosecution may choose to retry the defendant.

7. Name and define the three main perspectives from which the criminal justice system can be viewed.

The criminal justice system can be viewed from at least three perspectives:

- A social system that encompasses all levels of society, from the legislature that enacts the penal code to the citizens whose acts are governed by those laws
- A body of legal rules, which is the primary focus of subsequent chapters in this book

- An administrative system, in which the criminal justice system is the official apparatus for enforcing the criminal law. It consists of law enforcement agencies, prosecution and defense attorneys, courts, and correctional institutions and agencies.

8. **Name the different types of departments in which police work, and give some examples of federal agencies.**

Police work in police departments in cities, sheriff's departments in counties, state police agencies, state bureaus of investigation, and federal law enforcement agencies. Some examples of federal police agencies are the Federal Bureau of Investigation (FBI), the Drug Enforcement Administration (DEA), the Bureau of Alcohol, Tobacco, and Firearms (ATF), the Customs Service, the Immigration and Naturalization Service (INS), the U. S. Marshals Service, the Bureau of Postal Inspection, and the Secret Service.

9. **What are the duties of the prosecutor? Of defense counsel?**

A prosecutor's duties are to:
- take a case from the police and pursue it until the case terminates by trial, guilty plea, or dismissal.
- decide whether to pursue a formal charge and, if so, what crime to charge.
- conduct any plea negotiations.
- decide whether to dismiss charges.
- try the case.

A defense counsel's duties are to:
- zealously represent the criminal defendant from the point of interrogation through the trial process.
- demand that the prosecution respect the defendant's rights, treat the defendant fairly, and meet the burden of proof beyond a reasonable doubt in the event the case goes to trial.

10. **What is jurisdiction? What is the jurisdiction of federal courts?**

A court's jurisdiction is the scope of its power or authority to act with respect to any case before it. Jurisdiction is a concept that can also apply to police and others involved in the justice system.

The federal courts have jurisdiction over the entire United States and all of its possessions, but only to consider cases charging defendants with violation of federal criminal laws.

11. **Name three or four of the constitutional due process rights that apply to state prisoners.**

Answers can include any of the following:
- The right to trial by jury in cases involving serious offenses
- The right to assistance of counsel in any case in which a sentence of more than six months in jail or prison is imposed
- The privilege against self-incrimination, including a ban against comment by the prosecution on the defendant's failure to testify
- The presumption of innocence and requirement of proof beyond a reasonable doubt
- The freedom from unreasonable searches and seizures
- The right to silence and counsel during police interrogation
- The right to compel witnesses' attendance at trial, to confront them, and to cross-examine
- The right to a speedy and public trial
- Freedom from double jeopardy
- Freedom from cruel and unusual punishment
- Freedom from racial and sexual discrimination in substantive and procedural criminal law

12. **What are the general duties of a probation department?**

Generally, a probation department:
- investigates defendants prior to sentencing.
- provides a pre-sentence probation report to the court.

- provides supervision over those persons placed on probation after conviction.

Problem-Solving Exercises

1. WITNESS TREATMENT
   Answers could include the following:
   a. The prosecution and defense have agreed to a plea bargain, which makes a trial unnecessary.
   b. They may not have had a legal obligation, but were extremely rude to keep the witness waiting all day.
   c. Most students would agree that the witness should be angry at this waste of time and inconvenience.

2. DISCLOSURE
   Answers could include the following:
   a. Actually, the prosecutor needs to disclose evidence before it is presented so that the defense can have a fair opportunity to rebut it.
   b. It could cause legal problems for the prosecution because it is not legally acceptable.
   c. It is not necessary because the defendant was caught red-handed, and seems like an unnecessary risk.
   d. Many students will state that they will attempt to convince the prosecutor that this is not necessary and can create problems during the trial.

3. DRUG POSSESSION
   Answers could include the following:
   a. Although she seems unwilling to confess, the amount of drugs and her interactions with known drug dealers seem to make her guilty.
   b. The large quantity of drugs in her car would influence most students' decisions, along with the fact that she has been seen driving to drug dealers' houses. It would be helpful if there were witness testimony, such as by her roommates or those involved in her drug dealing.

Workplace Applications

1. THE LESSER OF TWO EVILS
   Answers could include the following:
   a. You should call for backup in any event. Many students will state that they can report the speeding car to another patrol car that is in the vicinity while continuing to observe the youths. This is because they may or may not track down the speeding car, but can continue to observe the youths and possibly see if they are committing any crimes. Others will choose to chase the car, since it is clear that the driver has committed a crime but there is not even probable cause against the youths.
   b. Either could be a great risk. The car could spin out of control and kill people, and the youths could kill people while burglarizing their homes. Therefore, either answer is fine, but student answers should present realistic possibilities to support their opinions.
   c. As stated above, you should call for backup to assist in both crimes.

2. TRIAL BY JURY
   Answers could include the following:
   a. The prosecution could make its closing arguments and the judge would then turn the case over to the jury to decide a verdict.
   b. It is somewhat unusual, and many would feel that the defense has not provided adequate counsel because they should have made some effort to counter the claims of the prosecution. You can point out that if the defendant was indeed guilty, this case could have been handled through plea bargaining to save everyone time and effort.
   c. He or she could, depending on the circumstances. If it turned out that the prosecution's case was so strong that the defense had no real case left, then the defendant has no legitimate complaint. If, however, the defense counsel was merely lazy or inept, the defendant has a valid complaint.

3. RELEASE AND BAIL

Answers could include the following:

a. Many students will agree to not set bail for him because he seems to have severe problems that make him a threat to the community. In addition, his mother's mental illness contributes to an unstable home life, which is another important factor when determining whether bail should be set.

b. All of the factors should be considered except the attorney's pleas. He is obviously not concerned about the risks posed by his client.

Internet Applications

1. Answers could include the following:

a. Answers will vary depending on the cases that are posted and the student's individual taste.

b. It depends. In their legal actions against tobacco companies, attorneys general chose to pursue class-action lawsuits. Whether students agree with their actions will vary, but their reasons should be based upon the available facts of the case.

c. Answers will vary depending on the case and its outcome.

2. Answers could include the following:

a. NAPSA's goals are to promote the establishment of agencies that provide pre-trial services, promote research and development in the field of pre-trial services, promote an exchange of information among professionals, and encourage professionalism among pre-trial service providers.

b. NAPSA provides a variety of publications on pre-trial issues such as bail and drug testing, links, diversion information, and employment listings.

c. They could help a defendant by providing information on the pre-trial process. A defense attorney could use this information to educate his or her client about the pre-trial process. A prosecutor could use this as a resource when considering plea bargains that focus on diversionary sentencing.

d. Most students will agree that NAPSA's specialized information would be helpful to those facing trial and the attorneys involved in their cases.

Ethics Issues

1. DEFENSE ATTORNEY

Answers can include the following:

a. Most students will not defend this person because his actions are morally reprehensible and they would not want to be involved in his case.

b. This may change the mind of some students, but not many.

c. Since the defendant is clearly guilty, any efforts to backtrack would be little more than lying. Although lying is not unusual for lawyers, this is a particularly egregious case.

d. This case is probably not winnable because of the strong evidence against the defendant. Students may agree that they have nothing to lose by defending this person, but still may feel reluctant to get involved.

2. PROSECUTION

Answers can include the following:

a. It can help convince them that he has a violent disposition, which could help to prove that he murdered his wife.

b. It depends. Although the prosecutor should not use his personal friendship with the judge to allow such character witnesses, students should also understand that recovered substance abusers might carry the same negative personality traits that they possessed during alcoholism. Therefore, although the defendant is a recovered alcoholic, he may still be violent and such character witnesses could provide useful testimony about his personality. Therefore, it may be perfectly legitimate to introduce such evidence without relying on unethical means.

Additional Activities

Advanced Web Research

1. INTERNET

HABEAS CORPUS

Help students understand how *habeas corpus* works by having them read *Texas v. Karla Faye Tucker* at **http://www.courttv.com/legaldocs/ newsmakers/tucker**. This execution was controversial because although Tucker was clearly guilty of violently murdering two people, she considered herself rehabilitated at the time of her death. Have students read the introductory page, including the Table of Contents/Summary of Writ (including the quote at the bottom). Then have students write a one- to two-page summary by answering the following questions:

- What are the claims made in the Summary of Writ? What provisions of the U.S. Constitution are cited?

- Do you agree with the request of the Writ? Why or why not? What about the quote at the bottom? Why or why not?

This exercise will introduce students to the writ of *habeas corpus*, which is an important legal document and one with which they should at least be familiar. Essentially, the claims were that the Texas death penalty system did not provide adequate safeguards against executing people who did not deserve it. This, according to the writ, violates the Fourteenth Amendment's due process protections against the Eighth Amendment's protection regarding cruel and unusual punishment.

Whether students agree with the writ will likely depend more on their opinion of Karla Faye Tucker than on their opinion of Texas's use of the death penalty. You may want to ensure that both issues get equal time in any classroom discussion on the subject. Some will agree that executing Tucker was cruel and unusual punishment. Others will feel that she deserved such a punishment and that her apparent rehabilitation should not be a prominent issue.

2. INTERNET

GRAND JURY

Have students read "Grand Jury Secrecy Rules" at **http://www.washingtonpost.com/wp-srv/politics/ special/clinton/stories/rule6e.htm**. Then have them answer the following questions:

- Briefly, what are the rules of secrecy regarding those involved in a grand jury?

- Are any reasons given for this secrecy? If so, what are they? If not, what do you feel the reasons are?

Students should be able to understand that nobody involved in any grand jury proceeding, whether as a grand juror or as a member of the courtroom workgroup, is allowed to "disclose matters occurring before the grand jury." This secrecy is apparently to prevent leakage of the grand jury's findings. Since grand juries have more responsibility than petit juries, they are held to higher levels of secrecy.

3. INTERNET

BAIL HEARING, BOND, RECOGNIZANCE

Have students check out the helpful Web site "Arrest to Trial Summary - Bail Hearing, Bond, Recognizance" at **http://lawsmart.lawinfo.com/ canada/criminal/arrest2trial.html**. Although this is a Canadian site, the basic information here applies to American criminal courtrooms as well; remember that Canada, like the United States, shares the same English legal heritage. Then have students answer the following questions:

- What factors will the judge consider when deciding whether a criminal can be released upon recognizance or is eligible for bail? Are these considerations adequate, too lenient, or too strict? Why?

- What possible conditions could a criminal face when released on bail? Give some examples, and explain why they exist.

There are several factors that a judge will consider, including the defendant's prior record, current employment, and family and community ties. Most students will agree that these factors cover everything, but some may feel that they are too lenient for certain types of criminals. You can point out that the judge is never required to grant bail, and that first-time offenders with good jobs can be held without bail if accused of heinous crimes.

While on bail, a person can face a variety of restrictions, such as being required to check in with the court, abstain from certain types of activity, and in general act in a law-abiding manner.

Extended Workplace Applications

1. Role Play

Give students the following scenario: You are a federal judge who is hearing the case of a state inmate who is seeking *habeas corpus* relief. He states that this conviction violates his constitutional rights because he was given ineffective counsel. He states that his public defender never contacted him, called no witnesses, and was once drunk in court. The judge who oversaw the case states that he is exaggerating about the first and third charges, but that the public defender provided minimal counsel for a complicated felony case.

- Do you feel that the defendant has a case? Explain your reasons.

- What other information would help you make your decision?

It should concern students that the defendant appears to be lying. If this is the case, his petition should be denied. If, however, what he is saying turns out to be true, his petition should be granted because the counsel sounds extremely ineffective.

Students should further question the original judge and also the defendant to learn more about what actually happened and when. Students can also question the public defender and his supervisor to learn more about his history.

2. Discuss

Give students the following scenario: You are a police officer who wants to arrest a man who has been hanging around a city part all day, trying to talk to people and acting suspiciously furtive whenever you walk by. You try to start a conversation with him, but he refuses to speak to you. After he tries to talk to a couple, you ask them what the man said to them and they reply, "Some strange spiritual stuff. We couldn't figure it out." Although he has not committed any crimes, he seems like he could be selling drugs, panhandling, or generally harassing people.

Next, lead the class in a discussion with the following question:

- Do you have the right to arrest him? Why or why not?

Most students should respond that they cannot arrest this person because they do not have probable cause indicating a fair probability that the suspect committed a specific crime. Although he is unusual and looks suspicious, he has not yet committed a crime. They would have to wait until he attempts to commit a crime to arrest him. If this does not appear likely, they may want to focus their efforts elsewhere.

3. Role Play

Give students the following scenario: You have just arrested two adults and a juvenile for trespassing and breaking and entering an abandoned building. You photograph the adults, then ask the juvenile to stand against the wall for his picture. He insists that juveniles cannot have their picture taken or be fingerprinted. You explain that juvenile laws have recently changed and that you are now allowed to take his picture. He states that this is unconstitutional and that he can sue you. You reply that you have every right to do this.

- Which of you is correct, and why?

Today, many aspects of juvenile law are changing, and juveniles do not have many of the same protections that they used to. Some jurisdictions now allow police to photograph and fingerprint juveniles when arresting them, and do not keep sealed records for juvenile offenders as they did in the past.

The U.S. Constitution makes no special provision for juveniles, so this claim is invalid. The juvenile can sue your department, but whether he will win is another story. Although you do have the right to do this, it is possible that a civil court will find your department liable for not providing traditional privacy rights that were created for juvenile offenders. Therefore, although you are legally in the right, and many students will agree that juvenile offenders should be photographed and fingerprinted, there is a slim chance of legal repercussions.

4. Analyze

Give students the following scenario: You are a public defender who attempts to provide solid, practical advice to the dozens of defendants in your caseload. Today, you are talking to a 35-year-old mother of two who is facing her third felony offense for drug possession with intent to distribute. Although your state does not face a three-strikes law, she could face a maximum sentence of 20 years. You explain to her that she could plea bargain and get her sentence reduced to no more than seven years. She refuses and insists that she have a trial, which she is convinced that she will win because, although she is clearly legally guilty, she thinks that the judge will feel sorry for her because she is a single mother.

Next, ask students to analyze the situation by answering the following question:

- What is wrong with her assumption, and how does the concept of legality relate to this issue?

Clearly, this defendant does not have an understanding of the concept of legality, which holds that if she is guilty of a crime, she must face trial and punishment. The fact that she is a single mother is legally irrelevant; all that matters is that she committed the crime and is clearly guilty. In addition, although she seems to feel that her single motherhood will win the court's pity, it may actually bother the judge and jury to see a parent involved in so much crime and thus creating such an unstable home life for her children.

Chapter 3

Constitutional Limitations on the Criminal Law

KEY TERMS

Bill of Rights	equal protection	fair notice	proportionality
procedural criminal law	bill of attainder	substantive criminal law	
due process	*ex post facto*	clear and present danger test	

Lecture Outline

3.1 CRIMINAL LAW AND THE U.S. CONSTITUTION

The Question of Constitutionality
The Bill of Rights

3.2 PROCEDURAL CRIMINAL LAW
Due Process and Equal Protection
Bills of Attainder and *Ex Post Facto* Laws
Fair Notice and Vagueness

3.3 SUBSTANTIVE CRIMINAL LAW AND INDIVIDUAL DUE PROCESS RIGHTS
First Amendment Rights
Second Amendment Rights
Eighth Amendment Rights
The Right to Privacy

In-Chapter Questions

3.1 Self Check page 56

How does the U.S. Constitution influence federal and state law?

It provides for certain rights and limitations that cannot be changed by federal or state law. All of the due process protections contained in the Bill of Rights affect federal laws. Most of the due process protections contained in the Bill of Rights affect state laws; the only two exceptions are the Fifth Amendment's provision for prosecution of serious crimes only by indictment and the Eighth Amendment's ban on excessive bail.

Campus Police Officer page 57
What qualities do you think a campus police officer ought to possess?

A campus police officer should have excellent communication skills because he or she will deal with a wide range of student beliefs and backgrounds. Additionally, he or she should be especially sensitive to the problem of drunk driving, which is frequently a problem around college campuses.

 Carnell v. Texas page 60
Do you think laws like this one and sex offender registry laws violate the federal prohibition against *ex post facto* laws?

Some students may feel that this is the case, but remember that sex offenses were already crimes when these changes were made. In addition, you may want to ask students about the intentions of these laws, and if the good they do for the community is a valid issue.

Criminal Law Online page 60

What services does the ABA provide for those who are not attorneys? What did you learn from visiting this site?

The ABA provides much general information for the public and for law students. Students should report that they found a lot of helpful resources for not just criminal law, but also other legal issues such as civil law.

Photo Caption page 61

How can such laws promote overuse or discriminatory behavior?

By not providing law enforcement with guidance on how to act, law enforcement officers are given excessive discretion that leaves them uncertain about what is appropriate.

 People v. Maness page 62
How did the Wrongs to Children Act fail to give fair notice?

If people are not aware that a formerly legal activity has been made into a criminal one, they may not have received fair notice and therefore are not criminally liable. You may wish to ask students if anything could have been done to make this case turn out differently.

 City of Chicago v. Morales page 63
How could this law be rewritten to be less vague and more constitutional?

Students will have a variety of answers. Be sure that their answers are not equally as vague as the one that they are trying to rewrite (this sometimes occurs), and that they have a clear sense of what is "constitutional."

3.2 Self Check page 63

1. Why are *ex post facto* laws considered unconstitutional? Do you agree? Why or Why not?

They are unconstitutional because they do not provide fair notice that a certain action is a crime by legally making it a criminal act. Most students will agree with this, although there are certain egregious situations (such as new types of Internet-related fraud or sexual offenses) that may make them feel that certain exceptions should exist.

2. How do due process and equal protection protect people's rights?

Due process ensures that suspects and defendants are innocent until proven guilty by a series of procedures; it provides protections that they will not lose their lives or liberty until their guilt has been proven beyond a reasonable doubt. Equal protection ensures that all citizens receive the same level of protection.

 Hatch v. Superior Court page 68
Do you think the defendant should still be found guilty even though he was actually sending harmful matter to an adult?

Most students will agree that he should be found guilty anyway, since by sending this material he willingly took a risk that it may fall into someone else's hands. Some, however, will feel that his intent should be a mitigating factor.

Photo caption page 69

What are some limitations of the right to freedom of assembly?

The right to freedom of assembly does not apply to violent protests, such as when people are harassed or attacked for entering a particular business; nor does it apply to assembly in which protestors use violent language to provoke others to riot or otherwise cause public harm.

Criminal Law Online page 69

Write a half-page report explaining the breadth of issues you read about, and how they are covered under Constitutional law. Don't forget to include the Amendments to which these issues pertain.

Answers will vary depending on the article chosen and the Amendments covered, but students should demonstrate a clear understanding of the Amendment(s) covered in the article, as well as what the article means and what significance it poses for criminal law.

3.3 Self Check page 73

1. Which Amendment of the Bill of Rights do you feel is most important to one's fundamental rights? Why?

Many students will state that the First Amendment is the most important, and many others will prefer the Fourteenth Amendment for providing for due process and equal protection.

2. Why is the right to privacy controversial in American society?

It is controversial because religious activists throughout the centuries have attempted (with some success) to impose their beliefs on others regarding their sexuality, right to bear a child, and other matters. Also, since the right to privacy is not explicitly provided for in the Constitution, its definition is somewhat open to interpretation.

Review and Applications

Review Questions

1. What is the difference between substantive and procedural criminal law?

Substantive criminal law defines what actions are criminal. It differs from procedural criminal law in that substantive criminal law defines criminal conduct and prescribes the punishment to be imposed for such conduct. Procedural criminal law outlines the official mechanisms through which substantive criminal law is enforced, such as the rules and laws to be followed from the investigative stage of a crime to the arrest, trial, and sentencing of the defendant.

2. Name at least five constitutional subjects relating to procedural criminal law.

Answers can include any of the following:
- Article I of the Constitution
- Protection against unreasonable searches and seizures (Fourth Amendment)
- Due process protection (Fifth Amendment)
- Protection from double jeopardy and self-incrimination (Fifth Amendment)
- Grand jury indictment in federal cases (Fifth Amendment)
- The right to counsel (Sixth Amendment)
- The right to a trial by an impartial jury (Sixth Amendment)
- The right to a speedy and public trial (Sixth Amendment)
- The right to confront opposing witnesses (Sixth Amendment)
- The right to compel the attendance of witnesses favorable to the defendant (Sixth Amendment)
- The right to notice of the nature and cause of the accusation (Sixth Amendment)
- Due process (Fourteenth Amendment)
- Equal protection under the law (Fourteenth Amendment)

3. Name the three possible definitions of an *ex post facto* law.

An *ex post facto* law is one that does any of the following:
- Makes criminal an act that is done before passage of the law and punishes such action
- Aggravates a crime, making it more serious than it had been when it was committed
- Inflicts a greater punishment than the law imposed when the crime was committed

4. What are two possible problems that can arise from vague criminal statutes?

Vague criminal statutes can have the following problems:
- Criminal statutes lacking clarity violate the fair notice requirement that people are entitled to know what they are forbidden to do, so that they may shape their conduct accordingly.

- Criminal statutes lacking in clarity are susceptible to enforcement in an arbitrary or discriminatory manner within the discretion of the police, prosecutors, and judges and juries.

In addition, they violate the due process clause of the Fourteenth Amendment.

5. Define the due process clause of the Fourteenth Amendment, and explain its relevance to criminal law.

This clause has been interpreted by the courts to encompass the multiple procedures and processes that must be followed before a person can be legally deprived of his or her life, liberty, or property. Many of these processes and protections are covered in the U.S. Constitution. One of these, also found in the Fourteenth Amendment, is the guarantee to equal protection under the law. This is relevant to criminal law because defendants must receive certain protections before facing conviction, punishment, and the stigma of punishment under the criminal justice system.

6. Name some examples of limitations on the First Amendment, as applied by the courts.

Restrictions of free speech are allowed, but "must be evaluated by the Court in light of the government's responsibility to meet the public's interest, as well as the individual's First Amendment guarantee of free speech." One typical prohibited form of speech is fighting words. Other areas of potentially unprotected speech include hate speech, profanity, libelous utterances, and obscenity.

Religious freedom claims are limited, and criminal convictions have been upheld for people found guilty of the following crimes (but who attempted to use their religions to justify them):
- Polygamy
- A Christian Scientist parent's withholding medical treatment for a child
- Handling poisonous snakes in religious ceremonies
- The use of peyote as part of a religious practice (although this is currently legal for Native Americans, which is discussed in further detail in Chapter 14)

Public assembly is limited when it may threaten public safety, peace, and order. Specific statutes that curtail the right to assemble under specific circumstances, such as when protesters try to block people from entering abortion clinics. In addition, the government has the right to impose reasonable restrictions on the time, place, and manner of assembly.

7. What are fighting words? How do these legally differ from hate speech or profanity?

Fighting words are defined as "those which by their very utterance inflict injury or tend to incite an immediate breach of the peace." They are a subcategory of unprotected speech that poses a clear and present danger because they threaten public peace or order by being provocative enough to induce a violent reaction.

Hate speech and profanity are types of speech that are potentially unprotected. Although provocative, they do not necessarily contain the same threats or inducement to fight or disrupt public order as fighting words do. However, hate speech and profanity may be used in fighting words.

8. What does the Eighth Amendment address, and how is this applied to criminal justice?

The Eighth Amendment to the U.S. Constitution prohibits the infliction of "cruel and unusual punishments." It also provides for proportionality in crimes, which is especially important in regard to consistency in sentencing and limitations on what kinds of offenders receive the death penalty. Proportionality means that the punishment inflicted for a criminal violation should not be grossly disproportionate to the crime committed.

9. How does proportionality affect the grading of offenses?

The proportionality requirement of the Eighth Amendment affects the grading of offenses regarding the consistency of sentencing, the assessment of the validity of terms of imprisonment, and the imposition of the death penalty. To ensure proportionality in the death penalty, for instance, the two following cases indicate restrictions placed upon who can receive the death penalty:

- In *Coker v. Georgia* (1977), the Court held that death was an excessive penalty for the rape of an adult woman.
- The Court has also ruled that the death penalty cannot be imposed upon a defendant who was less than 16 years old at the time of the killing offense.

10. Explain what "equal protection under the law" means, and how it applies in criminal law.

"Equal protection under the law" is a provision of the Fourteenth Amendment, which holds that no state shall "deny to any person. . . the equal protection of the laws." This means that a law that distinguishes between two classes of persons (e.g., men and women, wealthy and poor, minorities and non-minorities) is subject to attack if it does not provide equal protection to both groups. Today, all laws that make a distinction between persons based on race, ethnicity, gender, religion, sexual orientation, or national origin are subject to constitutional scrutiny, even when they are designed to rectify the discrimination of the past.

Problem-Solving Exercises

1. JUVENILE RIGHTS

At this point, the youths have not committed any crimes, so you do not have probable cause. The Fourth Amendment protects them from unreasonable searches and seizures, and the First Amendment provides them with the right to peaceful public assembly.

Point out that the one who is involved in a drug ring could perhaps be subject to a nuisance abatement order, which is an order issued by a civil court that requires known gang members to avoid certain unlawful and otherwise lawful activities that are related to their nuisance behavior, such as loitering in public.

2. FALSE ALARM

Answers could include the following:
a. The clear and present danger test could be applied, and most students would agree that this behavior would not be protected by the First Amendment. It is the equivalent of yelling, "Fire!" in a crowded theatre.

b. No. Because it produced the same endangerment to human life, it was obviously convincing enough to present a clear and present danger.

c. This was a prank, so criminal intent was not present. However, the student behaved recklessly in regard to human life. Students will have mixed feelings about how to handle their case. If these were first-time offenders, perhaps a combination of restitution, probation, and community service would be the best option. Others may wish to charge and punish them more severely.

3. ANTI-LOITERING ORDINANCE

Answers could include the following:
a. This ordinance may not be constitutional because it may be overly vague and broad, but it may legally and constitutionally apply to loitering on private property such as a strip mall.

b. You may prosecute the youths since their loitering took place on private property (the entire strip mall belongs to its owner, and is not legally public property like a street corner or city park), but since they committed no wrongdoing, it may be preferable to let them go or handle the case informally.

Workplace Applications

1. INCITEMENT TO RIOT

Answers could include the following:
a. Yes, because he is using fighting words, which are not protected under the First Amendment. His use of threats are basically an assault on the police officer.

b. Yes, especially since it appears that he is succeeding in provoking the crowd to a violent reaction. This is because he is using fighting words and may also cause substantial danger by provoking a riot.

c. Yes, he can be charged with inciting a riot, and may possibly be held liable for losses to life or property that result from his involvement.

2. THE BILL OF RIGHTS

Answers could include the following:

a. Most people cannot name seven of the ten Amendments in the Bill of Rights. They can usually name the first two, but may get confused after that. Student explanations for this will vary, but most will state that American citizens do not fully understand or appreciate their rights.

b. Students' levels of surprise will vary, depending on what they expected. Many will be at least somewhat surprised by other people's lack of understanding, especially if they meet anyone who cannot adequately define even the First and Second Amendments.

c. Most people have an inadequate understanding of the Bill of Rights, which can leave them open to abuses or mistakes when they encounter the justice system. It also will leave them at least partially unaware of their rights and responsibilities as American citizens.

3. ILLEGAL ASSEMBLY

Answers could include the following:

a. This statute appears unconstitutional because it requires a chaperone for college students, who are adults and can act independently, but more importantly because it requires the school's approval and thus may be subject to arbitrary restrictions. Many students will say that they will strike down this law. Although the university has every right to refuse to issue permits, as a state university it must provide for students' rights to peaceful assembly.

b. Those who will apply the law may decide in favor of the students because their case seems just, but a strict application of the law as it stands would require the judge to decide in favor of the university.

Internet Applications

1. GAY RIGHTS

Answers could include the following:

a. Gay marriage is simply not provided for in most states because traditional concepts of marriage do not recognize it. However, a few states have recently made gay marriage expressly illegal. Generally, religious special interest groups have funded campaigns to make gay marriage illegal.

b. Yes, such prohibitions are generally the work of religious special interest groups because their beliefs prohibit homosexual relations and thus consider gay marriage a sin.

c. This affects their constitutionality because such laws violate the First Amendment's provision for the separation of church and state.

d. Since it limits one's liberty to get married, which most reasonable Americans consider to be a fundamental right, it is not constitutional.

e. Students will have different feelings about this. Some will feel that individual courts representing the wishes of their jurisdictions should decide, and others feel that the U.S. Supreme Court should make a decision on it to settle the issue.

2. DEATH PENALTY

a. This exercise will show students the life, motives, and crimes of a man that was executed for the brutal murders of two elderly men. Answers will vary; students may state that they are generally against the death penalty, but not in this case.

b. Many will agree that Boggess seemed incapable of feeling genuine remorse.

c. It is clear that he did suffer some abuse and neglect, but students will probably be divided on whether this could be considered a mitigating factor. You can point out that he claims to have Fetal Alcohol Syndrome and see how the class responds. Finally, many students will agree that he is psychopathic.

> NOTE TO INSTRUCTOR: Encourage students to read as much of this as they can; the questions and answers listed above can be considered a minimum assignment. This could be converted into a fairly large long-term or extra-credit assignment if students are required to read more of the information that has been posted.

Ethics Issues

1. ETHNICITY AND THE LAW

    Answers can include the following:

    a. Yes. Even though this particular group is responsible for much of the crime that you have seen, making assumptions without probable cause violates the individual's due process rights and right to equal protection under the law.

    b. A good rule of thumb is to make sure that you have probable cause before taking an action such as arrest.

    c. You can set an example by refusing to participate in racial profiling, talk with them about it, and talk with your supervisor about educating people about it. If the behavior does not change, police-community relations will certainly deteriorate and possible lawsuits may follow.

    d. Racial profiling can affect one's sense of liberty regarding freedom of speech and assembly, and it may also make one subject to unreasonable search and seizure.

2. DOMESTIC VIOLENCE

    Answers can include the following:

    a. One possibility is that you can persuade lawmakers to add specific definitions to this ordinance so that such problems do not occur again. You can also talk to the chief of police to ensure that all officers understand the intentions of the law, and how your amendments will address those intentions. Finally, it would be a good idea to meet with all of the women who are dissatisfied and are considering lawsuits, or perhaps meet with someone representing them, and try to remedy the situation by having investigators meet with them and determine if charges can still be filed against their perpetrators.

    b. The police should be clearly educated on the meaning of this law and any amendments that you pass to clarify it. Although most of them are making a good-faith effort to enforce the law in the best way possible, it is also possible that some do not care about or understand the importance of dealing effectively with domestic violence issues. Because of this, it needs to be made clear that they could face future legal repercussions if these duties are not fulfilled properly.

Additional Activities

Advanced Web Research

1. INTERNET

DUE PROCESS

Have students read about the ongoing and controversial treason case of Lori Berenson at *http://www.freelori.org*. Berenson has been tried and convicted of treason in Peru, and is expected to serve a 20-year sentence. She strenuously denies her guilt. Ask students to read the main page, the FAQ section, and "20 Violations of Due Process," then have them answer the following questions:

- In your opinion, does Berenson appear to be guilty? Why or why not?

- What misdeeds appear to have been committed by the Peruvian criminal justice system, and how do they violate a defendant's rights?

- Do you believe that this could occur in an American court of law? Why or why not?

Student answers will vary regarding Lori's guilt. Some will feel that she knew the chances she was taking when she decided to work as a freedom fighter in Peru; others will feel that she is innocent. Still others will feel that regardless of her guilt, she needed more due process protections than the Peruvian government gave her.

Students should be able to understand that the main due process violations are that she has been subjected to double jeopardy in the criminal courts, and the civil proceedings are not staffed by proper judges, but by military officials and people wearing hoods. Therefore, the civil trials were clearly held in kangaroo courts meant to convict her. Most students will disagree that such trials happen in the United States today, but that they probably have in the past and could happen again if due process rights are not continually protected.

2. INTERNET

EX POST FACTO LAWS

Have students read "The Case Against Civil *Ex Post Facto* Laws" by Steve Selinger at *http://www.cato.org/pubs/journal/cj15n2-3-4.html*. Have them read the opening section and the section under *"Calder v. Bull,"* then assign them the following questions:

- Why has the Supreme Court applied the *ex post facto* violation to criminal cases, but not to civil ones? What is the essential problem with *ex post facto* laws?

- In *Calder v. Bull*, what were the circumstances of the case? What was the outcome, and why?

- How does the author of this article feel about this, and what are your opinions?

There is apparently no good reason why the Supreme Court has chosen to apply the prohibition against *ex post facto* laws against criminal cases, but not civil ones. As the article states, *ex post facto* laws are "unfair and unpredictable" and "mar the American legal system and create an abundance of problems."

In *Calder v. Bull*, Calder was appointed some property under the provisions of a will. The law soon changed due to this case, and the case was retried, with the probated court deciding in favor of Bull. Calder appealed to the Supreme Court on the basis that this violated the Constitution's provision against *ex post facto* laws, but the Supreme Court rejected his claim. Most students will agree that this is unfair and that the provision against *ex post facto* laws should apply to civil proceedings as well.

3. INTERNET

FBI MOST WANTED LIST

Students visit the FBI! Have students go to *http://www.fbi.gov*, and click on "Most Wanted" to reach the current Ten Most Wanted list. Ask them to read about the ten people listed, as well as their crimes, rewards, and countries of origin. When they are done, have students answer the following questions in a one-page summary:

- Who gets chosen, and why do think this is?

- Why does the FBI have jurisdiction over certain people from other countries?

- Do you think that criminals like this are commonly seen by local, county, or state law enforcement? Why or why not?

- Do the rewards match the severity of the crimes, and do they appear to be consistent among the Top Ten criminals? Why or why not?

Students are usually fascinated by the FBI, and the FBI's Ten Most Wanted list is always interesting reading. Students will see that the crimes are varied; some involve terrorist activities, and many involve crimes against law enforcement. They should understand that people who commit terrorist crimes against the United States come under the FBI's jurisdiction, although that may not be immediately clear from the information provided. Students should note that local, county, and state law enforcement will see some of these types of crimes (such as murder, attempted murder, and organized criminal activities), but that others such as terrorism are less common. Students will disagree about whether the rewards offered are appropriate or consistent. They will, however, probably agree with the higher rewards.

Extended Workplace Applications

1. Research

Have students go online or visit their local library to try to find a detailed definition of bills of attainder. Have them answer the following questions:

- Despite the constitutional prohibition against them, do they still occur either formally or informally? How, and in what form? Use your imagination.

Students should have a relatively easy time finding a more detailed description of bills of attainder. They should be able to find specific examples of ways in which citizens still suffer under informal bills of attainder, as there are many online sources that discuss this topic. Possible forms include tax penalties that are levied without a trial, the persecution of political activists, and racial profiling that denies people liberty without probable cause.

2. Interview

Ask students to contact their local prosecutor's office and have them ask the following questions:

- Are there any methods of prosecuting people who commit crimes before they are legally made into criminal acts, without violating *ex post facto* laws. Is there anything else they can do, or do they generally have to wait until the person commits the crime again?

Students will learn that since prosecutors cannot violate *ex post facto* laws, they must either find another crime with which to charge the suspect or let the suspect go until he or she commits a legally defined crime. Prosecutors may have stories about how they were able to prosecute people on other charges, but they cannot prosecute someone for a specific action in any way unless and until that action is made criminal.

3. Report

Have students contact their local police department and have them ask the following questions:

- What are the procedures to get a permit for a public assembly?

- What are the deadlines and what limits, if any, are imposed on the assembly?

- How long does it take to get a permit? Have they ever denied someone a permit, and for what reasons?

- How do they handle issuing permits for groups that are hateful and may cause unrest?

Students should report reasonable deadlines for getting permits for public assembly. Limits may include certain time parameters, as well as reminding the assembly that they may not trespass on private property, including people's lawns. Permits should not take more than a few days to process in small municipalities, but may take longer in large cities. They may have denied people permits because they did not meet deadlines, because they had previously violated limitations in previous gatherings, or because the gathering appeared to have an unlawful purpose. Hate groups or gangs may be issued permits, and generally are protected by First Amendment rights to public assembly, as long as it is clear that their assembly does not have an unlawful purpose.

4. **Report**

Have students contact two or three local people who own or sell guns (they may be known or unknown to students personally) and have students ask them the following questions:

- How do they interpret the Second Amendment?

- What does the Amendment mean?
- How do they define a "well-regulated militia."
- Do they agree with background checks and cooling-off periods? Why or why not?

Gun owners and dealers have varying issues on this topic. Most people, when asked to explain the Second Amendment, focus on the first clause referring to the right to "keep and bear arms," but generally neglect to discuss the second clause. Students may report that their respondents were not as articulate regarding this second clause as they were regarding the first one, and some may feel that it does not pertain to private firearms but to larger weapons such as tanks and airplanes. Most people agree that background checks should be conducted, but some feel that they should be conducted quicker, with no cooling-off period.

Chapter 4

Classification of Crimes and Elements of Criminal Responsibility

KEY TERMS

crime	*mens rea*	purposely with respect to attendant circumstances	cause-in-fact
tort	motive	knowingly causes a result	but-for test
felony	specific intent	knowingly with respect to conduct and attendant circumstances	proximate cause
misdemeanor	general intent	recklessly	
petty offense	transferred intent	negligently	
actus reus	purposely with respect to result or conduct		
omissions			
possessory offenses			

Lecture Outline

4.1 CLASSIFICATION OF CRIMES
Criminal, Civil, and Moral Responsibility
Felonies, Misdemeanors, and Petty Offenses

4.2 BASIC ELEMENTS OF CRIMINAL CULPABILITY

4.3 THE PHYSICAL ACT: *ACTUS REUS*
Voluntary Action
Thoughts Versus Acts
Omissions as Acts
Words as Acts
Possession as an Act

4.4 THE MENTAL STATE: *MENS REA*
Specific Intent and General Intent
Transferred Intent
Model Penal Code Classifications of Mental States

4.5 CAUSATION AND CONCURRENCE
Cause-in-Fact and But-For Tests
Proximate and Intervening Causes
Concurrence of Elements

In-Chapter Questions

Criminal Law Online page 88

How are petty offenses, misdemeanors, and felonies defined differently as offenses? How do their punishments differ?

A felony is any serious offense, but does not have to be violent; examples include murder, rape, and racketeering. A misdemeanor is a criminal offense that is not as serious as a felony; an example is shoplifting a small item. A petty offense is a very minor offense involving a minimum of misconduct; a common example is a traffic violation.

Felonies can be punished by one year or more of imprisonment and by death. In addition, fines can be added to the term of incarceration. Misdemeanors are generally punished by fines, penalties, or incarceration of less than one year.

Photo caption page 89

How are petty offenses usually punished?

Sometimes, they are punished by a brief jail term, such as 15 days or less. More often, they are punished by fines or community service requirements.

4.1 Self Check page 90

Give one example each of a felony, misdemeanor, and petty offense. In what important ways do these offenses differ?

Answers will vary. If students neglect to name any nonviolent felonies, remind them that nonviolent felonies do occur.

The salient differences among these crimes are the level of criminal misconduct involved and the severity of the punishment.

4.2 Self Check page 91

Explain why these five elements of criminal responsibility are required.

These five elements are necessary to show that the crime did occur by the defendant with the intent to commit the crime at the time of its commission, and also to prove that the criminal act did in fact cause harm.

Ethics in Criminal Law page 92

1. Is Bert criminally culpable for the death of Jimmy?
   No, because Bert is not Jimmy's parent.

2. Should Bert be criminally culpable for the death of Jimmy?
   Many students will agree that he should be held criminal culpable because the child could have been rescued with little personal risk on Bert's part (the fact that the child sank indicates that rapids were not present). The fact that Jimmy was a child can also be seen as an aggravating factor.

 People v. Decina page 93

What other involuntary acts can you think of that could result in a conviction for criminal negligence?

Answers may vary, and can include drunk driving, violent or otherwise criminal behavior resulting from voluntary alcohol or drug use, and driving a car that has a dangerous malfunction (such as bald tires).

 Jones v. United States page 94

Does Shirley Green have any liability in this case? If so, why?

Yes, because she was the child's mother and thus had a special responsibility to care for her child's needs. Since she lived in the same home as the child, she could have seen if the child were malnourished or lacking in any other type of essential care. Allowing the friend to watch the child does not excuse her from criminal culpability.

 People v. Beardsley page 95

Does a person who does have a legal duty to protect another person have a responsibility to prevent that person from committing suicide?

This is a sticky issue because suicide is not a crime and it is an individual's decision whether to commit suicide. However, students may feel that children and adolescents should be protected from attempting suicide by parents and guardians; and that, even if a legal obligation does not exist, a moral obligation does.

 Barber v. Superior Court page 96

In what situations should a doctor, working under a patient's family's wishes, be charged with a crime?

The operative word in this question is "should." Some students will feel that doctors who participate in pulling the plug before brain death occurs should be held liable; they may also feel the same way about assisted suicide, which is a separate issue and will be discussed in Chapter 8. Some students will feel that doctors should be given more leeway to end lives that are ruined by suffering or are characterized by a long-term "vegetable" state.

4.3 Self Check page 98

1. How can omissions legally be treated as the *actus reus*?

When a person has a legal duty to act or intervene in a certain situation, such as paying taxes or providing basic care for his or her child, this failure to take action causes a criminal result and therefore is a criminal action.

2. How can words legally be treated as the *actus reus*?

When words can constitute a threat or cause further physical actions that cause harm, they are considered to be the *actus reus* as a crime. Examples of this include yelling "Fire!" in a crowded theater, causing a stampede; threatening to kill another person; or giving a speech that incites a crowd to riot.

 ***United States v. Melton* page 101**

What crimes do you think a person could be prosecuted for without intent? Should there be more?

Students will likely agree that any crimes of negligence should be prosecuted, as long as harm occurred. They will probably agree that where any harm occurs as a result of someone's actions, criminal liability should be placed upon those responsible.

Photo caption page 102

How is transferred intent used by prosecutors?

The concept of transferred intent is used to prosecute defendants who, although possessing the intent to a commit a specific crime, were not able to complete the crime exactly as intended.

 ***People v. Scott* page 103**

If Jack Gibson had only been wounded in the shooting, would transferred intent still apply, considering the defendants' aim to kill?

Since the defendants could not be certain that they would succeed in killing Hughes, and since they possessed the requisite *mens rea* to commit serious harm against Hughes, the doctrine of transferred intent would likely still apply.

Criminal Law Online page 105

How did these extended definitions help your understanding of these concepts?

Students generally find that reading differently-worded definitions and examples help give them a more complete definition of a concept. They should have a greater understanding of these concepts after completing this exercise.

 Jury Coordinator page 106

List three things you would like about being a jury coordinator and three things you think you might not like.

Answers will vary. Some will like the human relations aspect more and others will prefer the administrative aspect. Still others will like being involved in the court system, but without the responsibility of a lawyer or judge.

4.4 Self Check page 106

1. Explain the doctrine of transferred intent. Though a "legal fiction," is this doctrine valid? Why or why not?

Most students will agree that it is valid because the necessary elements of a crime are present and harm has been done. Most will believe that although the intended victim is not harmed, the defendant should be liable for the harm caused by his or her actions.

2. How do purpose and knowledge differ in regard to liability?

Purpose refers to an actor's conscious object to commit a crime, and knowledge refers to a reasonable certainty that one's conduct will cause a particular result.

4.5 Self Check page 109

1. Explain how causation is tested.

There are two steps: The accused person's act must be the cause-in-fact of the result, and if it was, the accused person's actions must also be the proximate cause of the result.

2. What concurrence of elements is necessary to constitute a crime?

There are two components: The *mens rea* and the *actus reus* must occur simultaneously, and the accused must hold the motivation to commit a specific crime.

Review and Applications

Questions For Review

1. How can some actions be torts and crimes at the same time, and what is the essential difference between torts and crimes?

An act is a tort and a crime at the same time when it can be punished under both criminal and civil law. You can refer students to the example in the textbook, in which a drunken driver who kills a pedestrian can be liable for criminal punishment for the harm caused and also for civil damages for the expenses caused by such harm. Courts have supported cases in which defendants have been required to pay for medical and/or funeral expenses incurred by the harm they have caused.

The two main differences between a tort and a crime are as follows:

- A crime is committed against the community at large, but a tort is a wrong against specific individuals only. This is why civil suits have plaintiffs, but not prosecutors.

- The consequences of tort liability are less than the consequences of criminal liability because a party in a civil suit does not face the possibility of punishment, such as loss of liberty or life. Although many people would consider punitive damages a form of punishment, it is not considered equivalent to incarceration or the stigma of conviction.

2. What is a voluntary, willed act?

A voluntary, willed act is one in which the person who committed it possesses sufficient free will to exercise choice and be responsible for his or her conduct. Even if a person who has acted voluntarily later regrets the act, he or she is still held responsible. This requirement is consistent with the fundamental principle of individuality upon which the Anglo-American legal system is based.

3. What is the difference between thinking about committing an act and acting upon the thought?

This difference is essential to understanding how *actus reus* works. Although a person cannot be punished for thinking about committing a crime, if he or she actually acts on that thought and commits the physical acts connected to the thought, he or she will be liable for the crime committed. Everybody can think of times when they were angry with someone and wished that something bad happened to them. However, even if something bad did happen to that person, the person who only thought about harming him or her would not be criminally responsible.

4. How do *actus reus* and *mens rea* work together to create a criminal act?

They create concurrence, which is another element necessary for a crime to have been committed. The *actus reus* and the *mens rea* must occur concurrently for the defendant to be held criminally liable for his or her actions.

5. Why must an act be voluntary to be a crime, and how does this work in situations where a person commits a voluntary act with involuntary consequences (such as drunk driving)?

If an act is not voluntary in any way, then the person lacks the criminal intent necessary for him or her to be criminally liable. If, however, he or she voluntarily engages in an action that may cause harm, such as drunk driving, he or she will be responsible for any harm that results.

6. When does an omission constitute an act for purposes of criminal responsibility?

This can occur in two situations:

Where the definition of a crime specifically designates an omission as punishable. Examples of this include failure to register for the draft or failure to file an income tax return.

Where a person has an affirmative duty to act in some way but fails to do so, and such failure causes a criminal result. An example of this is child neglect.

7. When do words alone constitute a criminal act?

Words constitute a criminal act when they cause harm or the possibility of harm to others.

Common examples of this are yelling, "Fire!" in a crowded theater, threatening to kill someone, or making a speech that incites a riot. Other examples include hate speech or making a statement such as "He's got a gun!" in a crowd.

8. Explain the difference between motive and intent.

Motive, which is a term sometimes used to mean intent, usually means the emotion prompting a person to act. It is slightly different from intent, which is the mental state that a person possesses when they make a voluntary choice to commit a criminal act. Nonetheless, motive is often important as a matter of proof because it may help to identify the perpetrator of a crime or explain why a suspect may have acted in a particular way.

9. Explain the doctrine of transferred intent.

This doctrine holds a person criminally liable even when the consequence of his or her action is not what the actor actually intended. The transferred intent doctrine exists to ensure that a person is punished for his or her criminal culpability, even though the intended harm was directed at the wrong person accidentally. In other words, if a perpetrator is a lousy shot or steals from the wrong address, that should not make him or her free from guilt.

10. What is the difference between the MPC's definition of acting purposely and acting knowingly?

When a perpetrator acts purposely with respect to result or conduct, it is his or her voluntary wish to act in a certain conduct or produce a certain result. When a person acts purposely with respect to attendant circumstances, he or she is aware of conditions that will make the intended crime possible, or believes or hopes that they exist.

A person knowingly causes a result if he or she knows or is practically certain that his or her conduct will cause this result. A person acts knowingly with respect to conduct and attendant circumstances if he or she knows that his or her actions are criminal, or that attendant circumstances made an otherwise legal act a criminal one.

11. According to the MPC, when does a person act recklessly? What about negligently?

According to the MPC, a person acts recklessly if he or she voluntarily ignores a substantial and unjustified risk that a certain circumstance exists or will result from the reckless conduct. A risk is considered substantial and unjustified if a reasonable law-abiding citizen considers it a clear deviation from how a reasonable person would behave.

A person acts negligently if he or she should be aware that a substantial and unjustifiable risk exists or will result from the negligent conduct. As with recklessness, the risk involved for negligence must be substantial and unjustifiable. The difference between negligence and recklessness is that the reckless person consciously disregards the risk, but a negligent person's does so unknowingly.

Problem-Solving Exercises

1. HAZARDOUS WASTE
   Answers could include the following:
   - No, unless he was a responsible actor in this behavior before purchasing the company. If he was not previously involved, he cannot be retroactively involved in the company's misdeeds. He can, however, be held responsible for concealing evidence of past misdeeds if he committed any such actions upon purchasing the company.
   - Yes, because as owner of the company he is responsible for its operations. Even if he acts with willful blindness to the company's misdeeds, he is still ultimately responsible for its actions.

2. BATTERY
   Answers could include the following:
   - Yes, because his actions constitute an unlawful application of force when he held Brittany and refused to let her go. The *mens rea* is more complicated: Although he did not consciously intend to commit a crime, his actions still constituted a crime.

- Students will be divided on this. Some will feel that he should be charged, but others will feel that he should just get a warning. You could also suggest that Josh be charged with assault, which can be defined as offensive touching. This may suit the situation best.

Workplace Applications

1. DECIDING ON CHARGES

Answers could include the following:

a. The suspect's attitude is remorseful and he does not have a criminal record, which are factors that should mitigate (lessen) his charges. On the other hand, he has a weapon. Although he did not plan on using it, this is a serious issue because even an unloaded weapon may cause substantial fear. Many students will pick attempted burglary as a felony because it is a compromise: The weapon makes it too serious to be a misdemeanor, but his behavior and the situation makes it unlike other armed burglaries. Some students, however, may prefer the other choices.

b. Most students would charge him with aggravated attempted burglary if there were aggravating factors such as these.

2. DECIDING ON DEFENSE

Answers could include the following:

a. The elements of *actus reus* and *mens rea* are both present, and there is a unity of both factors. Although the defendant had abandoned her original plans when she met her aunt, what is important is that she possessed the intent to steal the jewelry at the time of the criminal act.

b. Yes, because the jewelry was stolen by a defendant who had no apparent intention of returning it.

Internet Applications

1. TAKE THE ROLE OF THE PROSECUTOR

Answers could include the following:

a. Many students would agree that the ship captain and any other responsible individuals should be charged with criminal negligence, and that Exxon should be sued in civil court.

b. As mentioned in the last answer, they could be prosecuted either way. You may want to explain that individuals are generally prosecuted and companies are held responsible for civil damages.

c. Some students may feel that Exxon was not sanctioned strongly enough for the *Valdez* crash, especially since they did not pay for the entire clean-up. Some will feel that the sanctions were adequate.

d. Most students would state that they should be solely responsible for the clean-up cost, but that the government or a disinterested third party should manage it.

2. RESEARCH LIABILITY OFFENSES

Answers could include the following:

a. Students need to realize that all that is needed to impose criminal liability is a fulfillment of the elements of that particular crime. In other words, if the defendant has committed an act that contains all of the elements of a crime, he or she can be charged with it. Civil action can be used in tandem with criminal prosecution, or in instances where the evidence cannot be proven "beyond a reasonable doubt."

b. Most students will agree that they would impose strict liability, although some would allow for special circumstances, such as when a vessel unexpectedly hits another object. You can ask students how strict liability would work as a general deterrent and as a specific deterrent. (They should remember these concepts from their Introduction to Criminal Justice course; if not, you can refresh their memories.)

c. If they can prove charges other than negligence, yes. If they cannot prove anything else, and the negligence charges will not stand up to scrutiny in a criminal court (due to lack of hard evidence or otherwise), the best option may be a civil action.

3. THE KITTY GENOVESE CASE

Answers could include the following:

a. Although an estimated 38 people heard her cries, nobody called the police or attempted to physically stop the attack. One neighbor did yell at her assailant to stop, but it did not help.

b. The neighbors generally gave poor, selfish excuses, such as the woman who stated that her English was not good and she is not the police. Most students will show disgust at their excuses. If any students feel that they were justified, ask them why they did not at least call the police.

c. After this crime was committed, the rest of the United States was outraged at the neighbors' refusal to help Kitty. However, the focus was less on whether to make this behavior a crime and more on the need for American communities to be more caring and cohesive. Ask the students which is more important, and which would work best if such a situation happened again.

Ethics Issue

CHILD NEGLECT

Answers can include the following:

a. Since the child's life has been severely endangered, and the mother is unable to change her mental infirmity, it would be best to place the child in foster care. However, since the mother lacks intent, imprisonment may constitute cruel and unusual punishment for her. Most students will agree that the child should be removed from the home, but many will also agree that the mother should be punished.

b. No, she does not appear to possess the *mens rea*, even for negligence. This should be a key factor in determining the sentence she receives. Although her lack of *mens rea* should affect her punishment, it does not change the fact that the child has been neglected. Indeed, her mental condition makes it fairly certain that the child would be neglected again if he were returned to her care.

Advanced Web Research

1. INTERNET

MODEL PENAL CODE

Have students check out "Penal Law: A Web" at *http://wings.buffalo.edu/law/bclc/web/cover.html*. Be sure to tell them to bookmark this site for future reference. Under "Statutes and Other Penal Norms," have them click on the "Analytical Structure" section under the Model Penal Code. Ask students to read this outline, then answer the following questions:

- How do the provisions of the Model Penal Code break down the elements of a crime and the behavior related to the elements of the offense? Does this make sense to you? Why or why not?

- What questions and issues are covered under the "Illegality" section? How does this section affect the penal code, and why is it important?

This breakdown may be hard for students to understand. Show them how it covers the jurisdiction requirements, the elements of crime and whether the behavior fits the required elements, and defenses based upon justification and excuse.

Under the Illegality section, the questions that are first asked are meant to confirm whether the behavior is actually legal and a crime has actually been committed. After that, it breaks down the justifications into general and specific ones, as well as mistakes.

2. INTERNET

PETTY OFFENSES, MISDEMEANORS, AND FELONIES

Have students visit "Petty Offenses, Misdemeanors, and Felonies–What Class am I In?" at FreeAdvice.com, located at *http://criminal-law.freeadvice.com/offenses_misdemeanors.html*. Assign students the following questions:

- Why is the class of a crime important?

- Do petty offenders have the same amount of protections as felons? Why or why not?

Students should be able to understand that the class of a crime is important because it affects the type of punishment that the defendant receives. Petty offenders usually receive fines, but not loss of liberty. Misdemeanants may lose their liberty for a short time, and felons may lose their liberty permanently, either through a life sentence or death.

Petty offenders do not have the same protections as felons because they do not stand to lose as much if convicted of the charge(s) against them.

3. INTERNET

TRANSFERRED INTENT

Have students read the brief discussion of transferred intent as it applies to the New York State court system, at *http://www.courts.state.ny.us/cji/art125ti.htm#2*. Have students answer the following questions in a class discussion:

- If a court determines that transferred intent applies to the charge in question, explain in detail what the court should provide.

- Under what circumstances does it not matter whether the intent was transferred? Why do you think this is the case?

Students should express an understanding that if the court determines that such a charge applies, it should provide a transferred intent charge, which should make clear the statutory requirements which relate to the intended victim or the defendant's intent.

It does not matter whether intent was transferred if the victim is a police or correctional officer. This is because such officers work together as a unit and represent the same common cause; therefore, any attack on one is considered an equally serious crime.

Extended Workplace Applications

1. Interview

Have students contact their local prosecutor's office, whether at the county or state level. Have students ask them the following questions:

- Does their jurisdiction provide for any crimes that can be tried as felonies or misdemeanors, depending on the circumstances? (It does.)

- What are some examples?

- What factors determine whether an offense is charges as a felony or misdemeanor?

Students should be able to name several different offenses that can be tried as misdemeanors, such as different types of theft, larceny, and violent offenses such as assault and battery. Factors that determine differences in how these crimes are charged include the defendant's age, prior record, attitude, and level of remorse, as well as whether the defendant carried or used a weapon.

2. Group Activity

This is a good small-group exercise: Have students get together with three of four other students and, without them looking at each other's papers, have each student write a definition of *mens rea* in their own words. Then, have students compare their definitions with each other, and question each other about any differences in meaning. Next, students must agree on a single definition and share it with the rest of the class, explaining why they defined it in the way that they did. If time permits, students may debate their definitions with other groups.

This exercise illustrates the difficulties in understanding the true meaning of intent. Although intent appears to be a simple concept, different people have different concrete definitions of it. However, most students' definitions should come close to the correct definition. If any are incorrect or overly vague, you can refer them to the textbook definition and ask them to explain what that means.

3. Research

Have students contact their local prosecutor and ask if their local penal code categorizes *mens rea* in the traditional way (by labeling it as different forms of intent, such as general intent) or according to the Model Penal Code's classifications regarding purpose and knowledge. Students should ask them why they consider this particular system preferable in defining intent, and what problems arise when defining intent in vague situations, such as when a person shows willful blindness while transporting drugs.

This exercise will help students understand the reasoning behind why some jurisdictions model certain statutes after the Model Penal Code, but not others. Regardless of which style this jurisdiction has chosen, the reasons will be the same: ease and clarity. Lawmakers seek laws that are easy to understand and that lack vagueness.

Regarding situations in which intent may be hard to define, prosecutors may use circumstantial evidence or may try to catch the defendant in making a lie or giving contradictory testimony.

4. Interview

Have students contact their local police department and ask to name the most common petty offenses that they handle. Then have students ask them the following questions:

- Why do these offenses occur so often?

- How do they treat misdemeanors differently from petty offenses?

- Are people ever arrested for petty offenses?

Student answers will vary, but most will name various traffic violations, jaywalking, and littering, among several other petty offenses. These offenses occur frequently because people either do not care about what they are doing or do not realize that they are going to get caught for it. In essence, all of these offenses occur because it is more convenient for the defendant to drive a little faster, cut across the street before reaching the crosswalk, or throw something away before finding a trash can. These offenses are generally handled through a ticket, and misdemeanors are generally handled through police reports. People are generally not arrested for petty offenses.

Parties to a Crime

Chapter Resources

For the Instructor
Instructor's Resource Manual, pp. 41–52
Additional Activities, p. 50
PowerPoint Presentation and ExamView Pro Testbank
  CD-ROM for Chapter 5
cl.glencoe.com Web site

For the Student
Student Edition, Chapter 5, pp. 116–157
Review and Applications, p. 152
Tutorial with Simulation Applications
  CD-ROM for Chapter 5
cl.glencoe.com Web site

KEY TERMS

accomplice
aid and abet
accomplice liability
principal
accessory
principal in the first degree
principal in the second
  degree

constructive presence
accessory before the fact
accessory after the fact
criminal facilitation
agent provocateur
entrapment
natural and probable
  consequences doctrine

innocent agent or
  instrumentality
nonproxyable offense
conspiracy
agency theory
Pinkerton doctrine

Lecture Outline

5.1 THE ROLE OF THE ACCOMPLICE
Common Law Distinctions
Modern Parties to a Crime

5.2 *ACTUS REUS* OF ACCOMPLICE LIABILITY
Affirmative Acts
Acts of Omission
Accountability

5.3 *MENS REA* OF ACCOMPLICE LIABILITY
Purpose and Knowledge
Agents Provocateurs and Entrapment

5.4 EXTENT OF ACCOMPLICE LIABILITY
Natural and Foreseeable Consequences
Negligent Acts

5.5 RELATIONSHIP BETWEEN THE PRINCIPAL ACTOR AND THE ACCOMPLICE
Innocent Agent or Instrumentality
Feigning Primary Party
When the Principal Actor is Acquitted

5.6 ISSUES IN ACCOMPLICE LIABILITY
Limitations of and Defenses to Complicity:
  Abandonment
Accomplice Liability versus Conspiracy:
  The *Pinkerton* Doctrine
How Far Should Accomplice Liability
  Reach?

In-Chapter Questions

5.1 Self Check page 121

1. What is the difference between a principal in the first degree and a principal in the second degree?

   A principal in the first degree is usually the primary actor or perpetrator of the crime. A principal in the second degree is one who intentionally assists in the commission of a crime in his or her presence; in other words, he or she is an accomplice.

2. What is constructive presence? How is someone who is constructively present at a crime scene charged?

   Constructive presence occurs when an individual is within the vicinity of a crime and is able to assist the primary actor if necessary. For example, one who waits in the getaway car, or who acts as a lookout, is constructively present at the scene of the crime. People offering constructive presence to a crime are charged as principals in the second degree.

Criminal Law Online page 123

Explore this site and determine how child abuse laws and American society's awareness of child abuse is changing—and still needs to change.

Students should report that Americans' awareness of child abuse and tolerance of excessive corporal punishment have changed greatly, and that children have more rights and protections than in the past. Sadly, though, much child abuse still goes unreported or improperly handled by the justice system.

People v. Stanciel page 123

If there were no court order requiring Burgos to keep Stanciel away from her child, would she still be found liable as an accomplice? Why or why not?

Yes, she still would be found liable as an accomplice because, as the child's parent, she had a special responsibility to protect that child from abuse.

Photo Caption page 125

How do these two people demonstrate the *actus reus* of committing a crime?

The principal actor, is demonstrating the *actus reus* of committing this robbery by actually committing the robbery. The accomplice, is demonstrating the *actus reus* of committing this robbery because he is physically present to aid and facilitate the robbery by watching out for police.

5.2 Self Check page 126

Under the MPC, what are the three factors that, individually or together, determine if a person is an accomplice?

The MPC provides that a person is an accomplice if he or she:

- solicits another to commit a crime.
- "aids or agrees or attempts to aid such other person in planning or committing" a crime.
- has a legal duty to prevent the commission of a crime, but "fails to make proper effort to do so."

State v. Gladstone page 128

To what extent should people be liable to prevent crimes from occurring?

Legally, people who do not fit the definitions of principals or accomplices, and thus have no interest in the outcome of a crime, are not obliged to attempt to prevent crime. Many students, though, will feel that people have a moral obligation to do so. Whether this moral obligation should be a law is a controversial issue.

Ethics in Criminal Law page 130

1. What can such an officer do to make sure that the suspect already has the intent to commit a crime without the officer's assistance?

   An officer can avoid making statements that encourage the commission of criminal acts not already contemplated by the suspect, focus on crimes that the suspect is planning and wishes to commit regardless of the officer's involvement in them, and avoid providing materials and assistance that are needed for the crime to take place. Students will likely think of several other suggestions.

2. How can the officer be sure that the suspect would be committing the criminal acts regardless of the officer's involvement?

Again, the officer has to let the suspect's own statements indicate an independent desire to commit this crime, regardless of the officer's involvement in it. In addition, the officer should not supply anything that is necessary for the crime to take place because he or she should not take any efforts that will make the crime actually occur.

3. What, if any, are a prosecutor's options when it appears that entrapment has occurred?

Depending on the circumstances, a prosecutor may still be able to charge the defendant with conspiracy or with other crimes in which the officer did not entrap the defendant.

 Wilson v. People page 131

Should private citizens be allowed to use the defense of agent provocateur if they are trying to "get even" with someone?

Many students will feel that such behavior is a manipulation of the justice system. However, the nature of the role of agents provocateurs is that they do not inspire the idea to commit a crime; they are simply posing as accomplices to someone who already wanted to commit a particular crime. Therefore, even if the agent provocateur's motive is a petty one, he or she could be a valuable aid to law enforcement by providing eyewitness testimony.

 United States v. Twigg page 132

What implications does the *Twigg* decision have for law enforcement?

It shows that law enforcement may not create crime for the sake of arresting and convicting suspects. The defendant in *Twigg* went far beyond the role of an agent provocateur and showed clearly what types of behavior will constitute entrapment.

5.3 Self Check page 133

1. What is the difference between purpose and knowledge?

Purpose, which is the mental state of intent, makes one liable as an accomplice. Mere knowledge that one's act may facilitate a crime, on the other hand, does not necessarily prove

accomplice liability if the defendant lacks the required mental state of purpose to advance the commission of the criminal offense.

2. Define an agent provocateur, and explain how an agent provocateur differs from one who commits entrapment.

An agent provocateur, or feigning accomplice, wishes to set up the principal and intends for the principal to fail in his or her illegal venture. Because of the causation factor, such an individual is not an accomplice.

The difference between the agent provocateur and the entrapper is that an agent provocateur will get involved with the criminal actions of a suspect who would have carried on his or her criminal activity anyway, but an entrapper will induce a person to commit a crime that this person would not have or could not have committed the crime without the officer's aid or involvement.

 People v. Luparello page 134

In this case, of what crime is the murder a "natural and probable consequence"?

Although it is not clear, it seems that Luparello wished to harm his ex-girlfriend; indeed, it seems odd that Martin would have been killed if Luparello only wished to speak with her or wish her luck. If this is the case, the original planned crime could be attempted battery, attempted aggravated battery, or attempted murder.

 Echols v. State page 136

Why do you think the prosecutor chose to charge Arthur as an accomplice if she could have been convicted as a principal?

Although it is not certain that Arthur Echols would have been convicted as a principal, the fact remains that the intent requirement would have been better satisfied and a conviction was a strong possibility. Perhaps the prosecutor was used to charging nonabusing but criminally liable parents as accomplices, since it is reasonable to see their role as such. Perhaps he or she did not have the time or resources to consider other options.

5.4 Self Check page 137

1. For what does the natural and probable consequences doctrine hold an accomplice liable?

   This doctrine holds an accomplice liable for the offense he or she intended to facilitate or encourage, and also for any reasonably foreseeable offense committed by the person he or she aids and abets. Therefore, liability may also reach beyond the crime planned or intended if additional acts (such as shooting someone who tries to call the police) are committed in the normal course of a crime.

2. What is a natural and foreseeable consequence?

   Although "natural and foreseeable consequence" is a vague term, in general, any additional criminal act that is necessary to accomplish the criminal goal will be considered a natural and foreseeable consequence.

 ### United States v. Walsar page 140

What are some other scenarios where a person can be charged with another actor's nonproxyable offense?

Other possible examples listed in the textbook are rape and being drunk and disorderly in public, although both of these may be interpreted either way.

 ### Vaden v. State page 142

Did the Department of Fish and Wildlife officer commit entrapment? Why or why not?

No, because the idea of having Vaden facilitate illegal hunting practices did not originate with the officer. Vaden was already committing this illegal behavior when the officer approached him.

Photo caption page 143

Is this undercover officer, who is posing here as a drug dealer, guilty of entrapment if he succeeds in selling drugs to this person? Why or why not?

Most people would agree that the officer would be guilty of entrapment because the girls are clearly initially uninterested in buying drugs. If they change their minds and buy drugs, a jury could reasonably believe that it was solely due to the persuasion of the undercover officer.

 ### Undercover Police Investigator page 145

What kind of special training should undercover officers receive?

They should receive specialized training in surveillance techniques and espionage, and should have a full understanding of ethical issues such as entrapment, corruption, and the ethical management of informants before beginning their undercover work.

 ### People v. Eberhardt page 146

Would the husband in this case have been found guilty as an accomplice under common law?

No, because under common law, when the principal was acquitted the accomplice generally escaped criminal liability as well.

5.5 Self Check page 146

1. What is a feigning primary party?

   The feigning primary party is a principal who pretends to have the required intent to be culpable of a crime, but does not actually possess this intent. In the case of undercover police work, a feigning primary party can set up willing accomplices for arrest by pretending to commit any type of crime.

2. Why have the laws changed for convicting accomplices in cases where, for whatever reason, the principal is acquitted?

   Although an accomplice will usually escape liability if the principal is acquitted, modern laws enable the prosecution of individuals for aiding and abetting another in the commission of a crime as long as the prosecutor could prove that a crime was actually committed. This is to prevent accomplices who are clearly guilty from escaping punishment due to different individual circumstances that led to the principal's acquittal.

Criminal Law Online page 147

Should accomplice liability be imposed on a company that sells a dangerous product if it can be proven that it is likely that that product will be used to injure or kill someone?

Many students will agree that such companies should be required to screen all potential customers to ensure that they do not have a criminal record, and many will agree that all potential customers should have a "cool-down" period before being allowed to purchase such an item. This is commonly the case with weapons purchases. If the companies do not fulfill these requirements, students will likely agree that they should face criminal prosecution.

 Regina v. Richards page 147

If the two men had killed the husband, what crimes would each of the parties involved be charged with?

Students will probably answer that the defendant should still be convicted of felony assault, since that was her intent, and the two men that she hired should be convicted of murder. However, you should explain to students that (as they will learn in Chapter 8, Criminal Homicide), people who intend to cause another person "grievous bodily harm" but end up being responsible for that person's death are generally guilty of possessing implied malice aforethought, which generally results in a second-degree murder charge. Since the two men also possessed this level of malice, they would likely be charged the same way also.

 Pinkerton v. United States page 150

Should co-conspirators be charged for crimes that they have no knowledge of? Why or why not?

Student answers will vary. Some will feel that this is unfair because a person should not be responsible for all of the actions of their co-conspirators, but others will feel that those who willingly engage in criminal conspiracies should share equal responsibility for that conspiracy.

5.6 Self Check page 151

1. What must a person do to legally abandon an agreement to commit a crime and end his or her liability as an accomplice?

The accomplice must clearly inform the principal of his or her intent to withdraw support and communicate the lack of a shared common intent for the crime to be committed. Additionally, the accomplice must attempt to make ineffectual any aid given to the principal that facilitates the commission of the offense,

such as by taking back any maps, tools, or weapons that were to be used in committing the offense.

2. What is agency theory, and how does it relate to the *Pinkerton* doctrine?

Agency theory holds that all conspirators act as the agent of (or represent) the other conspirators involved in the criminal scheme and are liable for all criminal acts committed by other co-conspirators. The *Pinkerton* doctrine holds a person associated with a conspiracy culpable for any criminal act committed by a co-conspirator if the act is within the scope of the conspiracy and is a foreseeable result of the criminal scheme. Therefore, the *Pinkerton* doctrine provides some definition for which acts co-conspirators may be liable under agency theory.

Review and Applications

Questions For Review

1. What are the two categories of accessories and principals?

The two categories of each are: principal in the first degree and principal in the second degree, and accessory before the fact and accessory after the fact.

2. How are accessories after the fact treated differently than principals under modern law?

Accessories after the fact are generally charged with lesser offenses because they did not participate in the commission of the crime, but only have aided and abetted the principal(s) and accomplice(s) after the crime was completed.

3. How significant must one's actions be for one to be culpable as an accomplice?

Like the principal, the accomplice must fulfill the *actus reus* requirement of criminal liability. A person may be culpable as an accomplice if he or she physically helps with the commission of a crime, or if he or she does as little as offering words of encouragement. What makes a person liable for any such action is his or her intentional participation in the criminal goal, voluntary identification with the primary actor, and willing consent to the same liability.

4. What is the difference between an agent provocateur and one who commits entrapment?

The difference between the agent provocateur and the entrapper is that:

- An agent provocateur will get involved with
the criminal actions of a suspect who would
have carried on his or her criminal activity
whether the agent provocateur had never
been involved. Therefore, the idea of the
crime did not originate with the agent
provocateur.

- An entrapper will induce a person to commit
a crime that this person would not have or
could not have commited without the officer's
aid or involvement.

5. What is the nonproxyable offense theory of
doctrine of innocent agency?

One instance in which the doctrine of innocent instrumentality is difficult to apply occurs
where the nonproxyable offense theory applies
instead. A nonproxyable offense is a crime that
can only be performed by the person himself or
herself, not through an agent of any kind.
However, this theory runs into problems of its
own, such as when a person places a drunk
person in public without the drunk person's
consent or when a person compels another to
rape somebody.

6. Can an accomplice still be convicted even when a
principal is acquitted? Why or why not?

Yes, in some circumstances. Some examples
are:

- The principal is a feigning primary party. In
such instances, if entrapment cannot be proven,
any accomplice to this feigning primary party
will be liable and may be convicted.

- The principal has a legal excuse that allows
him or her to avoid liability by virtue of a
condition that the accomplice lacks. Such
excuses include duress, insanity, infancy, and
involuntary intoxication.

Acquitting the principal in such situations is
acceptable because the principal does not possess the required *mens rea* or because he or she
is part of a class of people that are legally
excused, such as the underaged. However, these
personal excuses do not apply to accomplices,
so accomplice liability still applies.

7. What is the difference between a feigning accomplice (agent provocateur) and a feigning primary
party?

When primary actors receive assistance from
someone who actually wishes to set them up,
this type of accomplice is known as a feigning
accomplice (or agent provocateur). Such an
accomplice actually *intends* for the principal to
fail in his or her illegal venture, and is therefore
not an accomplice because he or she does not
intend that the underlying crime be completed
successfully. A feigning primary party is a principal who pretends to have the required intent
to be culpable of a crime, but does not actually
possess this intent. In the case of undercover
police work, a feigning primary party can set up
willing accomplices for arrest by pretending to
commit any type of crime.

Both types of feigning parties are often chal-
lenged when defendants claim that they have
been entrapped, which is sometimes true.

8. How can an accomplice abandon an agreement to
aid a crime?

To effectually sever a criminal agreement, the
accomplice must clearly inform the principal of
his or her intent to withdraw support and communicate the lack of a shared common intent
for the crime to be committed. Silent renunciation is not enough; the intent to abandon must
be communicated clearly in writing or in
words, in such a way that the co-conspirator(s)
will receive and understand them. The accomplice must also take back or render ineffectual
any aid given to the principal that facilitates the
commission of the offense, such as by taking
back any maps, tools, or weapons that are
needed to commit the offense. Ideally, the
accomplice should also contact the police if he
or she believes that the crime will still occur
without his or her involvement.

9. What is a conspiracy?

Basically, a conspiracy is a partnership in
crime; it is also called a common criminal enterprise. Either way, this means that it is an agreement between two or more people to achieve a
criminal purpose or to achieve a lawful purpose
using unlawful means. This usually involves an
ongoing, organized criminal activity, such as illegal gambling, distribution of drugs, or a series of

robberies. Criminal liability for co-conspirators differs from that for standard accomplices because, to be guilty of conspiracy, the co-conspirator must actually agree to the ongoing criminal enterprise, not only to single crimes.

10. What are agency theory and the *Pinkerton* doctrine?

Agency theory is a form of extended conspiratorial liability, which holds that all conspirators act as the agent of (or represent) the other conspirators involved in the criminal scheme and are liable for all criminal acts committed by other co-conspirators.

The *Pinkerton* doctrine is a variation of agency theory. It holds a person associated with a conspiracy culpable for any criminal act committed by a co-conspirator, if the act is within the scope of the conspiracy and is a foreseeable result of the criminal scheme. The theory of prosecution is not based on a claim that the conspirator assisted the perpetrator in the planning or commission of the offenses; rather, the conspirator's liability is based on his or her prior agreement, as a conspirator, to the perpetrator's criminal activity.

Problem-Solving Exercises

1. ACCOMPLICE OR NOT?
   Answers could include the following:
   a. Yes, she can be convicted. She may also be liable as part of a conspiracy, or continuing criminal enterprise.

   b. She can be convicted as an accomplice because she had knowledge of the ongoing crimes and physically aided him in selling drugs.

   c. No, because her actions were substantial enough in aiding Ron in his drug transactions.

2. AN ABANDONED CRIME?
   Answers could include the following:
   a. Tim is not really an accomplice because he clearly abandoned the crime. However, giving his friend an unregistered weapon, even if it was years ago, is a crime in its own right and one for which he is legally liable. Although Tim clearly forgot about the gun

or did not think it would be used in the robbery, he is still responsible for giving it to Paul. Therefore, a prosecutor may still opt to charge him as an accomplice, although Tim could fight this and gain an acquittal.

b. Tim clearly shows a lack of intent to aid in the commission of this crime. However, the unregistered gun poses other problems that may affect his liability.

c. Tim should be charged with having possessed an unregistered weapon and giving it to Paul, and Paul should also be charged with being in possession of such a weapon (in addition to his robbery charge). Many students will agree that Tim should not be charged as an accomplice because he clearly made a good-faith effort to avoid being involved in the crime.

3. GUILTY OF CHILD ABUSE
   Answers could include the following:
   a. Since the husband has a special duty as the child's parent to report any child abuse of which he has knowledge, he is guilty.

   b. It is not adequate as an excuse for not calling the police, although battered spouses are sometimes psychologically unable to take responsible actions to end the abuse of their children. However, depending on the size and personality of the wife in relation to the husband, it may be an adequate excuse for why a spouse may not physically intervene while a beating is taking place. This may not stand up in this case, because the husband's decision to engage in recreational drug use indicates callousness toward the situation.

Workplace Applications

1. ACCOMPLICE LIABILITY
   Students may be divided as to whether she should be charged. Those who are in favor with charging her would likely point out that she would have been informed by her employer that she should not give out confidential information, and that this was common sense. They also would doubt that being a teller is an important position worth bragging about. On the other hand, some students may feel that

she was genuinely naïve and did not realize what she was doing. In any event, you may want to suggest to the students that they need to question others at the bank to see if she has been acting suspiciously, or question her further to see if she contradicts herself or cannot stand up to more detailed questioning.

2. DEFINING AN ACCOMPLICE
Answers could include the following:
a. Jurisdictions that choose to hold people with knowledge of crimes liable do so as a preventive measure. Those that choose to not hold such people liable are usually trying to avoid net-widening, because sometimes people hear about criminal plans but do not think that they will actually occur or do not believe what they hear about crimes that have already occurred.

b. Answers will vary, depending on the emphasis on punishment and law enforcement found in that jurisdiction. A jurisdiction that is committed to low crime and a high level of law enforcement service may be more satisified with holding people with knowledge of a crime liable than would be a jurisdiction that is more concerned with maintaining the status quo and taking a "hands off" approach to lesser criminals.

c. Most place will agree that their law could use further modifications for special circumstances, although not all such circumstances will be foreseeable and thus cannot be addressed until they occur.

3. PRINCIPAL IN THE SECOND DEGREE
Answers could include the following:
a. Students will give different opinions of this. For instance, why did the defendant greet Recia? Out of carelessness, because he didn't think about committing the crime until the moment it occurred, or as a signal to her that he was present? Also, why would Recia be afraid of pressing the secret alarm unless she knew that he was already aware of its existence? Several other questions will probably come up.

b. Ideally, it would be best to further question Recia, question the witnesses to see if Recia could have pressed the button at any time

without the defendant seeing her, and question the defendant about his relationship with Recia. If Recia lied about her relationship with him, she could be charged with perjury and as an accomplice.

Internet Applications

1. **Work on Key Terms**
Answers could include the following:
a. Students usually like Nolo.com because its topics are easy to read and understand. They will generally state that they liked reading about these concepts in a slightly different context, and that it helped give them a more well-rounded understanding of the key terms.

b. Answers will vary, but given Nolo.com's emphasis on basic legal knowledge, they should not be unusually difficult questions or answers.

c. Many students will state that it is more complex than they imagined, but you can ask them if it isn't actually *simpler* for them to have an understanding of how the law works than to labor under the myths and misunderstandings that surround criminal legal issues. Some students will anticipate such a question and state that criminal law has become easier for them to fathom than before.

Ethics Issues

AIDING AND ABETTING
Answers can include the following:
a. Many students will agree that it would be best to play along with the sister to avoid arousing her suspicions and perhaps provoking the nephew to go into hiding, but to report the case to law enforcement anyway. Some will feel that it is best to keep quiet since the nephew will receive a harsh sentence, and others feel it is best to be honest to the mother and contact the police.

b. Yes, she is aiding and abetting her son. She is also liable for attempting to lure the aunt into aiding and abetting him. Her actions are known as misprision of a felony, a crime that is discussed in Chapter 15.

Additional Activities

Advanced Web Research

1. INTERNET

MENS REA

Have students read about *People v. Russell* at Cornell University's Legal Information Institute at *http://www.law.cornell.edu/ny/ctap/comments/i98_0003.html*. Tell them to read the entire article, including the Commentary. Then have students write a paragraph to answer the following questions:

- What was the main issue in this case?

- What did the court find, and how did it reach this conclusion?

Students should understand that the main issue was whether all three of the defendants were equally guilty in the shooting murder of a school principal whom they shot simultaneously. The court found all three defendants guilty of second degree, depraved indifference murder. Students should understand that the court reached this conclusion because it was clear that the defendants had the requisite *mens rea* for committing this crime and intentionally aided each other.

NOTE TO INSTRUCTOR: The Legal Information Institute at Cornell University is an excellent resource for all students. You can point out to them that the site's main page can be found at *http://www.law.cornell.edu*, and encourage them to visit and explore it.

2. INTERNET

CONSPIRACY

Have students read Alabama's criminal code regarding criminal conspiracy, which is covered under Section 13A-4-3, at *http://www.legislature.state.al.us/CodeofAlabama/1975/13A-4-3.html*. Have students write down any questions they may have regarding the terms or concepts and discuss them in class. Then have students answer the following questions:

- When is a person guilty of criminal conspiracy? Of accomplice liability?

- How are conspiracies charged in relation to the crimes that a person conspires to commit (see the list at the bottom of the page)?

- Why do you think that Alabama charges conspirators in this way?

According to the statute, "A person is guilty of criminal conspiracy if, with the intent that conduct constituting an offense be performed, he agrees with one or more persons to engage in or cause the performance of such conduct, and any one or more of such persons does an overt act to effect an objective of the agreement."

Students should be able to understand that conspiracies are generally one step lower than the crimes themselves. Therefore, conspiracy to commit a Class A felony results in a Class B felony charge, conspiracy to commit a Class B felony results in a Class C felony charge, and so on down to conspiracy to commit a Class C misdemeanor, which is a violation (petty offense). Apparently, Alabama charges people in this way because its lawmakers feel that conspirators do not hold the same level of liability as single criminals acting alone, but that their liability should be as close as possible to that of the single criminal.

3. INTERNET

ACCOMPLICE LIABILITY

Have students read "Wong Says He'll Win" at *http://starbulletin.com/1999/04/13/news/story1.html.* Several crimes are alleged against this defendant, and one of them is criminal conspiracy. Tell them to answer the following questions:

- What are the crimes that have been charged against Wong and his cohorts?

- How does criminal conspiracy play a role in this? What other accomplice liability issues are apparent here, in relation to either Wong or his cohorts?

Wong was charged with first-degree theft, perjury, and conspiracy. Wong's wife, Mari, was indicted for criminal conspiracy and for hindering prosecution. Wong's brother-in-law, local developer Jeffrey Stone, was charged with commercial bribery, criminal conspiracy, and serving as an accomplice to theft.

Students should show an understanding of, apparently, how all three of the defendants were involved in a kickback scheme "from his brother-in-law Stone through a series of complicated real estate transactions." Other accomplice liability issues are Mari Wong's hindering of prosecution by lying for her husband.

Extended Workplace Applications

1. Research and Analyze

Have students go online or to their local library to find recent cases of felonies that involved accomplice liability. They should find two or three cases to analyze and write a report by answering the following questions:

- How were the accomplices involved in the crime? How were they charged and convicted?

- Based on what you have learned, were the charges appropriate?

- Did the sentences seem just?

- Why or why not?

This exercise will help students see how accomplice liability works in the real world. Students should be able to explain what the

accomplices did to create liability. Depending on the circumstances, they may or may not feel that the charges were appropriate. You can explain to them that inappropriate charges or convictions may be the result of ineffectual counsel or plea bargaining. The sentences will reflect the charges and usually the plea bargaining process; some students may complain that the punishments are too lenient.

2. Interview

Have students interview two or three people they know who have children, and have students ask them to imagine the following scenario: In the last year, your child (assume that the child is 16 years old for the purposes of this discussion) has begun to hang out with a tough crowd and has had several run-ins with the law. You continuously try to reprimand your child, but he or she will not listen and is repeatedly running away and committing crimes such as petty theft, joyriding, and underaged drinking. This week, you learned from overhearing a phone conversation that your child was involved in an armed robbery that took place last week. You know from a previous conversation with a police lieutenant that as soon as your child is involved in any type of violent crime, they will be forced to charge him or her as an adult. It appears that nobody other than you and the people directly involved in the crime know who did it; even the victim of the robbery does not know, since they were wearing ski masks.

- What are your options, and what will you do about this situation?

- Explain your situation.

Answers will vary. This exercise provides a moral quandary for many parents: Although every parent wants to make sure that his or her child obeys the law, many are reluctant to turn the child over to law enforcement when a crime has occurred–especially if it appears that the child will not get caught. Some parents will point out that the armed robbery could have resulted in someone's death, and that it is apparent that their child is graduating to more serious crime; they will likely call the police. Others will insist that they could rehabilitate the child "on their own" and will not call the police. Many will find themselves in a moral gray area of, "I would call the police if such-and-such were the case: if it were clear he or she was going to get caught, if they wouldn't try him or her as an adult, if he or she were really a bad kid." You can ask students who get responses like this what they feel about such responses, and if they sound like denial. What, if anything, can be done about parents who protect their children in such a way?

3. Role Play

Give students the following scenario: "Your roommate has been acting suspiciously lately. She isn't attending classes as often as she used to, and she comes in and out of your apartment at odd hours. Today, while cleaning the hallway, you move a bag of hers. It falls open as you set it down, and you see several bags of drugs. You confront her, and she insists that she knows nothing about the drugs; that this bag was left in her car and she just brought it in because it was taking up too much space." Then have students answer the following questions:

- What are your options, and what do you think you will do?

- What possible problems could arise from your choice?

Students should understand the two basic options of either calling the police or not calling the police. If they opt to call the police, they may wish to do so anonymously or openly. If they do not, they may wish to let the matter slide entirely or warn their roommate to never bring home drugs again. If they choose to contact the police, their roommate will probably know that it was them whether or not they give their name, and they may face possible physical threats or violence from the roommate or her co-conspirators. If they choose to not contact the police, they could face

further crime problems at their home and also be indicted as an accessory for failing to report the crime.

4. Evaluate

Give students the following scenario to evaluate: "You are a local police officer investigating a domestic disturbance. As you leave the house, you find two children next door playing with a crack pipe. They do not have any drugs on them and it is clear that they are not using any drugs at this time, but the pipe has residue and appears to have been used very recently. You ask the children where they found this. At first, they do not say anything, but eventually they tell you that the pipe is their father's. You ask if their mother knows about it, and they tell you that she helps him sell and deliver drugs. You enter the home and find that it is a filthy mess, and there is no food in the fridge. The father is passed out on the couch, and the mother has been absent all day." Then have them answer the following questions:

- With what drug charges could the parents be charged? What about child endangerment?

- In which case do you find accomplice liability for one of the parents?

Most students will agree that the parents are guilty of drug possession and distribution. However, it is still not certain whether the mother is a co-principal or an accomplice. The officer will need to further investigate this situation before making a decision about this. It is clear, however, that the children are living in an unfit home and that the parents are equally guilty in this regard. Most students will agree that they should be removed from this home because of the squalor and the incident with the crack pipe.

Regarding accomplice liability, it is probably the drug crime in which one of the parents is only an accomplice. Again, however, this is not certain.

Incomplete Crimes

Chapter Resources

For the Instructor
Instructor's Resource Manual, pp. 53–64
Additional Activities, p. 61
PowerPoint Presentation and ExamView Pro Testbank
  CD-ROM for Chapter 6
cl.glencoe.com Web site

For the Student
Student Edition, Chapter 6, pp. 158–197
Review and Applications, p. 192
Tutorial with Simulation Applications
  CD-ROM for Chapter 6
cl.glencoe.com Web site

KEY TERMS

inchoate crimes	indispensable element test	"hybrid" legal impossibility
attempt	unequivocality test	genuine legal impossibility
last act test	substantial step test	abandonment
physical proximity test	factual impossibility	solicitation (incitement)
dangerous proximity test	legal impossibility	conspiracy

Lecture Outline

6.1 ATTEMPTED CRIMES
   The Six Stages of Committing a Crime
   Historical Development
   Mens Rea of Attempt
   Actus Reus of Attempt
   Other Elements and Issues

6.2 DEFENSES TO ATTEMPT
   Impossibility
   Abandonment

6.3 SOLICITATION
   Mens Rea of Solicitation
   Actus Reus of Solicitation
   Defenses to Solicitation

6.4 CONSPIRACY
   Mens Rea of Conspiracy
   Actus Reus of Conspiracy
   Defenses to Conspiracy

In-Chapter Questions

Criminal Law Online page 161

What are the elements of stalking? What acts are punishable as cybercrimes?

   Essentially, stalking is the unlawful act of harassing a person through repeated unwanted contact.

   Stalking is a common cybercrime, as are fraud (particularly credit card fraud), obscenity (including child pornography), and copyright violations (such as providing free downloads of copyrighted music).

Photo caption page 163

Can anyone considering a criminal plan be liable for this crime?

   No. Mere thoughts or even intentions to commit the crime are not enough. At the very least, one must physically prepare to commit the crime.

Regina v. Eagleton page 166

Do you think the last act test is a good way to determine attempt liability? Why or why not?

Most students will feel that it is not, because it does not extend liability to people who have taken actions toward committing an offense but have not managed to do so before being caught. Some may feel that it is good because it is provides liability only to those who are undoubtedly attempting a crime.

People v. Rizzo page 167

What flaws and benefits can you find in the dangerous proximity test?

Many students will like the dangerous proximity test because it covers those who are very likely to succeed in committing the crime and have clearly taken positive steps to that end. Some, on the other hand, may dislike that it does not focus more on intent, such as the unequivocality test. A few may prefer the last act test because it completely eliminates doubt that a crime has been attempted, whereas the other tests do leave some doubt (but extend liability to more guilty parties).

People v. Vizcarra page 168

Do you think that the defendant's actions met the requirements of the dangerous proximity test? Why or why not?

Most students will agree that carrying a rifle and behaving in such a suspicious way outside the store was enough to indicate that the defendant was in dangerous proximity of success, because all that he had to do was enter the store to commit the armed robbery.

People v. Orndoff page 169

What substantial step was missing from the defendant's actions?

Because the scheme required a substantial step in which the victim withdrew the money from the bank and gave it to the defendant, the act did not proceed beyond mere preparation and therefore did not fulfill the substantial step test.

People v. Kraft page 173

Do you think the defendant had the necessary *mens rea* to be convicted of attempted murder?

Many students will feel that the appellate court's overturning of the conviction was a miscarriage of justice, and that the defendant did possess the necessary *mens rea* but offered a poor alibi. Many students will feel that his behavior was inappropriately aggressive, but some will feel that such erratic behavior could be possible if a person were under severe depression; you can ask the latter group if this mitigates the defendant's responsibility in any way.

6.1 Self Check page 00

1. Why are inchoate crimes considered criminal behavior?

Because they are behaviors that lead to other crimes, and thus have elements of intent and *actus reus* that contribute to criminal behavior.

2. In your own words, how does the MPC define attempt?

Student answers will vary. Basically, according to the MPC, someone is guilty of attempt if he or she acts as though the crime will be completed, acts or fails to act in such a way that would normally complete the crime, or acts or fails to act in such a way that furthers the crime attempt.

3. Why must the *actus reus* be accompanied by the *mens rea*?

Because to be criminally culpable, a person must possess criminal intent while committing a criminal act.

United States v. Thomas page 176

Do you think factual impossibility should be a legal defense? Why or why not?

Most students will agree that this defense should be used because it can have validity in certain circumstances, but they may also voice general concerns that legal defenses are overused by guilty defendants.

***United States v. Berrigan* page 177**

How does this case meet the requirements for the defense of legal impossibility?

A lot of students may not understand how this decision was reached. If he smuggled the letters, they may reason, what difference does it make if the warden knew? You can explain that because smuggling requires secrecy, it cannot occur if the authority in question is aware of the action. You may ask students if Berrigan still should be guilty of a crime, such as attempt, because of his *mens rea* and *actus reus.*

 ***Wilson v. State* page 179**

Under what tests for attempt liability do you think the defendant was originally convicted?

Perhaps the unequivocality test because it is clear that he possessed criminal intent when he committed this action.

Photo caption page 180

What types of materials must be retrieved when one legally abandons a crime plan?

Typical materials include firearms or other weapons that the co-conspirators were planning to use together, maps or drawings, tools to use for burglary or other crimes, and any other items that could be used in committing the crime.

 ***People v. Kimball* page 181**

Do you think the defendant's abandonment was voluntary or involuntary? Why or why not?

Students will be divided on this case because the defendant took substantial steps toward committing the robbery more than once, and it may not have been clear to the clerk (or any other reasonable person in a similar situation) that his abandonment was sincere. Others may feel that since the defendant abandoned the crime, he should not be considered guilty.

6.2 Self Check page 183

1. In your own words, what are the differences between factual and legal impossibility? Give an example of each.

Answers may vary. In factual impossibility cases, the defendant is mistaken regarding some fact that is critical to the success of the crime. A person who attempts to detonate a bomb containing no explosive material and an impotent man who tries to rape a woman are two examples of factual impossibility.

Legal impossibility occurs when the intended acts, even if completed, would not have amounted to a crime. For instance, if a defendant bribes a person because he or she wrongly believes that individual to be a juror, the defendant could not be convicted of attempting to bribe a juror.

2. What elements are generally required for a successful abandonment defense?

A successful abandonment defense can be used when the defendant has a change of heart on his or her own because of a sincere belief that furtherance of the act is wrong.

6.3 Self Check page 186

1. Why is solicitation considered a crime?

It is considered a crime because a deliberate inducement of another to commit a crime is sufficiently dangerous behavior to call for the imposition of criminal penalties.

2. Briefly, what are the *actus reus* and *mens rea* required for a solicitation conviction?

The *actus reus* of solicitation occurs when the solicitor takes any action, whether verbal or otherwise, to urge another to commit a crime. The *mens rea* is the desire that a specific crime be carried out, not merely a vague interest in seeing crime occur; solicitation is a specific intent crime.

FBI Special Agent page 187
What qualities do you think a good FBI agent should possess?

Answers will vary, and could include any of the following: FBI agents should be at least bilingual, if not multilingual. They should be intelligent, possess good memories, and be able to absorb and distinguish among many pieces of detailed information. They should also have strong communication skills and an ability to "read" others.

Criminal Law Online page 189

What offenses are most typical of large-scale conspiracies, and why?

Drug offenses, money laundering, and racketeering are typical large-scale offenses because they require extensive resources and can yield enormous wealth for those that commit these crimes successfully.

 United States v. Alvarez page 189
What kind of overt act do you think would have been necessary for the defendant's conviction to be upheld?

Although some students may feel that his agreement to unload the drugs was sufficient, many will feel that he would have needed to actually unload the drugs or take clear steps toward doing so to sustain his conviction.

6.3 Self Check page 191

1. How does this text's definition of conspiracy differ from your original conception of the crime? Why do you think that there is a frequent misunderstanding of it?

Most students think of conspiracies as assassination attempts or government corruption. In fact, it is much broader than that. This frequent misunderstanding occurs because these types of conspiracies are the best known and, perhaps, the most feared.

2. What factors help justify making conspiracy a crime?

The crime of conspiracy is an excellent aid to law enforcement because it allows them more leeway in arresting members of crime rings.

Review and Applications

Questions For Review

1. What is the six-stage process by which an actor commits a crime, and after what stage is a person liable for criminal punishment?

A crime is a six-stage process in which the actor:

- conceives of the idea of committing the crime.
- evaluates the idea, considering whether or not to proceed.
- forms the intention to go forward.
- prepares to commit the crime, for example, by obtaining a gun.
- commences commission of the offense.
- completes his or her actions, achieving the goal.

Under Anglo-American law, a person is liable for criminal punishment only after the third stage.

2. Explain the historical cases in which the crime of attempt was first recognized.

An English court first recognized the crime of attempt in *Rex v. Scofield* (1784). In this case, the defendant was charged with placing a lighted candle and combustible material in a rented house in a clear attempt to set it on fire. The court held that the defendant's intent turned an otherwise innocent act into a criminal one. In addition, the court found that the completion of a criminal act was not necessary to constitute criminality.

The idea that attempt was itself a crime was recognized in *Rex v. Higgins* (1801), in which a British court upheld an indictment charging an unsuccessful attempt to steal. After this case, the common law treated all attempts as a misdemeanor, even an attempt to commit a felony.

3. Your textbook names six of the various tests for the crime of attempt. How do they differ?

The six tests are:

- The last act test, which holds that an attempt occurs when a person has performed all of the acts that he or she believed were necessary to carry out the action that would constitute the underlying offense.

- The physical proximity test, under which the perpetrator need not have advanced so far as the last act, but the conduct must be "proximate" to, or very near, the completed crime.

- The dangerous proximity test, which incorporates the physical proximity test but is somewhat more flexible. Under this test, a person is guilty of attempt when his or her conduct is in "dangerous proximity" to succeeding at the crime.

- The indispensable element test, in which a suspect who has not yet gained control over an indispensable instrumentality of the criminal plan cannot be guilty of attempt.

- The unequivocality test, which does not look at how close the defendant came to succeeding, but at whether the defendant's conduct was indicative of his or her criminal intent.

- The substantial step test, which is the MPC's test for the *actus reus* of attempt. This test requires that the suspect must have done or omitted to do something that constitutes a "substantial step" in plans to commit the substantive offense.

4. How does the MPC define the mental element of attempt, and how is this different from other definitions?

The following is a direct quote from the MPC that is found in the students' textbook: "Definition of Attempt. A person is guilty of an attempt to commit a crime if, acting with the kind of culpability otherwise required for commission of the crime, he:

(a) purposely engages in conduct that would constitute the crime if the attendant circumstances were as he believes them to be; or

(b) when causing a particular result is an element of the crime, does or omits to do anything with the purpose of causing or with the belief that it will cause such result without further conduct on his part; or

(c) purposely does or omits to do anything that, under the circumstances as he believes them to be, is an act or omission constituting a substantial step in a course of conduct planned to culminate in his commission of the crime."

5. What are the similarities and differences between "hybrid" legal impossibility and pure legal impossibility?

Hybrid legal impossibility is a description given to cases in which the reasons for punishing unsuccessful attempts can be countered equally by the defense of legal impossibility and the defense of factual impossibility.

Pure legal impossibility exists when the law does not define as criminal the goal the defendant sought to achieve. Pure legal impossibility, therefore, is really just an application of the principle of legality.

6. What are some reasons why some jurisdictions recognize abandonment as a defense?

Some jurisdictions recognize abandonment as a defense to the crime of attempt do so for various reasons, which include but are not limited to:

- The defense may deter an actor from continuing the plan to commit a crime.

- By abandoning plans to commit a crime, a person has demonstrated that he or she does not threaten the safety of the public in the same way as someone who continued plans to carry out a crime.

7. Why is solicitation designated as a crime, and what are some of the criticisms of this practice?

Solicitation is a crime because it constitutes a deliberate inducement of another to commit a crime, which is sufficiently dangerous behavior to call for the imposition of criminal penalties. This has been criticized because:

- Since the crime requires an independent individual, who is capable of forming his or her own moral judgments, to act on behalf of the solicitor, it is always possible that the individual will refuse.

- It has also been argued that the solicitor manifests reluctance to commit the crime himself or herself, and thus is not "a significant menace."

- As with inchoate crimes in general, the ultimate criticism of solicitation is that an unsuccessful solicitation is so far removed from any actual societal harm that its punishment comes close to punishing evil thoughts or intentions alone, thus raising First Amendment issues.

8. How does the treatment of conspiracy as a crime help law enforcement efforts?

By criminalizing the attempt to commit crimes by conspiring to commit them, lawmakers provide law enforcement with more leeway in arresting members of crime rings, which, although they provide a great threat to society, are extremely difficult to detect.

9. What are all of the possible requirements to determine the *actus reus* of conspiracy?

Since the *actus reus* of conspiracy is the act of reaching an agreement, an agreement can be proven in the following ways:

- By direct evidence

- By either spoken or written words

- By proof of conduct of the defendants, often in the form of proof of their cooperation.

In addition, most jurisdictions require that the prosecutor must also prove that some overt act was committed in furtherance of the conspiracy. The purpose of the requirement of an overt act is to prove that the conspiracy has functioned to the extent that real crimes have been committed as a result.

10. How can the defenses of abandonment and impossibility apply to conspiracy?

Most courts hold that impossibility of any kind is not a defense to a charge of conspiracy, and the MPC also does not recognize impossibility as a defense to conspiracy charges. Although a few decisions exist that hold impossibility as a valid defense, it is generally not.

Almost all jurisdictions have applied the same test in determining whether a participant in a conspiracy has abandoned it early enough not to be convicted. Courts look for an affirmative act that will prove that abandonment was timely and effective, and expect the conspirator who is withdrawing to give notice to everyone involved. Some jurisdictions go even further and recognize withdrawal only if the defendant not only abandons the planned crime, but also talks his or her co-conspirators out of committing the act.

11. What does the MPC allow in regard to defenses to conspiracy?

The MPC does not recognize impossibility as a defense to conspiracy charges. On the other hand, it does allow abandonment (also called renunciation) to be an affirmative defense to conspiracy, but requires that the defendant may validly assert withdrawal as a defense only if he or she was able to stop the other co-conspirators from continuing plans to commit a crime. Some jurisdictions that follow the MPC's approach provide that withdrawal is a valid defense if a conspirator notifies police of the criminal activity as a way to prevent it from occurring.

Problem-Solving Exercises

1. PROSTITUTION RING
   Answers could include the following:
   a. Solicitation, because they did not succeed in their attempts at prostitution. You can also point out that they can be charged with pandering or pimping, depending on their exact relationship with the other prostitutes.

   b. They could be charged with solicitation as well, since they were present and available for prostitution.

   c. Most students would agree that Sandy and Luisa seemed very naïve and probably tipped people off when they were announcing their brothel to others.

2. DRUG TRAFFICKING
   Answers could include the following:
   a. Yes, according to the definition of this term that is found in the textbook.

b. Yes. Fred agreed to provide Raul with long-term help in his criminal enterprise.

c. It probably will, at least against Raul, although Fred could claim duress (a defense that will be covered in the next chapter) because he feared for his life if he did not cooperate with Raul.

3. **ATTEMPTED MURDER**
   Answers could include the following:
   a. This is a good question, and students would be intelligent to question the husband's honesty in this case. Perhaps a laboratory could test the woman's bloodstream or stomach lining for evidence of this same substance; if no trace of it could be found, this could indicate that the husband is lying.

   b. Although his crime may seem like attempted murder because he had the requisite *mens rea* of malice aforethought, attempted the *actus reus*–and, were the substance not poisonous, the elements of concurrence and causation would have been fulfilled–the fact that the substance was harmless creates a situation of legal impossibility. Therefore, he did not commit a crime because it was impossible to kill his wife with this harmless substance.

Workplace Applications

1. **SUBSTANTIAL STEP TEST**
   Answers could include the following:
   a. Yes, the driver could be charged with murder, and also perhaps with attempted murder or attempted aggravated battery toward any other children who were in the vicinity. Although his intent is not stated here, his *actus reus* showed a clear disregard for the choices, and he should be held liable for the fact that other children (and adults) could have been killed as well.

   b. The concept of substantial certainty holds that even though a defendant may not have desired or wanted a particular result, the defendant is still guilty if he or she acted with a substantial certainty that a certain result would occur.

c. He may state that he did not realize it was a school zone, but such zones are clearly marked with signs and speed limits, so this response would not be valid. If he claimed that he was in a hurry for some urgent reason, this is not a valid excuse either. You can mention to students that defenses based on excuses and justifications will be used in the next chapter.

2. **FALSE TESTIMONY**
   Answers could include the following:
   a. It would not be ethical to do so, especially since attempted murder can carry such a severe punishment. It would be best to have her renounce her false testimony and provide a truthful statement instead. If not, the defendant could sue your jurisdiction in civil court for unlawful imprisonment and concealment of evidence.

   b. Yes. Although this is risky in relation to gaining a conviction, it is the best option ethically.

   c. Yes. This would be the best choice, because this is the only crime for which there is truthful evidence to convict him.

3. **LAST ACT TEST**
   Answers could include the following:
   a. They would not qualify as guilty under the last act test, because although the bank employee had arrived to open up the machine and repair it, the three suspects still had not attempted to commit the crime. You can explain to students that this offers a clear example of why the last act test is no longer used: because it does not provide for people who are obviously planning to commit a crime, but have not succeeded in reaching the final step.

   b. This would be considered a crime of attempt under the dangerous proximity test because they were in dangerous proximity of succeeding, had not the officer caught them. Most students would agree that their failure was a matter of chance, and this vignette gives no clear indication that they were planning to abandon their criminal plans.

Internet Exercises

1. INCOMPLETE CRIMES

Answers could include the following:

a. Students should be able to easily name these offenses and provide basic examples of each.

b. No, because they have varying degrees of severity. Proportionality dictates that they carry different sentences.

b. Answers will vary, but students should recognize that violent crimes are usually the least common.

2. CONSPIRING

Answers could include the following:

a. Students' answers will vary. Some will want to investigate the Mafia connection, some will want to investigate the New Orleans-based suspects, and others will suspect Vice President Lyndon Baines Johnson and his allies (since the murder occurred in Johnson's home state of Texas and Johnson stood to gain the most from Kennedy's death). Some students will find the conspiracy theory to be rubbish, but all should find this to be interesting reading.

b. Most students would agree that all parties connected to the attempted murder should be indicted for conspiracy to assassinate the President. If they attempt to lie or conceal evidence, they should be tried for these crimes as well.

c. Since motive is related to intent, you could try to deduce the guilty parties by determining who gained the most from the President's death. You could then establish *mens rea* by determining what actions were taken to facilitate the President's assassination.

Ethics Issues

1. CONSPIRACY TO COMMIT MURDER

Answers could include the following:

a. You should definitely tell him because he not only willfully abandoned the plot, he reported it the police to help prevent the crime from occurring.

b. Since he willfully renounced his involvement in the crime and even went to the police, he will probably not be charged with any crime, regardless of the jurisdiction.

c. Most students will agree that he does not, but his friends should be charged with murder.

2. CHANGE FOR AN INCOMPLETE CRIME

Answers could include the following:

a. No, because he renounced the crime by his own free will, not out of fear of law enforcement or due to a technical error that would not let him commit the crime. However, some students will correctly point out that he is still culpable for possessing a firearm and pointing it at the cashier.

b. He abandoned the plan voluntarily.

Additional Activities

Advanced Web Research

1. INTERNET

INCHOATE CRIMES

Have your students visit "Inchoate Crimes" at *http://faculty.ncwc.edu/toconnor/293/293lect05.htm*. Ask them to read the first two sections, entitled "Attempt" and "Conspiracy," and answer the following questions:

- What, in essence, is criminal attempt all about, and what are its elements, according to this page?

- What are the three types of *mens rea* and the two types of *actus reus* of conspiracy, and how do they differ? Can you think of any others?

Criminal attempt is all about failure to commit the crime as planned. The elements of attempt are (1) specific intent, (2) an overt act toward commission, and (3) failure to consummate the crime.

The three types of *mens rea* relating to conspiracy are the unilateral rule, bilateral rule, and Wharton's rule. The two types of *actus reus* are the chain conspiracy and the wheel conspiracy.

2. INTERNET

ATTEMPTED MURDER

"Anti-Gay Minister Arraigned on Attempted Murder" can be found at *http://www.datalounge.com/datalounge/news/record.html?record=2584*. Ask students to read the brief article, then answer the following questions:

- What were the various motives behind Crossley's attempt to murder Waldo, and how did these appear to affect his intent?

- Was Crossley's bigotry a factor in this case? If so, and if he were found guilty, should it be considered an aggravating factor in his sentencing? If not, why?

Crossley was apparently angry at Waldo for being homosexual and also because of ongoing disputes with Waldo. His motive appeared to affect his intent because his hatred for Waldo led to his attempt to have him murdered.

Most students would agree that Crossley's bigotry served as a provocation and certainly exacerbated his sour relationship with Waldo. Most would also agree that it should be an aggravating factor in his sentencing, since it is clear that he used inflammatory and hateful speech on a regular basis. Some will feel that this was his constitutional right and that it should not be considered; however, you may want to ask them if this is not a clear indication of Crossley's motive.

3. INTERNET

IMPOSSIBILITY

Have your students read about the New York case *People v. Dlugash* at Penal Law: A Web. The Web address is *http://wings.buffalo.edu/law/bclc/web/nydlugash.htm*. Next, have them answer the following questions:

- With what crime was the defendant charged, and was he found guilty?

- What issues were at stake that made this case unusual, and why was its appeal unique?

- What was the defense offered for Dlugash's actions? Did this seem valid to you? Why or why not?

The defendant was charged with murder, and although the victim was possibly dead at the time of the shooting, the jury convicted the defendant of murder anyway because they believed "beyond a reasonable doubt" that defendant intended to kill a live human being. In other words, the defendant acted in the belief that the victim was alive at the time of the shooting.

What made this case unusual was that Dlugash claimed innocence by stating that he shot someone that was already dead, which the jury did not believe. His appeal was unique because it applied his intent to kill a live person to his shooting of a dead person.

Dlugash's defense was that he knew that Geller was dead already. Students who believe this will generally point out that you can tell when somebody is dead. Those who do not find the defendant's claim to be valid will ask why he bothered to shoot a dead person, especially five times point-blank in the face.

Extended Workplace Applications

1. Analyze

Have students analyze the following situation: Bob decided to rob the neighborhood store because he desperately needs money to pay his rent. While inside the store, he observes someone he knows and who may be able to identify him. He decides to take his chances anyway and hope that the person does not remember him. He points the gun at the cashier and demands the large bills. The cashier tells Bob that he needs to reconsider his actions and that he could go to jail for a long time. She tells him that she will not call the police if he simply leaves the store. Bob decides that she is right, and changes his mind because he might get caught and go to jail. He immediately leaves the store, but is arrested while walking to his car.

Next, ask students the following questions:
- Has Bob committed attempted robbery?
- Did he abandon his plan? Was the abandonment voluntary or involuntary?

2. Discuss

Tell students the following situation and lead the class into a discussion with the questions below: Serena, who is 19, decides to take her father's car without her parents' permission and drive to a local liquor store. There, she attempts to buy lemonade coolers, but does not present a license. When she is arrested and booked, she insists that she thought they were real lemonade, not anything containing alcohol. She states that she was puzzled when asked for I.D., but the clerk says that she acted furtive and tried telling him that she had bought alcohol there before. She has one prior sentence for under-aged drinking, and her parents are outraged that she took their car.
- What possible charges could be brought against Serena?
- How should her ongoing issues with drinking be handled–through punishment, treatment, or both?

Serena could be charged with attempting to purchase alcohol because her story does not sound very believable. If she has a prior record of under-aged drinking, she would know the difference between regular lemonade and lemonade coolers. In addition, depending on her parents' wishes, she could be charged with joyriding because she took their vehicle temporarily without their permission. You may want to mention that a prosecutor could bring both charges against her, then plea bargain to have her accept a sentence for underaged drinking.

Regarding the best possible treatment for her, it depends on her personality and willingness to take responsibility for her actions. Some students may feel that she has a drinking problem and should be given treatment, but others may feel that she is incorrigible and should be taught a lesson through a strict punishment.

3. Role Play

Give students the following scenario: You are a judge hearing a case involving an attempted breaking and entering. During a snowstorm, two teenagers who were walking home from school tried to break into an abandoned home to warm themselves and wait for the storm to calm before finishing their walk home. A police officer, who was just leaving a service call from down the street, saw them approach the house and then saw one start to push the other one through a window they pushed open. Just before the arrest, they changed their minds and decided to try to make it home. The arresting officer tells you that the teenagers are trouble-makers who should be punished. The teenagers say that they changed their minds before entering the house, and that they were justified because of the cold weather.

- In whose favor do you decide, and why?

Most people would say that, regardless of the police officer's dislike for the teenagers (which may be justified, depending on other circumstances that have occurred between them), the teenagers showed voluntary abandonment by their own free will and should be acquitted. In addition, although this is not discussed until a later chapter, breaking into a house during a snowstorm can be defended by using the necessity defense.

4. Role Play

Give students the following scenario: You are a juror hearing a case for arson and attempted murder in which the defendant is pleading impossibility. The defendant was angry at her mother for cutting her out of her will, and in her anger she set fire to the mother's vacation home on a Thursday night. In the 14 years that the mother has had a vacation home, she had never visited it except between Fridays and Sundays; however, because she was upset with her daughter and needed some peace, she states that she drove up early that weekend and was actually present when the fire was set, then drove home in a panic when she realized what was occurring. The defendant claims that she was not there because her car was not present, and no witnesses saw the mother arrive or depart. Although the defendant is pleading

guilty to arson, which she committed because she was angry at losing her inheritance, she insists that she did not intend to kill her mother and such a crime would have been impossible since she was not there.

Next, ask the following questions:
- Does it sounds like the defendant is guilty of attempted murder? Why or why not?
- Assume that the mother is telling the truth. How can she prove this?
- If she can prove it, will it automatically disprove her daughter's claims to not have intended to kill her?

Although the defendant is clearly guilty of arson, the attempted murder charge does sound sketchy because the defendant claims that the mother was not present, history indicates that she would not have been present on a Thursday, and no witnesses can corroborate the mother's story.

The mother would need to do more than find fingerprints or proof that she had been in the house, since she went to this house frequently. Credit card receipts, pay phone charges, gas receipts that clearly name her as the purchaser, and interaction with local residents or employees could indicate her presence in the neighborhood at that time. If she cannot prove she was there, this does not necessarily make her guilty of perjury (since there is no direct proof that she was lying), but it does make it nearly impossible to prove the attempted murder charge.

Even if the mother can prove she was present, prosecutors may not be able to prove that the daughter possessed intent to kill her if the daughter did not happen to see her mother's car and was genuinely convinced that she was not present. Her behavior may have been reckless, but it lacked malice aforethought.

Defenses to Crimes

KEY TERMS

defense	self-defense	duress	bifurcated trial
failure of proof	aggressor	coercion	*M'Naghten* test
true defense	deadly force	intoxication	irresistible impulse test
burden of proof	law enforcement	voluntary intoxication	MPC test
affirmative defense	defense	involuntary intoxication	federal test
justification	necessity	insanity	diminished capacity
excuse	consent	incompetency	defense

Lecture Outline

7.1 TYPES OF DEFENSES
Failures of Proof Versus True Defenses
Burden of Proof
Mitigating Versus Complete Defenses
Justification Versus Excuse as the Basis
    of a Defense

7.2 DEFENSES BASED ON JUSTIFICATION
Self-Defense
Other Defenses Based on Justification
Defense of Others
Defense of Property and Habitation
Defenses Related to Crime Prevention and
    Law Enforcement
Necessity (Choice of Evils)
Consent

7.3 DEFENSES BASED ON EXCUSE
Age/Infancy
Duress
Intoxication
Insanity
Diminished Capacity (Partial Responsibility)
Mistake
Entrapment
Specialized Defenses

In-Chapter Questions

7.1 Self Check page 204

1. In your own words, distinguish between failure of proof and a true defense.

   A defense based on failure of proof is valid when the prosecution fails to prove the cause of action in its entire scope and meaning, such as by failing to produce adequate evidence to prove each element of the crime. A true defense, also called an affirmative defense, is one in which the defendant admits his or her guilt, but offers one or more legally recognized reasons (such as necessity or duress) why he or she should nonetheless be acquitted.

2. Explain the differences between mitigating and complete defenses.

Mitigating defenses are also called partial defenses because they reduce a defendant's charges, rather than produce an acquittal as complete defenses do.

 People v. Goetz page 207

Do you think Goetz was justified in his actions? Why or why not?

Students will likely debate this one. Some will feel that Goetz was simply racist, and others will believe that he was reacting to uncontrollable crime in a large city. This polarity of opinions is seen in Goetz's acquittal and the subsequent civil judgment against him that provided restitution to the victim of the shooting.

Photo caption page 208

Under what circumstances is deadly force justified?

A victim can use deadly force if he or she reasonably believes that he or she will suffer death or great bodily harm if such force is not used.

 State v. Kelly page 211

Do you believe that battered women syndrome is a valid excuse to murder? Why or why not?

Many students believe that it should be a valid excuse, especially since battered women are often left unprotected by police or are offered protection but are too scared to escape their situations.

 People v. Young page 214

Do you think the defendant should have been acquitted in this case? Why or why not?

Many students will agree that although his intentions were honorable, his behavior was prejudiced and he should have tried to understand the situation before jumping in.

 People v. Caballos page 218

To what degree should a person be allowed to use force to protect his or her property?

Many students will agree that nonlethal force is acceptable, such as the use of electric fences, dogs, pepper gas, and perhaps stun guns.

 Tennessee v. Garner page 222

Do you agree with the Supreme Court's decision regarding the use of deadly force by law enforcement? Why or why not?

Many students will agree, especially since the use of deadly force in this case was not justified.

Criminal Law Online page 223

Is the use of force in police-citizen contacts rare or prevalent? Is it usually accompanied by provocative behavior on the part of suspects?

Although not extremely rare, it is much rarer than the news media would lead students to believe. In addition, it is usually preceded or accompanied by provocative behavior from suspects. Sometimes, this provocative behavior is obviously offensive, but sometimes its offensiveness is a matter of opinion.

 Regina v. Dudley and Stephens page 225

Do you think the defendants should have been acquitted? Why or why not?

Since the boy's death apparently saved two lives, it could conceivably be seen as the lesser of two evils. However, students may have a hard time reconciling themselves to the taboo of cannibalism; they may also state that it is impossible to know if the boy was truly sickly and whether or not he would have lived.

 United States v. Holmes page 226

Should the defendant have been acquitted based on the necessity defense? Why or why not?

Possibly, but the court's decision that the unnecessary crew members should have been sacrificed first may cause some debate among the students, who may feel that this is discriminatory and could be self-destructive if the crew were the only people who were able to navigate.

7.2 Self Check page 227

1. How can self-defense be used as a complete defense? As a mitigating defense?

To use self-defense as a complete defense, a defendant usually must prove the necessity of using force, the proportionality of the force to the threat, and the reasonableness of the belief that force was necessary.

A few states allow an unreasonably mistaken defendant to assert a partial or "imperfect" self-defense claim, in which case a murder offense will be mitigated to manslaughter. However, this defense is not usually accepted.

2. What are the two problem areas that arise from a defense based on the protection of another person?

The two problem areas are:

- Determining the category of persons who can be assisted

- Identifying situations in which the person defended had a legal right to act in self-defense

 ***People v. Unger* page 230**

Do you think duress should be a valid excuse to prison escape? Why or why not?

Many students will agree that not only is it a valid excuse, but that it should indicate to prison staff that certain inmates need more protection than others.

 ***State v. Toscano* page 231**

Should duress be a defense when danger is not imminent? Why or why not?

Such a concept appears self-contradictory, although it is valid when used in crimes such as extortion or blackmail. Therefore, it could be a defense, and many students will agree it would be valid in this case.

 Clinical Social Worker page 237

What qualities do you think a good clinical social worker should have?

Students will name several traits, which may include: intelligence, organizational skills, decision-making skills, compassion, communication skills, and perceptiveness.

Photo caption page 239

What is your opinion of the insanity defense?

Student answers will vary. Some will feel that it should be used; others, that it can be used, but with more restrictions; and some will feel that it should be abolished altogether.

 ***State v. Cameron* page 241**

Do you think the defendant in this case deserved the verdict not guilty by reason of insanity? Why or why not?

Be sure to explain to students that a person can also be found guilty but insane, and that insanity can also be used as a defense that leads to institutionalization rather than incarceration.

 ***United States v. John Hinckley, Jr.* page 242**

Do you agree with those states that implemented the "guilty but mentally ill" verdict? Why or why not?

The guilty but mentally ill verdict is still a controversial subject. Many students will feel that this verdict can guarantee punishment for those who would otherwise get off on a not guilty by reason of insanity plea. Others may feel that the mentally ill should not be held responsible for crimes that they could not control. And some may feel that there should be no insanity defense whatsoever.

 ***People v. Evans* page 244**

Should the defendant in this case have been convicted? Why or why not?

Since rape is such a controversial and personal issue, students may have strong opinions about this case. Some will feel that the defendant should have been convicted because the college student did not want to have sex with him. However, some students may say that the defendant did not meet the force element of rape.

1. Explain the differences between insanity and diminished capacity.

Insanity is established as a complete defense when a criminally accused person is suffering from mental disease when the crime occurred and thus may be relieved of criminal responsibility. This defense is rarely used, probably because even if successfully used, it does not lead to the freedom for the accused but instead leads to commitment in a mental hospital until he or she is no longer dangerous.

Diminished capacity may be used as a failure of proof defense like insanity, but may also be used as a partial or mitigating defense. It is used by accused persons who, at the time of the act charged, were suffering from a mental condition insufficient to support a successful insanity defense but who might nonetheless be able to introduce evidence of their mental condition on the question of whether they had the mental state required for conviction of the crime charged.

2. Explain the elements that must be in place for entrapment to occur.

In entrapment, the defendant is tricked or otherwise induced by law enforcement agents to commit an illegal act that he or she would not otherwise have committed.

Review and Applications

Questions for Review

1. Explain how the burden of proof defines the prosecutor's task, and how defenses shift the burden of proof to the defendant.

In criminal cases, the prosecutor's job is to produce evidence and prove beyond a reasonable doubt the existence of the defendant's criminal culpability. In addition, if a particular defense falls into the "failure of proof" category, not only must the prosecution introduce its own evidence of the defendant's guilt, it must also disprove the defendant's failure of proof claim beyond a reasonable doubt.

True defenses, on the other hand, sometimes require that the defendant (via his or her attorney) introduce evidence of the claimed defense and bear the burden of persuading the jury of the facts establishing the defense. The burden of proof on the defendant's part is a preponderance of the evidence, which is the same level of proof required in civil cases and is lower than "beyond a reasonable doubt." Once the defendant has met that burden, it becomes the responsibility of the prosecutor to disprove the defense beyond a reasonable doubt.

2. What is considered to be a reasonable defense of habitation and property? When can deadly force be used?

A person may use force to prevent another from dispossessing him or her of real or personal property or to regain possession of property immediately after dispossession. An actor can never use deadly force solely to protect property, but if the threat is against habitation (a person's residence), the actor may be justified in the use of deadly force.

Some jurisdictions allow the use of deadly force to protect habitation only when the actor believes that the intruder intends to injure the actor or another occupant and deadly force is necessary to repel the intruder. Other jurisdictions require that the actor reasonably believes that the intruder intends to commit a forcible felony in the dwelling or to kill or seriously injure an occupant, and deadly force is necessary to repel the intrusion. The MPC limits the use of deadly force to instances in which there is a substantial risk to the person.

3. What are the MPC's three requirements in order to maintain non-deadly mechanical security devices?

The MPC provides that an individual can use non-deadly force to protect his or her property if three conditions are met:
- The other person's interference with the property must be unlawful.

- The property owner must have possession of the property in question or must be acting on behalf of someone who is in possession of the property.

- Force must be immediately necessary to protect the property.

4. Under what four conditions may police officers use non-deadly force?

The following four conditions allow non-deadly force by law enforcement:

- To stop and arrest someone who is committing or who has committed a crime
- To prevent an escape from custody by someone subject to arrest or who has been arrested
- To prevent the commission of a crime
- To suppress riots and disorders

5. Are citizen's arrests legal? If so, under what circumstances? If not, why?

At common law, private citizens could make an arrest for a felony or for a misdemeanor involving a breach of the peace, if the crime actually occurred and the citizen reasonably believed the suspect committed the offense. A citizen's arrest for other misdemeanors in the citizen's presence is also authorized.

6. Give some examples of cases in which the necessity defense would be valid.

Under this defense, a person is considered legally justified in acting unlawfully if his or her actions were a necessity designed to prevent some greater harm. This defense has been recognized in a variety of situations, such as:

- A parent who keeps a child home from school due to long-term illness is not guilty of violating the law compelling school attendance.
- A person who drives on a suspended license to take a loved one to the hospital in a dire emergency would not be guilty of driving without a license.
- A police officer who plays cards to catch and arrest a gambler would not be guilty of violating the gambling laws.
- A person who kills one person in order to save two or more would not be guilty of homicide.

The above list comes from the FYI box on page 227, to which you can refer students.

7. Compare the MPC's choice of evils defense with the common law necessity defense.

The MPC's choice of evils defense, which has influenced over half of all American states to adopt statutes recognizing it, is a broader version of the common law version. With respect to homicide, the MPC recognizes the sanctity of human life but then notes that it is sometimes necessary to take one life to save many others. It does not apply to situations in which an actor kills one person to save one other, because this is a choice of equal, not lesser, evils–which is not protected by law.

The common law necessity defense holds that a person is justified in violating a criminal law if the following six elements are present:

- The actor must be faced with a clear and imminent danger.
- The actor must expect, as a reasonable person, that his or her action will be effective in abating the danger sought to be avoided.
- The actor may not successfully claim the defense if there is an effective legal alternative available.
- The harm caused must be less than the harm avoided.
- The legislature in the state must not have decided the balancing of the choice and legislated against it.
- The actor must not have wrongfully placed himself or herself in the situation that requires the choice of evils.

In addition, the common law rule has some further limitations.

8. Under what noteworthy situations does the MPC, but not the common law, allow the duress defense?

Duress is a choice of evils created by human threats. The MPC has broadened the defense in a number of ways, including the following three noteworthy situations, which would not be accepted at common law:

- A person who is "brainwashed" or "coerced" over time into committing an illegal act by responding to earlier threats that have rendered the actor submissive

- An escape from prison to avoid an intolerable condition or circumstance
- When a battered woman "commits a crime at the 'suggestion' of her abusive partner"

9. What is a bifurcated trial, and how is it used in a trial where the insanity defense is raised?

A bifurcated trial is a criminal trial that is divided into two parts. It is used in trials to determine insanity and also in trials for which the death sentence can be imposed.

In a trial where the insanity defense is raised, it is used as follows:

- In the first trial, a jury decides whether the defendant is guilty or not guilty. If the verdict is not guilty, the person is acquitted and the proceedings end. If the defendant is found guilty but asserts the insanity defense, the fact finder (whether that be a judge or jury) will hold a separate trial after the verdict to determine whether to enter an additional verdict of not guilty by reason of insanity.

- In the second trial, the evidence introduced, principally expert psychiatric testimony, will relate solely to issue of the defendant's mental health.

10. Explain the two ways in which the diminished capacity defense may be used, and give an example of each.

Diminished capacity can be used to describe two circumstances in which a mental condition will acquit the defendant or lessen his or her sentence:

- Where the accused raises the condition as a failure of proof defense, negating an element of the crime, a *mens rea* use of the defense

- Where the defense is a true partial defense, in which the crime of murder can be mitigated by the defense to manslaughter

Problem-Solving Exercises

1. DURESS DEFENSE
Answers could include the following:
a. The defendant's story does not fulfill either the common law or MPC requirements of the duress defense. At common law, the threats must be immediate or imminent at the time the actor commits the crime, which is not the case because the person making the threats lives on another continent. Under the MPC, the person being threatened must be "unable to resist" the threat. Since this threat is not imminent and the person can be reported to the authorities in Ecuador and the United States, the defendant is able to resist him.

b. The officer can look for any reasonable excuse for using such a defense. For instance, perhaps the person making the threats has traveled out of the country before to harm other peoples, or has harmed people close to the defendant.

c. If the threat were made in person and the defendant were in imminent danger, he would likely have a valid defense.

2. VOLUNTARY INTOXICATION
Answers could include the following:
a. Since voluntary intoxication is rarely a basis for a defendant's acquittal of criminal charges at common law, it is unlikely that this will work.

b. He should be able to present it, but an acquittal is rare.

c. They should consider all relevant evidence, but some students may believe that some of his evidence will be irrelevant.

> NOTE TO INSTRUCTOR: See *Montana v. Egelhoff,* 518 U.S. 37 (1996) for a real-life case involving similar circumstances.

3. INSANITY DEFENSE
Answers could include the following:
a. Although he was clearly provoked, he cannot claim any type of self-defense or defense to his reputation. In addition, he may not even have a good reason to claim provocation, because all the person was doing was spreading false rumors about him.

b. Although he may feel justified in his killing, most students will agree that he should be charged with murder. The provocation can serve as a mitigating factor, but it is not guaranteed that a jury will be sympathetic to it.

Workplace Applications

1. INVOLUNTARY INTOXICATION
   Answers could include the following:
   a. Students should investigate the crime scene thoroughly to ensure that the driver's intoxicated state was definitely the cause of accident.

   b. Most students will ask why the driver was not given a blood alcohol test just in case he was lying. They will probably also state that the next place that the officer should visit, with back-up, is the scene of the party. Although the party is probably over by now, students will likely feel that the location of the party holds some clues. If the people who threw the party convincingly testify that the suspect had a lot to drink or took drugs voluntarily, you can focus your investigation on the suspect. If, however, their story is unconvincing, you should continue to focus on the scene of the party. If people were being drugged, there were likely other victims in this case.

   c. Again, he should have been tested for blood alcohol content, just to confirm that he was definitely not drunk. In addition, he should be questioned and requestioned. Finally, he should be able to provide witnesses who were also at the party and could confirm his story.

2. DIMINISHED CAPACITY
   Yes, he can use this defense because his low I.Q., Fetal Alcohol Syndrome, and low emotional development indicate that he is unable to control himself as would a normal adult.

3. SELF-DEFENSE
   Answers could include the following:
   a. Yes, because he was quite larger than she and probably much stronger. She had reason to fear for her life because some rape cases end in murder.

   b. The fact that he entered her habitation and threatened her with a forcible felony that caused her substantial risk would make her self-defense justified in almost any, if not every, jurisdiction.

Internet Exercises

1. NECESSITY DEFENSE
   Answers could include the following:
   a. They can be valid justifications when self-defense is a valid issue, and they can be valid excuses when necessity or duress force a person to leave a dangerous prison environment.

   b. Answers will vary, but inmates who leave because of death threats and sexual abuse are generally considered to be justified in their actions.

   c. Escapes in which the inmates did not face real harm, or were in a relaxed correctional environment with helpful staff, will generally not be considered valid.

2. STRATEGIZING A DEFENSE
   Answers could include the following:
   a. Student answers will vary widely. As some examples, the amount of evidence raised by the prosecution is very important, as are careful jury selection, understanding and managing public opinion, and attempting to portray the defendant as a victim who has somehow been framed.

   b. Answers will vary depending on the information provided in the previous answer.

c. Students will likely state that they will present such evidence aggressively, to throw doubt on the prosecution from the beginning.

d. Generally, juries from the same demographic background as the defendant may be more sympathetic, but ones who see the defendant as different or strange may be less sympathetic. A less aggressive prosecution may be seen as weak, but an assertive and rational prosecution may undermine the defense's drama. Judges can vary in their opinions due to their political beliefs and, sometimes, prejudices.

Ethics Issues

1. **DEFENSE OF HABITATION**

   It is clear that the homeowner overreacted and killed the intruder too hastily, then lied to cover up his misdeed. Some students will agree that the burglar got what he deserved and that the homeowner should not be punished for overreacting to a crime threat. Others will feel that his actions were reprehensible and that he should not be rewarded with an acquittal for clearly illegal behavior.

2. **DEFENSE OF DURESS**

   Answers can include the following:

   a. It is unlikely because, although she was compelled to steal money for her boyfriend, she agreed to take and use half of this money.

   b. Most students will agree that it does because it shows that she agreed to split the profits from the thefts. Indeed, many students will not find her story believable.

NOTE TO INSTRUCTOR: These additional activities are exclusive to this IRM. They are designed to meet the special needs of your students. If you or your students cannot access a Web site referred to here, go to *cl.glencoe.com* for the latest updated links.

Advanced Web Research

1. INTERNET
INFANCY DEFENSE
Ask your students to read the brief "Guide to Defaulted Student Loans" at *http://www.ed.gov/offices/OSFAP/DCS/disputes/infancy. html*. Next, have them answer the following questions:

- How does it appear that the infancy defense has been used by people who have defaulted on student loans?
- Do you agree with the government's position on using the infancy defense? Why or why not?

It appears to have been used to excuse young students who signed off on student loans, then claimed to not be responsible for them because of their age when signing for them.

Most students, although they would probably like an excuse to get out of their own student loans, will agree with the fairness of the government's position. A college student should not be entitled to an infancy defense.

2. INTERNET
USING DURESS AS DEFENSE
Refer your students to "Defense: Duress" at the Tennessee District Attorneys' General Conference site, located at *http://www.tndagc.com/ juryinst/40_03.htm*. Ask students the following questions: Under which four conditions is

duress a valid defense? What are the differences in meaning among "present," "imminent," and "impending"?

Duress is a valid defense when:
- The defendant is threatened with harm that is present, imminent, impending and of such a nature as to induce a well-grounded apprehension of death or serious bodily injury if the act is not done.
- The threatened harm is continuous throughout the time the act is being committed.
- The harm is one from which the defendant cannot withdraw in safety.
- The desirability and urgency of avoiding the harm clearly outweigh the harm sought to be prevented by the law proscribing the conduct.

"Present" means existing right now and relating to the present time. "Imminent" means near at hand or on the point of happening. "Impending" means imminent and threatening.

3. INTERNET
PLEADING INSANITY
Have your students read "Successful Insanity Defense Rare Here" at *http://www.yorkdispatch. com/spechold/skul_attack/010206e.html*. Then ask the class the following questions:
- Why is the *M'Naghten* defense being used in this case? How successful has it been in the past, and why?
- How are the *M'Naghten* defense and the "burning bed" defense similar, and why?

Students should be able to understand that the defense in this case wished to show that the defendant was at least temporarily insane during his recent criminal attack on an elementary school. However, one defense attorney could not recall "any such successful defenses in York County trials in the past 20 years."

The *M'Naghten* defense is similar to the "burning bed" defense because in both instances, the traditional concepts of right and wrong have been suspended and this is legally justifiable. Under the *M'Naghten* rule, they are suspended because the person is insane and cannot tell right from wrong; under the burning bed defense, the concepts are suspended because the defendant suffered from temporary insanity.

Extended Workplace Applications

1. Analyze

Give students the following situation: Janice and Tom had been married for ten years and are the parents of three children, ages two, seven, and nine. Several months after their wedding, Tom began to slap Janice occasionally during arguments. After their first child was born, they started to fight more often, and Tom began to beat up Janice several times a month. However, he always apologized and told her that he loved her and had just "lost control." She had to seek emergency medical treatment several times but did not press charges against Tom. Eventually Tom's attacks on Janice became more violent, and on two occasions, he slapped their oldest child across the face. Janice begged Tom to go with her for counseling, but Tom refused. On a number of occasions, he threatened to track down Janice and the children and kill them if they attempted to leave.

Janice believed the threat and felt that she had to get out of this violent marriage. Most of all, she felt that she had to protect her children. Finally, several days after a fight during which Tom again threatened to kill her if she left, Janice fatally shot Tom while he was sleeping.

The prosecution has charged Janice with first-degree murder. Ask students to analyze this situation by answering the following questions:

- If you were her defense attorney, what approach would you take?

- Does a defense of justification (self-defense, defense of others) or a defense of excuse (diminished capacity, insanity, duress) seem most relevant?

- How would you respond to the claim that such defenses would make Janice's act one of "legalized revenge"?

Most students will state that they would raise the defense of battered woman's syndrome, which is a type of duress defense that is allowed under the MPC.

An excuse defense of duress seems most appropriate.

Students may respond that it is not a case of revenge, but self-defense.

2. Discuss

Lead the class in a discussion with the following situation: Courts have become increasingly willing to try juveniles as adults when the crime committed is especially heinous. Suppose that a 13-year old has shot and killed a teacher and a fellow student at her school.

- Under what conditions, if any, should she be tried as an adult?

- How would your answer change if the girl was eight years old?

Although thirteen is young, some students will agree that this defendant should at least receive blended sentencing, to ensure that she receives a serious punishment and will enter the adult correctional system upon reaching adulthood. If the defendant were eight, few, if any, students would agree that she should be tried as an adult, and the case would become more complex because some states provide that persons under ten are too young to be tried even as juveniles (because they are assumed to be too young to form intent).

3. Evaluate

Ask students to write a one- to two-page response to the following scenario: Police officers often come upon perpetrators who are under the influence of drugs or alcohol. Many convicted felons are required to abstain from alcohol as a condition of their release from prison on probation or parole. Often, intoxicants cause a person to become violent and emotional, so it is important for the officer to act with caution and to stay calm in these situations so as not to ignite or fuel such aggression.

- What criminal charges should an officer consider when arresting someone who appears to be intoxicated?

If the person is merely being obnoxious but not violent, he or she could be tried for disorderly conduct or for being a public nuisance. If they are violent, they should have to face charges for their violent crimes. If they are on probation or parole, there is a strong chance that it will be revoked.

4. Role Play

A suspect for murder quickly confesses to the crime, but insists that voices in his head told him to commit the crime. He insists that he is insane, but when his public defender explains to him that an insanity defense will not result in his freedom, but institutionalization in a mental hospital, he states that he is not insane and that he wants to recant his testimony. You are the public defender for this defendant.

- Should he rely on any defenses?
- How will you advise him to approach his trial?

Since it is clear that the defendant is not insane but was only lying, other defenses may not be very convincing, especially since they will seem to have been concocted after the fact.

Most students will state that he should simply admit his guilt, plea bargain, and attempt to get leniency through the plea bargaining process.

Criminal Homicide

Chapter Resources

For the Instructor
Instructor's Resource Manual, pp. 77–86
Additional Activities, p. 84
PowerPoint Presentation and ExamView Pro Testbank
   CD-ROM for Chapter 8
cl.glencoe.com Web site

For the Student
Student Edition, Chapter 8, pp. 254–299
Review and Applications, p. 294
Tutorial with Simulation Applications
   CD-ROM for Chapter 8
cl.glencoe.com Web site

KEY TERMS

homicide	murder	mitigation
criminal homicide	manslaughter	adequate provocation
malice aforethought	year-and-a-day rule	imperfect self-defense
born-alive rule	malice	involuntary manslaughter
feticide	felony murder rule	negligent homicide
brain death syndrome	inherently dangerous felonies	vehicular manslaughter
premeditation and deliberation	capital murder	
corpus delicti	voluntary manslaughter	

Lecture Outline

8.1 HOMICIDE
   The Beginning of Life
   The End of Life
   Right to Die

8.2 ELEMENTS OF CRIMINAL HOMICIDE
   Corpus Delicti Requirement
   Actus Reus
   Mens Rea
   Causation
   Without Lawful Justification or Excuse

8.3 TYPES AND DEGREES OF CRIMINAL HOMICIDE

8.4 MURDER
   Malice Aforethought

The Felony Murder Rule
Reckless Disregard for the Value of
   Human Life
The Division of Murder into Degrees
Defenses to Murder

8.5 MANSLAUGHTER
   Voluntary Manslaughter
   Involuntary Manslaughter

In-Chapter Questions

 Keeler v. Superior Court page 259

How do you think this case would be
tried today in California? In Iowa?
   In California, it would be considered a criminal
homicide and Keeler would be tried for murder. In

Iowa, it would be considered a feticide and Keeler would face serious criminal charges for his actions.

Criminal Law Online page 262

Do you think the act should be adopted in other states? Why or why not? Should only doctors be exempt from criminal liability in assisted-suicide cases? What about family members?

This is a controversial topic, and students may have different opinions about it. Regardless of their answers, be sure to emphasize that they need to provide objective reasons for their opinions. Many will believe that doctors should be able to provide this service, but will have mixed opinions about family members, especially since elder abuse is common and people may seek to hasten the death of a relative to receive insurance money or inheritance.

8.1 Self Check page 263

1. Why are the definitions of the beginning and end of life so important in criminal homicide cases?

Because, by definition, a criminal homicide requires the killing of a human being. This requirement raises issues about when life legally begins, such as in the case of an unborn child, and when it legally ends.

2. If you could change one or two elements of the current definitions, what would be the legal consequences of such changes? Why?

If students chose to change the elements of the definition of birth, liability for the unlawful death of fetuses would change greatly. If students chose to change the elements that define death, that could have serious consequences for doctors, families, and law enforcement.

Photo Caption page 265

Why is a defendant's testimony not enough?

A defendant's testimony is not enough because police must objectively link the accused to the victim's murder through physical and circumstantial evidence. In addition, people sometimes confess to crimes that they did not commit.

 People v. Kimes and Kimes **page 266**

Suppose no evidence had been recovered but Kenneth Kimes had simply confessed to the crime upon the suspicions of a neighbor. How would the case be different? Why?

Because of the evidence requirements regarding murder cases, a confession alone would not be enough to sustain a conviction. Students may point out that this confession may yield some information about where evidence could be found.

 People v. Newton **page 267**

Pretend you are the first investigator to have arrived at the scene, and now the defense attorney is hearing your testimony in court. What questions do you think he or she might ask of you?

He or she may try to make you contradict yourself, question your honesty, or question the quality of the evidence discovered. In short, defense attorneys do whatever they can to undermine the prosecution's credibility.

 Forensic Scientist page 269

What qualities do you think a forensic scientist should possess?

A forensic scientist should have scientific education and experience, should be meticulous and detail-oriented, and yet should also be creative enough to understand parallels regarding different pieces of evidence.

Criminal Law Online page 270

Are homicide victims most likely to be killed by someone known or unknown to them? What are the implications of the correct answer?

People are more likely to be killed by people already known to them. This means that the greater danger of homicide does not lie within strangers or the unknown, but with spouses, rivals, and blood relatives.

APPLICATION CASE

Kibbe v. Henderson page 273

What do you think the student was charged with? What would his defense be?

Some students will express surprise at the idea that he should be charged with anything, considering the unusual circumstances of the case. His defense may be that he had no way of expecting such an occurrence late at night, and that because of the darkness the victim was impossible to see.

8.2 Self Check page 275

1. Why is the concept of *actus reus* or voluntary action crucial in proving criminal homicide?

As with all criminal offenses, the act that causes the harm (in this case, death) must be voluntary. The *actus reus* can be a voluntary act or an omission. In the case of criminal homicide, if the accused has a legal duty to act on behalf of another but fails to do so, and death results, the accused can be prosecuted for murder.

2. If the *actus reus* of a crime can also prove *mens rea*, have you then proven criminal homicide? Why or why not?

Yes. Since people rarely confess to murder, and since a confession alone is not enough to lead to a conviction, police and prosecutor must rely on circumstantial evidence surrounding the death to prove that the *actus reus* indicated the *mens rea* at the time of the crime.

8.3 Self Check page 276

How do common law and modern laws differ in regard to criminal homicide?

The common law definition of criminal homicide provides that, unless there are circumstances that excuse or justify the killing, all killings with malice are murder and all killings without malice are manslaughter.

The modern definition has many more factors. They are primarily related to the actor's mental state, which can be used to distinguish between different levels of culpability (and the punishment deserved) in homicide cases. The various types and degrees of homicide include murder, voluntary manslaughter, and involuntary manslaughter.

APPLICATION CASE

People v. Stamp page 279

Imagine that you are the first police officer to arrive at the robbery scene. Write in your report.

Important information would be what was stolen, how the robbery was conducted, clear evidence of the use of force or fear, and whether a weapon was used.

APPLICATION CASE

Taylor v. Superior Court page 281

Explain why the accomplice was charged with first-degree murder.

When accomplices can be shown to play a material role in crimes that result in another person's death, they are held accountable to those crimes and not to lesser charges. Most students will agree that this is just.

APPLICATION CASE

People v. Anderson page 283

Do you feel that this charge was appropriate, or was there evidence to support a first-degree charge? Is a preconceived design or motive necessary for such a charge? Why or why not?

Some students will feel that the charge was appropriate because of the intent issue, but others will feel that this is a good example of a case where a first-degree charge should have been given despite the specific requirements of the elements.

8.4 Self Check page 286

1. Why do you think provocation can be a mitigating factor in a case of voluntary manslaughter?

Because it can lead otherwise rational people to emotional extremes, leading them to commit acts that they would not commit under normal circumstances.

2. Do you think that the felony murder rule should be used in all states or rejected by them (as in Michigan)? Why or why not?

Many people favor the felony murder rule because it ensures that serious criminals with a disregard for human life are punished appropriately. Others feel that it does not allow for mitigating circumstances, but you can point out to them that *any* defendant to the charges of murder may use any of the valid defenses discussed in this chapter.

State v. Gounagias
People v. Berry page 288

What do you think about the contrast between the decisions for these two cases? If you were the judge, how would you have handled each claim of provocation?

Many students will feel that they are inconsistent and thus unfair. Some will feel that both defendants were justified; others, that both were guilty. Regardless, the inconsistency is a serious issue.

State v. Law page 290

What type of evidence would have allowed the defendant to be found guilty of voluntary manslaughter as opposed to murder? Explain why and give examples.

Proof that malice was lacking in the defendant's intent would have reduced his charges, since it was clear that he intended to murder the intruder. Also, if the defendant mistakenly believed that the victim was trying to cause him serious harm, he would have a successful partial defense. Students should be able to think of other partial defenses, as well as some complete defenses that would have applied in slightly different situations.

Montana v. Egelhoff page 291

What type of evidence and statements do you think were excluded from consideration by the Montana court?

Perhaps evidence of his blood alcohol content and any previous treatment for alcoholism were excluded, since the court found that voluntary intoxication was not a valid defense.

Photo Caption page 292

If the driver of this car is intoxicated and crashes the car, with what crime should he or she be charged? Why?

Most people would answer that the driver should be charged with vehicular manslaughter, since this covers "causing a death while operating a motor vehicle in either a grossly negligent manner, or while under the influence of alcohol or other drugs." However, if the driver was wantonly reckless (for instance, driving 80 mph with bald tires), he or she could be charged with murder.

8.5 Self Check page 293

1. What elements of the *mens rea* of criminal liability apply to voluntary manslaughter? To involuntary manslaughter?

The *mens rea* of voluntary manslaughter is killing without malice aforethought. This includes if the actor had intent to kill or cause great bodily harm under certain mitigating circumstances, such as provocation, and the imperfect self-defense.

The *mens rea* of involuntary manslaughter is an unintentional killing while acting in a criminally negligent or non-wantonly reckless manner, which is defined as creating a high and unreasonable risk of death or great bodily harm. This is different from recklessness as a *mens rea*, which requires that the defendant must be aware of the risk of harm but nonetheless disregard it. A defendant can be held liable under a gross negligence *mens rea* standard even if he or she did not specifically consider the possible harm that would result from his or her conduct–if an ordinarily careful person would have, under the same circumstances.

2. How do you differentiate wanton recklessness, negligence, and mere recklessness?

Wanton recklessness that leads to a death will result in a murder conviction. Negligence, or criminal negligence, that leads to a death will result in a conviction of involuntary manslaughter; the same applies for mere recklessness.

Questions For Review

1. What is malice aforethought, and how does it distinguish murder from manslaughter?

Malice aforethought is the *mens rea* (or mental state) of the accused at the time that he or she commits a murder. It is the element that distinguishes murder from manslaughter.

2. What is feticide?

Feticide is the illegal killing of an unborn fetus. Modern statutes that allow prosecution for the death of fetuses generally include four primary types of fetal homicide. These are defined by the stage of fetal development at which the death occurs:

- Viability, when the fetus is developed enough to survive outside the womb; usually about five to six months after conception

- Quickening, or the first movement, of the fetus; usually about four to five months after conception

- Seven to eight weeks after conception, or when an embryo (an earlier stage of pregnancy) becomes a fetus

- Conception

3. What is the difference between the common law and modern definitions of death?

At common law, a person was considered dead when there was a permanent cessation of respiration and heartbeat. Under modern laws, death is defined as complete brain death syndrome, which consists of:

- Absence of receptivity and unresponsiveness to externally applied stimuli and internal needs

- Absence of spontaneous movements or breathing

- Absence of reflex activity

- A flat electroencephalograph reading after a 24-hour period of observation

4. What is the difference between express and implied malice?

Express malice occurs when the actor causes death with the specific intent to kill another human being. Implied malice occurs when the actor causes death without intending to kill, but with a state of mind that is extremely dangerous to other persons. Three examples are:

- The intent to inflict grievous bodily injury or harm upon another

- The intent to act in a manner that shows extreme reckless disregard for the value of human life

- The intent to commit a felony that results in the death of another human being

5. Explain the difference between the felony murder rule and the misdemeanor-manslaughter rule.

The common law felony murder rule created murder liability for all deaths that occurred as a result of the felony participants perpetrating, attempting, or fleeing the felony. Today, this rule imposes a form of strict liability: It applies as long as there was intent to commit the felony and a death resulted.

Under the misdemeanor-manslaughter rule, which can be thought of as a lesser form of the felony murder rule, an accused can be convicted of involuntary manslaughter if an unintentional death occurs from the commission of a misdemeanor or non-forcible felony.

6. What is the Model Penal Code's definition of murder?

The MPC defines murder by specifying its *mens rea* as purposeful, knowing, or reckless. Therefore, killing done purposely, knowingly, or with extreme recklessness is murder. In addition, murder is any killing accomplished during the perpetration of typical enumerated felonies, such as robbery and rape.

7. What is a capital offense, and are all murders capital offenses?

A capital offense is a charge of murder with the maximum punishment of death. It can be, as these various definitions of first-degree murder illustrate:

- An intentional killing that is aggravated by premeditation and deliberation

- Unintentional killing committed by poison, torture, ambush, or bomb

- A killing occurring during the commission of specifically enumerated or inherently dangerous felonies (felony murder rule)

- Where the death penalty is allowed, first-degree murder is usually a capital offense, but second-degree murder is not. Therefore, not all murders are capital offenses.

8. What are the possible defenses to murder?
   Common complete defenses are:
   - Soldiers who kill enemies during wartime

   - A warden who approves the lawful electrocution of a convicted serial killer

   - A person who kills an armed assailant in self-defense, if he or she is rightfully protecting self or family

   In addition, a mitigating factor (partial defense) may justify a reduction of the charge from murder to voluntary manslaughter. Two partial defenses are provocation and imperfect self-defense.

9. What role does negligence play in determining whether a killing is voluntary or involuntary manslaughter?

   An actor is guilty of involuntary manslaughter if he or she causes an unintentional killing while acting in a criminally negligent or non-wantonly reckless manner, which is defined as creating a high and unreasonable risk of death or great bodily harm. Criminally negligent conduct is also referred to as *culpable negligence* or *gross negligence*. Mere negligence, or carelessness, is sufficient to create civil liability, which could result in a lawsuit, but insufficient to create criminal liability. For criminal negligence, the defendant's conduct must be so different from that of the ordinary careful person that it shows an indifference to the consequences. This is different from recklessness as a *mens rea*, which requires that the defendant must be aware of the risk of harm but nonetheless

disregard it. Rather, a defendant can be held liable under a gross negligence *mens rea* standard even if he or she did not specifically consider the possible harm that would result from his or her conduct–if an ordinarily careful person would have, under the same circumstances. Therefore, like provocation, criminal negligence is measured against an objective standard.

10. What are negligent homicide and vehicular manslaughter?

    Some states have a category separate from involuntary manslaughter called negligent homicide. One who is guilty of negligent homicide is said to have acted in such a manner that he or she did not exercise the degree of care that an ordinary person would have exercised under the same circumstances. In addition, some states have also created a separate category of homicide termed vehicular manslaughter which imposes criminal sanctions for causing a death while operating a motor vehicle in either a grossly negligent manner, or while under the influence of alcohol or other drugs.

Problem-Solving Exercises

1. PROM MOM: CRIMINAL HOMICIDE?
   Answers could include the following:
   a. Most students will agree that she should be charged with criminal homicide because she appeared to have caused the baby's death and took great care to conceal the body.

   b. Mitigating circumstances could include her age, immaturity, and fear of getting caught. Aggravating factors could include the fact that there were other options available (e.g., adoption, abortion, or leaving the baby where he could be safely found), the fact that she went to such lengthy efforts to discard the body, and anything in her attitude or testimony that shows a lack of remorse.

c. She could claim temporary insanity. Due to her youth and the fact that she was clearly unprepared for this birth, this may work as a complete or partial excuse.

2. Evidence of a Crime?

Answers could include the following:

a. Peter could be charged with murder in the first degree, since the murder appears to be premeditated and carefully planned, and circumstantial evidence points to an express malice toward David.

b. The love letter provides a motive, and the floor plan and crowbar provide insight regarding the *actus reus*. Both types of evidence help prove criminal intent.

c. It would be helpful, but since murder cases rarely have confessions and confessions alone cannot convict somebody of murder, prosecutors generally rely on circumstantial evidence to prove guilt in such cases.

3. School Violence

Answers could include the following:

a. Although Colin did not have express malice toward Joshua, his reckless behavior made Joshua's death highly likely and was its actual cause. Therefore, students may say that he should be charged with second-degree murder due to his recklessness. If any feel that he should be charged with manslaughter instead, ask them how the *mens rea* requirement of recklessness fits into their equation.

Colin could provide a provocation defense to show that Joshua's repeated harassment drove him to his reckless behavior.

b. Student answers will vary. Many will believe that his age and apparent lack of a prior record should be mitigating factors. Indeed, you can share with the class that many juveniles who are waived to adult court receive lenient sentences because of their youth and because it is their first time in adult court.

c. It could be, but the timeline is not clear in this example. Also, the harassment of Colin may have caused him to build up uncontrollable enmity toward Joshua. Again, the provocation defense may be feasible in Colin's case.

Workplace Applications

1. Police Investigation

It appears that the murder occurred while the perpetrator was committing an armed burglary. Many students will agree that the perpetrator could be charged with first-degree murder according to the felony murder rule, provided that the jurisdiction in which this occurred uses this rule.

2. Decisive Factors

Now it appears that the killing was premeditated because of the perpetrator's past history with the victim. Although the belongings that were taken may have legally belonged to him, his entry into the house was still illegal due to the restraining order. Students will be divided on how to charge him. Some may say that he could claim a heat of passion defense, and many others will state that his behavior was premeditated and was an act of express malice. In the latter case, the perpetrator would again face a first-degree murder charge.

Internet Applications

1. Homicide on the Internet

Yes. Some statistics measure it by reported homicides, others by conviction rates, and still others use different criteria to determine homicide rates. You can ask students which is more important to measure—the number of possible homicide victims, the number of certain homicide victims, or the number of cleared cases. Students will likely state that the number of certain homicide victims is most important.

2. AMERICAN BAR ASSOCIATION

Answers will vary, but many victims are given greater advocacy and a greater voice in the justice process. In addition, victims of certain crimes have special protections that pertain to the specifics of the crime: For instance, rape victims today are protected during rape trials by rape shield laws. Student answers regarding the comprehensiveness of these rights will vary, because many people feel that the justice system provides more for the rights of defendants than for the rights of victims.

Ethics Issues

1. INFANTICIDE, FETICIDE, OR NEITHER?

   a. Since it is clear that the parents caused the death, regardless of whether or not it was before or after the baby was thrown into the dumpster, it may not seem necessary to students. However, since this is a homicide case and the criminal liability can be great, it is advisable to examine all findings.

   b. That the child was born alive and that he died while in the care of his parents. In addition, the medical examiner can find out exactly when and where he died.

   c. Yes.

Additional Activities

Advanced Web Research

1. INTERNET

MANSLAUGHTER

Ask your students to check out "The 'Lectric Law Library's Lexicon on Manslaughter" at *http://www.lectlaw.com/def2/m013.html*. Then ask them the following questions:

- Name all of the differences between murder and manslaughter that are discussed in this article.

- What are the five general situations in which manslaughter can occur, according to this article?

The main differences are that murder requires malice aforethought and manslaughter does not; and manslaughter can have no accessories before the fact because there was no time for premeditation.

The five general situations in which manslaughter can occur are: provocation, mutual combat, resistance to public officers, killing in the prosecution of an unlawful or wanton act, and killing in the prosecution of a lawful act, improperly performed, or performed without lawful authority.

2. INTERNET

JURY INSTITUTIONS

Refer your students to "The Problem of Jury Instructions" by Professor Peter M. Tiersma of Loyola Law School, located at *http://www.tiersma.com/Juryinst/aaasfull.html*. Tell them to scroll down to the section entitled "Defining the Crimes" and read that section in full. Next, have them answer the following questions:

- Why is it important for judges to explain legal definitions of crimes and the elements of a crime in detail? What might happen if this does not occur?

- What suggestion does the author make for providing jurors with understandable information?

Students should understand that it is important because so many legal terms, such as mayhem, larceny, and assault, are either not understood or misunderstood by the public. For example, mayhem is generally used to mean "havoc," not a felony in which a person loses a limb or an eye. If judges do not spell out the proper meanings of these terms and the elements of a crime properly, jurors will misunderstand their duties and convict people incorrectly.

The author suggests providing jurors with a "roadmap or flowchart" that they can follow to reach a verdict. If all elements are met, the crime has been committed and guilt may be established.

3. INTERNET

ILLINOIS V. AUGUST SPIES ET AL.

Have your students visit the Chicago Historical Society's coverage of *Illinois v. August Spies et al.* (1886) at *http://www.chicagohs.org/hadc/transcript/volumeo/000-050/0001-010.html*. Tell them to read the brief section entitled "Instructions on the part of the People," which shows the instructions that the court gave the jury during this trial. Then, have students write a report by answering the following questions:

- What parts of the instructions are specific enough for jurors to clearly understand their meaning? How does this help jurors?

- Which parts are more vague and open to interpretation? Why is this a problem?
- Why is this especially important in murder cases?

Students should be able to express that the examples of how an unlawful killing may occur are specific, and this helps jurors by giving them examples of what constitutes the crime of murder.

Most of the instructions are rather vague and open to interpretation. What is "the peace of the people," "with malice aforethought," or "an abandoned or malignant heart"? Such terms can confuse jurors as to their specific meaning, leaving different people with different perspectives on the crime.

This is especially important in murder cases because of the serious punishments involved, including the death penalty, and the complicated nature of some murder trials.

Extended Workplace Applications

1. Vote

Give students the following scenario: You are a juror in a murder trial in which the defendant, who is 17, acted with express malice beyond a reasonable doubt but claims that he should be given leniency because he had an abused childhood and faced a lot of prejudice while growing up. The court has two decisions to make: whether to find him guilty of first-degree murder, which is characterized in your state as murder committed with express malice, and whether to sentence him to death.

- How will you vote in each decision, and why?

The defendant is clearly guilty of first-degree murder, so unless the jury engages in jury nullification, the facts have established that he is guilty of this crime. Regarding the death penalty, this may be where students would want to show him some leniency, provided that they feel that his excuses are valid and not merely an attempt to manipulate the jury. Although the U.S. Supreme Court has provided that the death penalty is valid for offenders aged 16 and older, students may have mixed feelings about whether to sentence him to death due to his age and personal issues.

2. Investigate

Give students the following scenario: You are a police officer investigating the death of a child. You know the parents because approximately three years ago, their first child died under suspicious circumstances. Although the case was eventually closed because it appeared to be an accident, you always believed that the parents were guilty. In this case, the suspects' three-year-old daughter was playing in the backyard when she allegedly slipped and fell into a six-inch mud puddle, where she was found face down and drowned. The mother claims that she attempted to use mouth-to-mouth resuscitation, but it did not work. In investigating the corpse, the medical examiner finds no trace of the mother's saliva around the child's mouth, nor does he find that the mother's fingerprints are anywhere on the child's face. In addition, he finds several bruises of different sizes on the child's body, which indicate serious injuries but which the parents cannot explain. At the crime scene, you find no evidence that the child slipped and fell, and the medical examiner does not see any bruises on the child's knees or hands that would indicate a fall.

You believe that the parents drowned the child deliberately, and that the child was subject to abuse before the killing.

- What evidence do you have that would help you prove first-degree murder?
- Which additional information would help, and how would you obtain it?
- Could you reopen the previous case and try the parents for that as well?

Students should be able to point out that the evidence on the child's body indicates that the mother was lying about trying to resuscitate the child, and that the child did not accidentally slip and fall. Evidence at the crime scene seems to back this up. Moreover, it is highly unlikely that a child playing outside would drown herself in a small mud puddle, and the prosecutor could use this fact to make the parents' story seem unlikely.

A confession would help, but seems unlikely and is not necessary. Past records of abuse, or information regarding child abuse from character witnesses, would be helpful and could be obtained through further investigation.

Since the parents have not yet been tried for the death of the first child, there are no restrictions to re-opening the case and possibly trying them for the murder of that child as well.

3. Murder on Campus

Give students the following scenario: In your second year of college, someone in your apartment complex is robbed and murdered outside his home. Immediately after his death, rumors begin to circulate that he was involved in drug dealing, which led to his death. Shortly after his death, you see someone with a key enter his apartment and take a carload of belongings. Since he had a key, you think nothing of it until the next day, when his family comes to pick up his belongings and finds most of his valuables missing. Also missing is a secret stash of cocaine that his sister knew he kept hidden in his closet. You can provide a description of the man who entered the apartment, and a general description of his car.

- How could this information be helpful to police?

This information could be helpful because this person may be related to the man's killing. He was aware of where the victim hid his drugs, and he somehow had a key to the victim's apartment. In addition, he committed a burglary and must at least answer for that; while in custody, police could interrogate him about the murder. Students will likely think of other ways in which this information may be helpful.

4. Prosecute

Give students the following scenario: You are a prosecutor who is preparing to try the case of a 16-year old who has killed seven people at his school. The defendant has a long history of mental illness and erratic behavior, and the defense is asking for a plea bargain based on his diminished capacity. They state that because he lacked malice aforethought, but reacted blindly out of an emotional reaction, he should be charged with manslaughter instead of murder. The defendant does appear to possess enough mental illness to warrant such a plea bargain, but the public outcry against him demands that he be tried and convicted of murder, which you could do because of the overwhelming evidence against him. It is really up to you to decide how to charge him.

- What do you do?

Many students would choose to charge him with murder because, even though he may have labored under diminished capacity during the commission of his criminal act, he is clearly capable of committing multiple heinous crimes. It is also not guaranteed that his capacity was too diminished to foresee the result of his offenses. Also, even though this is not a legal consideration, prosecutors face much political pressure and tend to lose public confidence if they are seen as lenient; as a result, public confidence in their community may suffer and fear of crime may rise.

Some students will charge him with manslaughter due to his age and mental infirmity. You can suggest to them that he may be subject to trial as an adult and/or to blended sentencing, which is when a juvenile's sentence begins in a juvenile institution but ends in an adult one, to which he is transferred upon reaching adulthood. Therefore, even with the diminished capacity defense, he can still experience a lengthy sentence.

Crimes Against Persons: Other Offenses

Chapter Resources

For the Instructor
Instructor's Resource Manual, pp. 87–96
Additional Activities, p. 94
PowerPoint Presentation and ExamView Pro Testbank
   CD-ROM for Chapter 9
cl.glencoe.com Web site

For the Student
Student Edition, Chapter 9, pp. 300–340
Review and Applications, p. 334
Tutorial with Simulation Applications
   CD-ROM for Chapter 9
cl.glencoe.com Web site

KEY TERMS

battery	rape	criminal abortion	elder abuse
aggravated battery	statutory rape	feticide	false imprisonment
assault	spousal rape	viability	shopkeeper's rule
conditional assault	rape trauma syndrome	child abuse	kidnapping
aggravated assault	child molestation	spousal abuse	
mayhem	Megan's Law	battered woman's syndrome	

Lecture Outline

9.1 PHYSICAL CRIMES
   Battery
   Assault
   Mayhem

9.2 SEX CRIMES
   Rape
   Child Molestation

9.3 CRIMES AGAINST THE PERSON IN THE HOME
   Criminal Abortion
   Child Abuse
   Spousal Abuse
   Elder Abuse

9.4 FALSE IMPRISONMENT AND KIDNAPPING
   False Imprisonment
   Kidnapping

In-Chapter Questions

Photo caption page 306
How can you distinguish assault from battery?
   Assault can be either offensive touching, such as shoving somebody, or the intentional scaring of another person. Battery is more serious, and is defined by an actual physical attack.

9.1 Self Check page 308
1. What is the difference between assault and battery, and why are the two sometimes confused with each other?
   Assault is an incomplete battery that is characterized by offensive touching and/or the intentional frightening of the victim. Battery is more serious than assault because it involves the use of direct force. The two terms are

sometimes confused because they are very similar, and because most people mistake battery for assault.

2. Describe the trend to eliminate mayhem.

In many jurisdictions and under the MPC, the concept of mayhem is considered outdated and has been replaced with aggravated battery.

 People v. Keenan page 309

Do you believe that a person is disfigured only if it can be publicly seen? Explain.

Most students will agree with the court in *People v. Keenan* and agree that disfigurement is disfigurement, regardless of where it occurs on a person's body. In any event, the scarring that happened to the woman in this case may be visible in swimwear, or at a locker room or shower at a gym; therefore, it is possible that it could be seen publicly, despite the defendant's claims.

Criminal Law Online page 311

1. How does this information and the 800 number help victims?

This 800 number helps victims because they can call it from any phone at any time, regardless of their financial resources. The additional information provides women with the knowledge that they can do something to deal with their situations.

2. How could criminal justice and medical professionals benefit from such information?

They could benefit from the statistics and other general information because it gives the reader greater insight regarding the enormous problem of sexual abuse in the United States.

 Rusk v. State page 313

Should defendants be found guilty of rape only if some form of force is applied? Why or why not?

No, because rape can be committed through involuntarily intoxication of the victim, through coercion without use of force, and through sexual relations with someone who is mentally infirm and cannot resist for that reason.

 Buckey v. County of Los Angeles page 317

What types of safeguards can help prevent slanderous accusations from damaging people's reputations?

People who commit slanderous accusations are legally liable for their actions, and can be punished for such accusations. Although this should act as a deterrent, it does not always succeed in doing so.

9.2 Self Check page 319

1. How have recent laws changed the ways in which rape victims are treated at trials?

Recently, rape shield laws have been created to forbid prosecutors from asking rape victims questions about their sexual past. This is because such questions are irrelevant, but have been used in the past to sway juries into believing that the rape victim "deserved" it.

2. How does Megan's Law protect a community from recidivism among sexual offenders?

By allowing a community to know about the existence of its sexual offenders, Megan's Law enables them to take protective measures to keep their children away from such offenders.

 State v. Horne page 322

In this case, how is the *mens rea* requirement fulfilled for feticide?

Since the man's intent was grievous bodily harm to someone who was obviously in the final stages of pregnancy, his intent constituted malice and would be considered sufficient to make him responsible for any deaths that resulted.

Ethics in Criminal Law page 323

1. Along with the requisite lack of consent, the use of threats, fear, and intoxication indicate that this crime has occurred.
2. No, because that does not mean that she consented to have sex with him. This is an important distinction, but still needs to be made clear to some students.

State v. Williams **page 325**
Do you think the conviction of man-slaughter is too severe? Why or why not?

Most students will feel that it is not too severe, since their negligence caused the child's death. In addition, some students will probably feel that it is not severe *enough*.

Criminal Law Online page 326

1. What does CDF mean by "A Healthy Start," "A Head Start," and the other items that you see listed on the main page?

The CDF uses these headlines to discuss the ways in which proper childrearing is necessary to create healthy and happy children. The CDF supports child nutrition, early childhood education, and other programs that enrich a child's life.

2. Overall, what is the goal of the CDF?

The basic goal of the CDF is to ensure that children are in safe and happy homes and are protected from abuse and neglect.

Photo Caption page 327

How prevalent do you think elder abuse is in nursing homes?

Most students will feel that it is fairly prevalent, and that negligence may be a bigger culprit than malicious abuse because of the understaffing, low staff quality, and emphasis on maximized profit that characterize most nursing homes.

9.3 Self Check page 328

1. How does viability affect the prosecution of feticide cases?

This depends on the stage of pregnancy at which the law provides for feticide charges. Many jurisdictions state the feticide has occurred in homicide cases involving fetuses that have already reached viability.

2. What are the differences in how social workers and prosecutors treat emotional abuse, physical abuse, sexual abuse, and neglect of children?

Emotional abuse is generally handled informally, such as by requiring the parent to take parenting classes. Physical and sexual abuse are generally considered the most serious and are subject to criminal charges; neglect can be equally serious and also result in criminal charges, although if it has less serious consequences it can be handled informally. Physical and sexual abuse, as well as child neglect, can lead to a child being removed from the home.

In the Matter of the Welfare of R.W.C.
page 330

Is the "tradition" defense a viable one? What other traditions could lead to criminal prosecution?

No, "tradition" is not a viable defense to criminal behavior. Actions that are criminal remain criminal regardless of whether people choose to create traditions around them. You could explain to students that serious crimes, such as hate crimes, can be seen as "traditions" by certain groups of people, and that this can be a very misleading concept.

Examples of "traditions" that can lead to criminal prosecution in this country are female genital mutilation (a tradition practiced widely in Africa, and to a lesser extent among immigrants in the United States), lynching and other forms of intimidation against minorities, and gang activity among people who live in neighborhoods where gang membership is common enough to be considered a tradition.

Certified Victim Assistance Specialist
page 332
What issues do you think certified victim assistance specialists must deal with in their jobs?

Student answers will vary, and may include any of the following: victim depression, rape trauma syndrome, victim phobias, substance abuse as a result of psychological problems resulting from the victimization, lowered job performance, and psychosomatic illnesses (such as headaches).

9.4 Self Check page 333

1. How have laws changed regarding kidnapping?

At common law, kidnapping was a misdemeanor that referred mainly to taking people outside the country. Today, it is a serious felony that involves the unlawful abduction of a person to any location, even if it is down the street.

2. Explain the Parental Kidnapping Prevention Act.

The Parental Kidnapping Prevention Act requires states to enforce child custody decisions entered by a court of another state if the custody decision is consistent with provisions of the act.

Review and Applications

Questions for Review

1. Name some ways in which assault and battery differ from mayhem.

Assault and battery, in their simplest forms, are less serious offenses than mayhem, which involves the loss of an eye or limb. In addition, assault and battery appear in all jurisdictions, but mayhem is considered outdated in some places and is being replaced by aggravated battery. Assault and battery range from misdemeanor charges to serious felony charges (as aggravated assault and aggravated battery), but mayhem is solely a serious felony charge. Students will likely be able to think of more differences.

2. How do aggravated assault and aggravated battery differ from simple assault and simple battery?

Aggravated assault is a felony in most jurisdictions and can be defined as any assault with intent to kill, rob, or rape, or as assault with specified deadly weapons. Aggravated battery involves conduct accompanied by intent to kill or rape; it is usually a specific intent crime and carries greater penalties than simple battery.

3. Why is rape considered a general-intent offense?

Rape is a general-intent offense because the defendant is not required to have the specific intent to have non-consensual sex in order to

be guilty of rape. Instead, he is guilty "if he possessed a morally blameworthy state of mind regarding the victim's lack of consent."

4. Explain how the laws regarding statutory rape have changed over time.

At common law, sexual intercourse between a man and a "woman child under the age of ten years" was considered rape regardless of whether consent was given. Today, this would be considered child molestation and the age of the victim for statutory rape has generally been raised to approximately 13 to 17, with some variation from state-to-state. Many states divide statutory rape offenses into two categories, and statutory rape involving a girl in her early teens usually carries a stiffer penalty than cases involving girls in their late teens.

5. Define spousal rape and explain recent legislation to outlaw it.

Spousal rape can be defined as "non-consensual sexual acts between a woman and her husband, former husband or long term partner, and… any unwanted, humiliating and painful sexual activity." Lack of consent can be determined by the use of intimidation or threats.

Currently, all 50 states and federal territories consider spousal rape a crime. In most places, it is a crime only when accompanied by force. As another legal option, a wife may also sue her husband in civil court for pain, suffering, and medical and other costs incurred as a result of spousal rape.

6. Name some reasons why child molestation frequently goes unreported.

Unfortunately, there are several reasons for this. The most common are:
- A desire to protect the molester, who is often a family member or close family friend
- A feeling that they were at fault, especially if they have been taught to look up to the molester
- Fear of punishment
- Difficulty in verbally expressing what has occurred

7. Why are parents and guardians more liable for child abuse than others?

Parents and guardians are more liable and are held to a higher degree of responsibility because they have an inherent duty that no other person has to care for, protect, and provide for their child. If the parent is the abuser, an observer of the abuse, or knows that the child is being abused but fails to intervene, that parent will be punished by the child abuse laws of any state.

Like many states, Maryland requires that in order to be convicted of felony child abuse in the first degree, the abuser must be either a parent, a person acting as the parent (a legal responsibility referred to as *in loco parentis*), or another person responsible for the supervision of the minor child.

8. What are some ways that social workers can respond to child neglect? To child physical abuse? To child emotional maltreatment?

Neglect can have serious consequences and result in criminal charges, although if it has less serious consequences it can be handled informally. Physical and sexual abuse are generally considered the most serious and are subject to criminal charges. Physical and sexual abuse, as well as child neglect, can lead to a child being removed from the home. Emotional maltreatment is generally handled informally, such as by requiring the parent to take parenting classes.

9. Who is usually the perpetrator in elder abuse cases, and why?

Elder abuse usually occurs in the home by the victim's spouse or children. Such abuse often occurs because when an older person requires another to take care of him or her, he or she is at the mercy of the caregiver and cannot fight back. In addition, the burden is often overwhelming and the elder does not get the care and attention he or she needs.

10. How did the MPC affect laws regarding false imprisonment?

Prior to the adoption of the MPC in the 1960s, few states considered false imprisonment

a crime. After the introduction of the MPC, many states revised their penal codes and a majority of them included the offense for the first time.

11. Explain how the shopkeeper's rule works. What are its limitations?

The shopkeeper's rule is a form of lawful restraint that provides that a shopkeeper, who is defined as an owner or manager of a store or restaurant, may restrain a person if the shopkeeper possesses a reasonable belief that the customer has not paid a bill or has shoplifted an item. In this situation, a shopkeeper may be able to restrain the customer in order to ascertain whether the bill or item was paid for. The limitations are that the restraint may not last an inordinate amount of time or involve physical force.

12. Name and define the two legal responses to child abduction that are discussed in this chapter.

Recent legislation regarding child abduction is the Parental Kidnapping Prevention Act, which requires states to enforce child custody decisions entered by a court of another state if the custody decision is consistent with provisions of the act. The other federal law that involves child kidnapping is the Lindbergh Act, which specifically addresses kidnapping (of adults or children) for ransom or reward when the victim is transported to another state or to a foreign country.

Problem-Solving Exercises

1. **ASSAULT AND BATTERY**
   Answers could include the following:
   a. He is the victim of battery, mayhem (or aggravated battery, depending on the jurisdiction), and gang-related violence (if the jurisdiction has separate charges or sentence enhancers for gang-related crimes).

   b. He has committed battery and gang-related violence (if the jurisdiction has separate charges or sentence enhancers for gang-related crimes).

c. Since the victim's injuries appear more serious than his rival's, students may want to recommend that the rival receive prosecution, but not the victim. Others may wish to see both prosecuted.

2. SPOUSAL ABUSE

Since the couple engaged in mutual fighting for a long time, and both were apparently to blame for this, battered woman's syndrome does not sound like it would be a successful defense. On the other hand, provocation may work as at least a partial defense, since it is clear that this couple provoked each other into violent fights.

3. SEX CRIMES AND FALSE IMPRISONMENT

Most students will not agree that she has been kidnapped because she agreed to get into the car, but false imprisonment might apply and rape certainly does. At the very least, he should be charged with forcible rape.

4. ASSAULT

Answers could include the following:

a. Students may feel inclined to revoke his parole because he was intoxicated in public and acting unpredictably. They should, however, indicate that they would consider other issues, such as his original conviction and other possible parole violations, before making their decisions. If this parolee has a completely nonviolent record and no other parole problems, it could be preferable to simply add more restrictions to his parole than to send him back to prison.

b. Yes, the arrest was justified because he was drunk in public and waving around a bone, which grazed somebody's head. He could be charged with public intoxication and assault; however, if the prosecutor does decide to press charges, it would be easier for everyone involved to simply revoke his parole and send him back to prison.

Workplace Applications page 00

1. CHILD ABUSE

Answers could include the following:

a. You could ask the mother what specific punishments are occurring, and why, checking her story for contradictions or lies. You could also ask what schooling they are receiving during this time, and how their home-schooling will be implemented.

b. You should ask to see the children and examine them for signs of abuse, neglect, or emotional maltreatment. If necessary, you can ask to speak to the children alone and individually to find out if they are doing well.

c. If there are clear signs of abuse, yes, the mother can be charged with child abuse. If the signs of abuse are ambiguous, you can continue to visit with follow-up calls to make sure that the children are well.

d. Careful interviewing of the mother, children, neighbors, and the children's school will help determine if child abuse has occurred. It will also alert the community to be aware that abuse may be occurring, so that they will watch for any signs of it.

2. DOMESTIC VIOLENCE

Student answers will vary, but should indicate at least some of the following: Typical services include shelter for battered women and their children, counseling, placement services for jobs and housing, and basic education for women who have never had a checking account or been on their own before. Typical outcomes vary from shelter to shelter, but many will report that the majority of women do not return to their husbands. In most shelters, the majority of women have children, which can make it harder for a woman to leave an abuser for emotional and financial reasons.

3. CRIME ON CAMPUS

Answers could include the following:

a. The roommate can be charged with false imprisonment, robbery, and battery.

b. Although the victim's story sounds very legitimate, it is best to make sure that the story checks out before making an arrest. It would probably be best to take fingerprints, have the victim repeat her story at least once to check for inconsistencies, ask if there were witnesses, and see if the roommate can be easily located for questioning.

Internet Applications

1. LEARN ABOUT ELDER ABUSE

Answers could include the following:

a. The goal of APE is to ensure safe and humane caretaking in nursing homes, which are fraught with elder abuse.

b. Elderly people face physical abuse such as beatings, starvation, and not receiving medication; sexual abuse; and emotional maltreatment.

c. People can educate themselves, support groups like APE, and contact their political representatives to lobby for more laws and law enforcement regarding the mistreatment of elderly people in nursing homes.

2. THE LINDBERGH CASE

Answers could include the following:

a. Various clues pointed to Hauptmann's guilt, but the main one was the handwriting sample.

b. The FBI looked for proof that Hauptmann was involved in the kidnapping and ransom efforts, and most students will agree that they amassed enough evidence to collect, even today.

c. Student answers will vary, but most will also agree that the FBI did a very good job of building a case from almost no leads.

d. Most students will agree with the charges, and most will agree with the severity of Hauptmann's sentence.

Ethics Issues

1. ABUSE

Answers can include the following:

a. Most students will agree that the mother is physically and emotionally abusing her child.

b. She should contact the police or her local child protective services agency immediately.

c. Since she is not the child's guardian and the living arrangement is informal, she does not have the same duty as a parent or guardian. However, some students will agree that she should be held as an accomplice if she continues to provide food and shelter for them without interfering in some way.

d. If the woman reports the abuse now, she will probably escape liability. However, the mother could be held criminally liable for the physical abuse that has occurred to date.

NOTE TO INSTRUCTOR: These additional activities are exclusive to this IRM. They are designed to meet the special needs of your students. If you or your students cannot access a Web site referred to here, go to *cl.glencoe.com* for the latest updated links.

Advanced Web Research

1. INTERNET

SEX CRIMES INVESTIGATORS

Have students check out the Web site for the Colorado Association of Sex Crimes Investigators at *http://www.casci.net* and read "About CASCI." Then have them answer the following questions:

- How does CASCI try to improve knowledge and information sharing among professionals?

- How do they try to improve sexual assault investigations, and what else do they do to promote professionalism in this area?

CASCI provides and encourages information sharing among sexual assault investigators by establishing an atmosphere of cooperation and by trying to understand sexual assault victims more thoroughly.

Students should be able to understand that their general goals are to ensure consistent high standards in sexual assault investigations and treatment of offenders, to encourage integrity in all sexual assault investigations, and to provide low cost, high quality training seminars and conferences related to all phases of sexual assault investigations.

2. INTERNET

CHILDREN'S SERVICES AND PROGRAMS

Have students visit the Web site for Children's Institute International at *http://www.childrensinstitute.org* and read the first page, "Programs and Services." Then have them write a summary by answering the following questions:

- What programs and services do they provide? Does this list seem comprehensive? Why or why not?

- What family violence and dysfunction issues do these programs and services attempt to address, and how do these issues make child abuse more likely?

Students should show an understanding of how these programs operate and that they include, but are not limited to, "child and family assessment, sexual abuse treatment, domestic violence intervention, family treatment, Early Head Start program, therapeutic day care, child health clinic, long-term foster care, and substance abuse treatment and prevention services." Most students will agree that their support programs are fairly comprehensive because they seem to cover all major family issues. Some students may have suggestions for additional programs that would help at-risk families.

Students should understand that these programs address issues such as parental substance abuse, domestic violence, and a lack of paternal responsibility, which indicates that many dysfunctional families suffer from these problems.

3. INTERNET

CHILD ABDUCTION

Have students visit the U.S. Department of State's page for The Office of Children's Issues, located at **http://travel.state.gov/children's_issues. html** and click on "Office of Children's Issues." Have them read the sections on that page entitled "International Abduction," "What the State Department Can Do," and "[What the State Department] Cannot Do," and answer the following questions:

- How can the U.S. State Department get involved to help parents find internationally abducted children?

- What international resources can they use in their efforts?

- What limitations do they face in trying to retrieve abducted children? Why do you think this is the case?

Students should be able to understand that the U.S. State Department can provide a point of contact for the parent whose child was abducted, list the child in a passport look-out database, monitor judicial or administrative proceedings overseas, and assist parents in contacting local officials in foreign countries or contact them on the parents' behalf. Parents can fill out applications with foreign authorities for the return of the child, and in some cases work through Embassies and Consulates abroad in an attempt to locate, visit, and report on the child's general welfare.

The U.S. State Department has several limitations. They cannot re-abduct the child, help a parent to violate host country laws, pay legal expenses or court fees, provide legal representation, or give refuge to a parent involved in a re-abduction. This is because they are not a law enforcement agency, nor do they have the right to supercede the laws or law enforcement of other countries.

Extended Workplace Applications

1. Report

Have students contact a local social services agency and have them ask the agency how they handle different types of child abuse, naming the four types discussed in the chapter (physical, emotional, sexual, and neglectful). Next, have students ask them how much heavy caseloads affect their ability to address all of the cases they receive.

Students should report a variety of options for responding to each type of abuse, depending on its severity, the age of the child, and the resources that are available at any given time. Most agencies will treat sexual and physical abuse as the most important, then neglect, and then emotional maltreatment. Heavy caseloads negatively affect the proper handling of child abuse cases in nearly all jurisdictions. Students may report that some people are reluctant to admit that this is a problem, but others are very open about it and will tell shocking stories about child abuse that is allowed to continue due to a lack of resources.

2. Interview

Have students call their local police department and ask how child abuse and neglect affect delinquency. Have students also ask how they handle children who are clearly becoming delinquents, but who are known to come from dysfunctional homes and need some kind of help.

Most police strongly believe that dysfunctional homes are the chief cause of delinquency and most departments are eager to involve themselves in crime prevention strategies that target younger, at-risk juveniles. However, students should understand that after a certain point if a juvenile does not respond to help and continues to act in a delinquent manner, police will stop sympathizing with them and will begin to treat them like criminals.

3. Summarize

Have students contact their local police department and prosecutor's office and have them ask the department how they distinguish the crimes of assault, battery, and mayhem. If this information is available online, have students get the URL from them and print it out with a summary explaining the law in their own words.

Student answers will vary. Most will find that assault and battery are defined in generally the same way as they are defined in the textbook. Some will report that the crime of mayhem does not exist in their jurisdiction, but has been replaced by aggravated battery. Others will report that mayhem is still on the books; be sure to get a complete explanation from them about how mayhem is defined in their particular jurisdiction.

4. Interview

Have students contact their local prosecutor's office or rape hotline and have them ask if spousal rape is handled through criminal courts or family courts. Then have students ask them why, and what types of convictions usually result.

Most jurisdictions handle spousal rape cases through family courts because they consider it to be a family issue, like domestic violence or child welfare cases. Some handle spousal rape through criminal courts because they recognize its seriousness as a crime and wish to prosecute it as any other rape. Students may report that jurisdictions that handle such cases through the criminal courts provide for lengthier sentences, but this is not always the case.

Crimes Against Habitation

Chapter Resources

For the Instructor
Instructor's Resource Manual, pp. 97–105
Additional Activities, p. 103
PowerPoint Presentation and ExamView Pro Testbank
CD-ROM for Chapter 10
cl.glencoe.com Web site

For the Student
Student Edition, Chapter , pp. 342–369
Review and Applications, p. 364
Tutorial with Simulation Applications
   CD-ROM for Chapter 10
cl.glencoe.com Web site

KEY TERMS

common law arson	modern arson	constructive entry	aggravated burglary
curtilage	common law burglary	nighttime	burglar's tools
will	modern burglary	sleep test	motor vehicle
malice	inner door	simple burglary	joyriding

Lecture Outline

10.1 ARSON
   Intent Required for Arson
   Elements and Degrees of Arson

10.2 BURGLARY
   Elements of Burglary
   Breaking and Entering
   Degrees of Burglary
   Possession of Burglar's Tools
   Vehicular Burglary

Answers to In-Chapter Questions

Criminal Law Online page 345

What is their focus, and how do they educate the public about arson?

   Their focus is on uncovering and investigating arson (as opposed to accidental fire) cases and educating the public about the dangers of arson and how to avoid being victimized by it.

APPLICATION CASE *Poff v. State* page 347

Would a summer home, which is only used seasonally as a place to sleep, be considered a dwelling house? Why or why not?

   No, because the sleep test requires frequent sleeping at a place in order for it to be considered a residence.

Photo Caption page 347

What are some of the clues that are listed in your textbook?

   Clues include: incendiary devices, fuel cans, broken door locks, or any other signs of forced entry; any financial instability, which might indicate a motive to collect on an insurance policy; any enemies of the owner or occupant, who might have set the fire for revenge; and any known firebugs (arsonists) in the crowd.

Fire/Arson Investigator page 350

What special skills or traits do you think a fire/arson investigator must have?

He or she must have an understanding of the different methods and materials used by arsonists to start fires; an understanding of the ways in which arsonists try to conceal clues; and an understanding of who the typical arsonist is and how he or she operates.

10.1 Self Check page 350

1. How have laws regarding arson changed since common law?

At common law, arson applied to habitations only. Modern arson is the malicious, willful burning, or attempted burning, of one's own or another individual's property; it is a violent crime against both habitation and property.

2. What are the steps that officers need to take to investigate a fire, in order to determine if it was accidental or intentional?

Some basic steps are:

- The officer should look for incendiary devices, fuel cans, broken door locks, or any other signs of forced entry.

- The officer should also interview all available witnesses at the scene, asking questions that will help to determine the financial stability of the building owner or occupants. Any financial instability might indicate a motive to collect on an insurance policy.

- The officer should also seek to learn of any enemies of the owner or occupant, who might have set the fire for revenge.

- Finally, the officer should scan the crowd for any known firebugs, or known arsonists. Many arsonists get a psychological rush by watching the fires that they have set and often are present at the fire.

Youthful Burglar page 352

Do you think the boys in this case should be prosecuted? If you were a prosecutor, how would you handle this case?

Most students will agree that they should be prosecuted because they were mature enough to plan the crimes and because they presented a threat to the community.

As long as they are not legally too young to be tried as juveniles, many students would favor adjudicating them for their crimes.

Criminal Law Online page 352

1. Which of these suggestions have you already implemented?

Answers will vary. Many students will report having proper locks on their windows and doors, proper lighting, and using a timer to turn on lights when they are gone in the evening.

2. Which should you implement to increase your safety?

Students will generally agree that most, if not all, of these suggestions are worth implementing, although some (such as an alarm system that connects directly to a police department) are rather expensive.

State v. Cochran page 355

Would Cochran have been convicted if the bedroom had been unlocked? What if he had entered a closet?

Yes, because he still would have had to turn the handle of the doorknob, which is an affirmative act to committing the crime. If the closet had a closed door, the same would apply.

People v. Czerminski page 356

Should police officers be held to a higher standard of conduct? Should they be punished more harshly when they commit crimes?

Many students will feel that officers should be watched carefully for criminal behavior, but that they should be punished no differently than anyone else. Indeed, some students will state that the issue is not whether to punish officers more severely, but only to ensure that they receive any kind of punishment and are not protected by the justice system for their crimes.

K.P.M. v. State page 356
How does this case meet the requirements of burglary?

It meets the requirements because the defendant took the items for less than their actual worth.

Photo Caption page 00

Do you think this person is committing burglary or breaking and entering?

The two crimes are so similar that it is difficult to tell which the person pictured is committing. Whether students say breaking and entering or burglary, make sure they realize that burglary requires a specific intent to cause a crime inside the structure while breaking and entering does not.

10.2 Self Check page 363

1. What are the differences between burglary and breaking and entering?

    Breaking and entering involves the illegal entry into a dwelling or building. Burglary contains these elements plus the additional one of possessing the intent to commit a crime inside.

2. What are the three general purposes of vehicular burglary?

    The three general purposes are stealing the vehicle, stealing something out of the vehicle, or joyriding.

Review and Applications

Questions For Review

1. What level of burning is required to constitute arson? What levels of burning do not constitute arson?

    At common law, charring of wood is required. Scorching, discoloration, or smoking of the wood did not and do not constitute arson unless charring also occurred.

2. Under modern law, what is the definition of dwelling structure in most jurisdictions?

    Modern arson is generally defined as the malicious, willful burning, or attempted burning, of one's own or another individual's property.

Today, most jurisdictions consider arson to be a violent crime against both habitation and property, not just habitations or places within one's curtilage as was the case at common law.

For example, the Model Penal Code provides that a person is guilty of arson if he or she "starts a fire or causes an explosion with the purpose of: (a) destroying a building or occupied structure of another; or (b) destroying or damaging any property, whether his own or another's, to collect insurance for such loss."

3. What are some of the differences between first-degree and second-degree arson?

    At common law, a building had to be an inhabited dwelling or within a person's curtilage in order for its unlawful burning to be considered arson. Today, the dwelling requirement exists in a much broader form to distinguish first-degree arson and second-degree arson. First-degree arson is generally defined as arson to any dwelling, any structure that is normally full of people such as a hospital or school, or "any other structure that the arsonist knew or had reasonable grounds to believe was occupied by a human being." Second-degree arson generally applies to arson against generally uninhabited buildings, such as warehouses.

4. State the common law purpose of the burglary law.

    Common law burglary protected against the violence that was likely to occur when a burglar broke into an occupied dwelling at night. The burglary laws were not to protect persons against unlawful trespass, or breaking and entering, which do not require the intent to commit a crime beyond the actual trespass or entering.

5. What is an inner door, and what is its meaning in relation to burglary?

    An inner door is any door that is inside a building but does not lead directly outside; one must already be inside to gain entry. If a burglar gains legal entry into a building through an open outer door, such as one in a retail establishment during normal business hours, breaking into an inner door of a building is still burglary. Courts have determined that a burglary has occurred if a thief enters an open outer door or window, and later turns a knob or key, or lifts a latch.

6. What is the difference between the common law and modern definitions of nighttime, and its relevance to the crime of burglary?

At common law and the current state laws that follow the common law definition of burglary, the act must be committed at nighttime, which is defined as the period between sunset and sunrise where there is not enough daylight to discern a man's face. For states following this common law definition, the time of day, amount of sunlight, and use of sunlight to see becomes important in establishing whether it is nighttime.

Under modern revised definitions, many states define burglary without a time requirement, so that it can occur during the day or night. The jury has the right to apply common sense and knowledge to determine when the burglary occurred.

7. What is the sleep test?

The sleep test is whether the dwelling is used regularly as a place to sleep. Occasional sleeping on the premises is usually not enough to satisfy the sleep test, and a building that is not inhabited for any variety of reasons will not satisfy it.

8. How can the offense of breaking and entering be used as a prosecutor's tool, and why?

The breaking and entering offense can be an effective tool for prosecutors to use because they may offer this charge to a defendant, rather than burglary, in the hopes of a plea bargain.

9. What are some general and specific definitions of a motor vehicle, as given in your text?

A general definition is "a vehicle proceeding on land by means of its own power plant and free of rails, tracks, or overhead wires." More specific definitions vary by state. For instance, a Michigan court decided that a van with flat tires was a vehicle because it could be easily repaired and that thousands of vehicles in need of repair sit in repair lots, yards, and garages,

yet are still considered vehicles. In addition, a Texas court found that a vehicle sitting in a car lot without an engine was still a vehicle under Texas statutory language, which defines vehicle as any device that could be moved, propelled, or drawn by a person in the normal course of commerce or transportation. The court found that the temporary condition of the vehicle was less important than its mechanism, design, and construction.

10. What is joyriding, and how can this offense be used as a prosecutor's tool?

Joyriding is defined as the illegal removal and driving of someone else's car, but with the intention of keeping it only temporarily.

Sometimes, and under certain circumstances, a prosecutor may reduce the original charge of vehicular burglary to joyriding. This is because although joyriding is a felony in many jurisdictions, it is not considered as serious as burglary and may be used to persuade a defendant to accept a plea bargain and not go to trial.

Problem-Solving Exercises

1. BURGLAR'S TOOLS
   Answers could include the following:
   a. This alibi does not check out. Although carpeting jobs do change frequently and employees often follow their supervisors to locations for one-day work stints, he still should have a basic idea of the place from which he just drove. More importantly, the tools do not exactly match those used by carpet installers. Although the pry bar and knives are valid, the flashlight and plastic gloves seem unlikely and the screwdrivers and crescent wrenches are completely unnecessary.
   b. You can ask him exactly how these tools are used in carpeting, and what kind of job he was doing. Even if he doesn't remember the exact location, he should be able to describe the place at which the job was performed. If he is lying, his contradictions will become apparent.

c. It is likely that he possesses burglar's tools, and the combination of his prior record and poor alibi should be enough to establish probable cause. Further questioning, as suggested in Answer B above, will reveal more information.

2. ARSON INVESTIGATION

Answers could include the following:

a. Most officers would be suspicious of the apparent firebug in the audience, especially since the owner appears grieved. Also, the owner will be easy to locate at a later time, but the firebug may depart when he sees people being questioned. Therefore, the firebug should be questioned first, followed by the owner, his wife, the neighbors, and the onlookers, in that order.

b. The owner could be a suspect because his business has been slow and he may have set the fire for insurance purposes. Even though he is grieving, he still could have set the fire out of financial need and be mourning the failure of his business. However, the firebug in the audience appears very suspicious and should also be considered a suspect. After some questioning, there may be others whom the officer considers suspicious as well.

c. As discussed in the textbook, the officer can do all of the following to initiate a solid preliminary investigation:

➤ The officer should look for incendiary devices, fuel cans, broken door locks, or any other signs of forced entry.

➤ The officer should also interview all available witnesses at the scene, asking questions that will help to determine the financial stability of the building owner or occupants. Any financial instability might indicate a motive to collect on an insurance policy.

➤ The officer should also seek to learn of any enemies of the owner or occupant, who might have set the fire for revenge.

➤ The officer should scan the crowd for any known firebugs, or known arsonists, and question them thoroughly.

Workplace Applications

1. BURGLARY STATUTES

Depending on the jurisdiction, a few or even none of these may be considered a dwelling. Although a motorcycle may be burglarized, it is not a dwelling because it does not have a cover or roof of any kind, like a car or trailer, and one cannot live in it. A doghouse generally does not house humans. An empty house does not pass the sleep test, so generally would not be considered something that can be burglarized. A tool shed may be burglarized, perhaps if it is part of an inhabited dwelling such as in many apartment buildings. A corncrib will probably not be considered a dwelling, again because of the sleep test.

2. THEFT OR BURGLARY

Answers could include the following:

a. The officer should further question the victim and his roommates to confirm that the report is valid. He or she may also wish to explain the possible penalties for filing a false report, and that they can take no investigatory actions if they are given false information. The officer may also wish to explain that if they lie to their insurance companies, they could face fraud charges.

b. He or she should probably not because of the reasons listed above, and because it would be a waste of his or her resources.

c. The officer should further question all of the roommates about exact times and locations of the theft, then should contact the neighbors to confirm that a party was occurring the night before.

Internet Applications

1. ARSON PREVENTION

Answers could include the following:

a. Among other suggestions, this site suggests that churches could make sure that they have adequate lighting and security systems, and that they avoid too much shrubbery or foliage behind which an arsonist could hide.

b. They could follow the suggestions for churches that have not yet faced arson problems, as well as establish stronger communication with the police and community to ensure that any possible future arsonists are detected before the crime occurs.

c. Fire departments can provide fire safety tips and arson awareness materials that can help people prevent arson in a variety of ways. They also can provide information about typical arsonist profiles, so that churches can be aware of suspicious characters.

2. BURGLARY CASES

Answers could include the following:

a. Students should provide the case name, the charge(s) against the defendant(s), the outcome of the case (if available), and some details about the specific crime(s).

b. Answers will vary, but students should be able to name at least some helpful clues.

c. Students should be looking for more specific information, such as more exact times, locations, and names, and further testimony.

d. Such information could perhaps come from witnesses, victims, and those peripherally associated with the case.

Ethics Issues

Blue Wall of Silence

Answers could include the following:

a. You could question your coworker about the missing watch and see how he reacts. Perhaps he will put the watch back, but perhaps he will either deny it or refuse to return it. There is also a slim possibility that he collected the watch for legitimate reasons because perhaps it contained unusual fingerprints or something else that could be used as evidence, but you may prefer to take any such excuses with a grain of salt.

b. Regardless of whether he returns the watch after you bring it up with him, it would be morally preferable to discuss this matter with your supervisor. Whether this is feasible without endangering your job is another matter (see Answer C).

c. Many police departments frown on police officers who report their coworkers' misdeeds, a stance which, although it is intended to protect the department from disgrace, actually contributes to corruption. You could face additional stress from alienation and harassment, and possibly find yourself without a job due to a technicality. When New York Police Department officer Frank Serpico, who had been involved in ongoing efforts to uncover corruption at all levels of his department, was shot by an assailant, his fellow officers neglected to help him or alert the rest of the department that an officer had been shot. Despite all this, you should act according to your conscience and report corruption whenever possible.

Additional Activities

Advanced Web Research

1. INTERNET

BURGLARY PREVENTION

Have students visit the Burglary Prevention Council at *http://www.burglaryprevention.org*. Then have them read "Quick Tips," and answer the following questions:

- Which of these tips did you find most helpful? Why?
- Were there any tips that you have not heard or thought of before? If so, which were they?

Student answers will vary. Many will say that all of the tips were helpful, although some were "no-brainers."

Answers will vary. Some people have never heard of tip #8, which warns against leaving a message on your answering machine that you are away from home. Many have never heard of asking someone to park in your driveway or parking space to create the illusion that you are home.

2. INTERNET

RECOVER STOLEN PROPERTY

Have students visit TraceIt4U.com, an English site helping people who have experienced burglary, at *http://www.traceit4u.com*. Then have them read "About Us," and answer the following questions in a one page summary:

- Why was TraceIt4U created?
- How does TraceIt4U help police and victims recover stolen property?

TraceIt4U was created "out of the knowledge that only a fraction of identifiable property recovered by the police forces around the country is reunited with its lawful owner." Students should comprehend that this is because most objects are not photographed or adequately described before their theft. In addition, police recover many stolen items, but these items "cannot be returned to their rightful owners because there is no documentation that would identify the victims."

They help police, victims, and also professionals such as antique dealers identify and recover stolen property by providing a national pictorial database. The police place pictures of their "identifiable stolen/recovered property held in police stores to be viewed by the public 24 hours a day, 7 days a week." Victims of theft may also send in pictures for the police and others to view.

3. INTERNET

WANTED SUSPECTS

Have students visit the Los Angeles Sheriff's Department's "Wanted Suspects" Web site at *http://la-sheriff.org/crime-bulletins/wanted_suspects. html*. Have them download the PDF files for Arson and Arson/Terrorist Threats. (Students will need Adobe Acrobat Reader to view these files. If they do not have Adobe Acrobat, they can download it from this site.) Ask students to answer the following questions:

- What information do these files provide about the suspects?

- What additional information could possibly help the public find these suspects?

These files provide the people's names, photograph, basic description, driver's license number, and the charge against them, along with some basic information about their interests and possible whereabouts.

Students may state that it might be helpful to know the circumstances of the crime and the criminal's apparent *modus operandi*, so that they know if it happens again. Students may also wish to know the motive and perhaps more information on the suspect's personality.

Extended Workplace Applications

1. Analyze

Have students contact their local police department, or go online to find their state's penal code, and ask them to find out what qualifies as a "dwelling" and a "vehicle" for purposes of burglary. Next, ask students if these definitions seem to cover everything? Why or why not?

Answers will vary depending on the laws of that particular state. Most definitions of dwellings do not include occasionally inhabited or not-yet-inhabited structures, which some students may dislike because such structures could contain valuable personal items. Most definitions of vehicles will include automobiles in various states of disrepair. Some students may disagree with this because they may feel that the car should at least be operable, but in fact such a car could have its functioning parts, such as the radio, burglarized.

2. Research

Have students go online or to their local library and find a recent arson case that is either facing trial or has been tried. Ask students to answer the following questions in a one- to two-page report:

- Under what circumstances was the arson set, and why?

- What evidence has been amassed against the defendant(s), and does the prosecution appear to have a convincing case?

- What were the charges (and, if applicable, sentence), and do you feel that they were appropriate?

This exercise will enable students to apply what they have just learned to an actual current case. They should be able to provide details about the arson such as the location and time at which it took place, the possible motives for setting it, and why the evidence points to the defendant(s). Students should also list and analyze the evidence against the defendant(s). Student opinions will vary regarding the charges and sentence. They may feel that the sentence was lenient, especially if plea bargaining takes place.

3. Interview

Have students contact their local prosecutor and ask the following questions:
- How is joyriding prosecuted for first-time adult offenders and juvenile offenders?

- Is it a felony? What is the range of sentencing options for adults? For juveniles?

Students should understand that adult offenders usually get more serious sentences than juvenile offenders, especially if the juvenile offenders are young and have no prior record. In many jurisdictions, joyriding is a felony because it involves taking an automobile, albeit temporarily. Sentencing options are probably different for adults; since probation is by far the most common sentencing option for juveniles, this will likely be a common choice for juvenile offenders.

4. **Role Play**

Give students the following scenario: You are investigating an arson case in a farmhouse. The entire house has burnt down, but the family has escaped unharmed. You know that this family has been experiencing hard times recently, but also know that they are devoted to their farm and have recently leased some new equipment. Near the house, just outside a storage shed, are several cans of oil and some rags, but the owner explains that those are for farming equipment and are used frequently. He does not know if they were a contributing factor to the fire.

- Does this sound like an accidental fire or an arson? Why?

- What additional information do you need to dismiss this as an accident or determine probable cause for arson?

This case poses many contradictions. Although the house has burnt down, the family seems to be interested in staying on their farm. The newly leased farm equipment may indicate their innocence or it may indicate that they are in need of cash to pay for this. The oil cans and rags definitely could be used for farm equipment, but they are also obvious arson tools. Therefore, students will be undecided about this one. To determine if this was an accident or a crime, they should question the family, contact the fire department to have them determine where the fire originated and how, and try to learn more from neighbors about any suspicious activity occurring before the fire.

Crimes Against Property

Chapter Resources

For the Instructor
Instructor's Resource Manual, pp. 107–115
Additional Activities, p. 113
PowerPoint Presentation and ExamView Pro Testbank
   CD-ROM for Chapter 11
cl.glencoe.com Web site

For the Student
Student Edition, Chapter 11, pp. 370–398
Review and Applications, p. 394
Tutorial with Simulation Applications
   CD-ROM for Chapter 11
cl.glencoe.com Web site

KEY TERMS

theft	embezzlement	extortion
grand theft	misappropriation	under color of authority or office
petty theft	false pretenses	blackmail
thief	receiving	bribery
larceny	constructive possession	forgery
larceny from the person	robbery	uttering
shoplifting	force	fraudulent making
abandoned property	fear or intimidation	
joyriding	armed robbery	

Lecture Outline

11.1 FORMS AND VARIATIONS OF THEFT
Theft
Larceny
Embezzlement
False Pretenses
Receiving Stolen Property

11.2 ROBBERY, EXTORTION, BLACKMAIL, AND BRIBERY
Robbery
Extortion, Blackmail, and Bribery

11.3 FORGERY AND UTTERING

In-Chapter Questions

Quarterman v. State **page 374**
Should the media be allowed to set up "bait" as the reporter in this case did? Should the police be allowed to?

Some will doubt the good intentions of the media, and many will agree that private citizens should not be allowed to set up crimes to advance their personal or professional interest. Most students, however, will agree that law enforcement should have this right, provided that entrapment does not occur.

Criminal Law Online page 374

What are the key differences, and by what criteria are they determined?

The key differences are that they are different types of theft, and they are distinguished by the circumstances in which the theft occurs.

Photo caption page 376

How does this differ from mere larceny?

The difference is the proximity of the property to its owner. Mere larceny, regardless of the degree or classification, generally refers to the taking of property that is not on the person or within his or her immediate control.

 Fingerprint Technician page 377

What skills and talents do you think a person needs to be a fingerprint technician?

Most students will agree that attention to detail, the ability to apply intense concentration, and a long attention span will help in this job.

 ***Fussell v. United States* page 378**

What crimes could the defendant be charged with in this case?

He could be charged with forgery for creating false subway passes.

 ***People v. Lorenzo* page 381**

Of what crime could the defendant in this case be convicted?

Under some shoplifting laws, switching price tags is a crime by itself.

11.1 Self Check page 383

1. What is larceny, and how is it distinguished from the other types of theft discussed here?

    Larceny is a type of theft that is defined by the taking and carrying away of the property of another without consent and with the purpose of stealing or permanently depriving the owner of possession.

    It differs from other types of theft because it involves tangible property, the intent to permanently deprive the owner, a lack of consent, and a lack of force or fear.

2. How is receiving stolen goods related to, but not a part of, theft?

    It is not an actual theft, but it is a crime that can occur as a result of theft. Professional thieves rely on fences to give them cash for their stolen goods.

Criminal Law Online page 388

What information does this Web site provide? How does it help investigators?

Bankguys.com provides helpful and detailed information on recent bank robberies in the Pittsburgh, western Pennsylvania, and West Virginia area. Because of its specialized focus, it can provide more information than a larger, more general Web site can. It helps investigators by publicizing the crimes and giving the public information on how they can help solve the cases.

 ***United States v. Jackson* page 389**

1. Which of the seven threats in the New Jersey statute did Jackson make?

    She would be guilty of threat C, which holds that one is guilty of extortion if he or she "expose[s] or publicize[s] any secret or any asserted fact, whether true or false, tending to subject any person to hatred, contempt or ridicule, or to impair his credit or business repute."

2. If she had told the "secret" to the media, what would have happened?

    Cosby would have likely suffered some disgrace, but some students will contend that, considering the sex scandals that have occurred in recent years, this could be seen as rather unimportant and may not have a large effect on the public.

Photo caption page 391

What can happen if an official refuses to accept a bribe?

An official who refuses the bribe can also press charges against the attempted briber. In this case, the briber will be liable for the attempted bribe, as well as whatever responsibility he or she was trying to avoid with the bribe in the first place.

11.2 Self Check page 391

1. How do you determine whether enough force or fear was used to justify a robbery, as opposed to a larceny or larceny from a person, charge?

   In some states, the determination between robbery and larceny is whether the force, fear, or intimidation occurred in order to take property or merely in an attempt to retain or escape with it. In others, there is a question of whether a robbery occurs when the property is obtained peacefully but force or fear is subsequently used to retain possession or allow escape. Finally, the Model Penal Code and some states define robbery as using force or fear at any time during the attempt or commission of theft, including the escape after committing the theft.

2. In your own words, how are extortion, blackmail, and bribery similar? How are they different?

   Extortion and blackmail are committed by a threat to do harm in the future, and all three crimes involve the illegal use of financial leverage toward another person.

   Their differences can be summed up by their definitions: Extortion is the gaining of property by threat of physical harm to a person or property by a public official by color of his or her office. Blackmail is a threat by a private citizen seeking *hush money*, which is payment to remain silent about a crime or a shameful act. Bribery is the payment by a person to a public official in order to gain an advantage that the person is not otherwise entitled to, in which case both parties are guilty of the crime.

Photo Caption page 393

How is forgery different than fraudulent making?

Forgery occurs when a person, with the purpose of deceiving or injuring, makes or alters a writing in such a way as to convey a false impression concerning its authenticity. Fraudulent making is forgery because it is the creation of documents that are not authentic and full of false statements

11.3 Self Check page 393

1. What, in your opinion, is the most common type of forgery? Why?

Many students will state that signing another person's name on a credit charge or sales slip is the most common. A variant of this is the use of credit card fraud on the Internet, which, although such transactions do not require a traditional signature, are fraud nonetheless.

2. Give an example of the crime of fraudulent making, and explain why this behavior satisfies the elements of a crime.

   A deed for a nonexistent piece of property is an example of fraudulent making. This will satisfy the definition of fraudulent making because the writing is full of false statements.

Review and Applications

Questions For Review

1. Name the different crimes listed under theft, and explain why there is so much confusion in distinguishing among these different crimes.

   Theft is a broad category that encompasses the following crimes:
   - Larceny
   - Embezzlement
   - Theft by false pretenses
   - Shoplifting
   - Robbery
   - Receiving stolen goods

   These crimes can be hard to distinguish because they all have some similarities, but each contains specific elements that make each crime slightly different. For instance, the difference between larceny and robbery is that robbery has an element of the use of force or fear.

2. What are the elements of shoplifting?
   The elements of shoplifting are:
   - the willful taking of possession of merchandise of another
   - without the consent of the seller, and
   - with the intention of converting the goods and without paying for the goods.

3. How can a person be convicted of larceny of "found" property?

Three conditions can lead to this conviction, if the "finder" does not fulfill his or her obligation to give the property back to the owner:

- The owner of the property can be identified.
- The item can be easily given back to the owner.
- The item has substantial value.

4. What is the difference between joyriding and larceny?

Joyriding is a lesser included offense of larceny involving a motor vehicle. The only difference is that joyriding has all of the elements of larceny except the intent to permanently deprive the owner of the vehicle. With joyriding, the offender only intends to take the car temporarily, sometimes for as briefly as a few hours.

5. State the difference between false pretenses and larceny.

Larceny is completed when the defendant takes property of another and has possession of this property without consent, but has not gained title to the property.

Conversely, false pretenses is completed only if the defendant gains title to the property from the owner with the owner's consent, but in a deceptive way that deprives the owner by illegal means.

6. List the essential elements of receiving stolen property.

The essential elements of offense of receiving stolen property are that the accused did all three of the following:

- Bought or received (came into possession of) the property;
- the property was stolen (some jurisdictions require proof that the property had been stolen by some person other than accused); and
- at time of possession of the property, the accused knew the property had been stolen.

7. How can a purse snatching be either a larceny or a robbery?

The snatching of a purse or handbag can be considered by court to be either a larceny or a robbery, and the difference between the two charges is as follows:

- The snatching of a purse that includes the use of force or fear is robbery.
- Without the force or fear, it is larceny or larceny from a person.

For example, if someone lifts a purse from a person who is sleeping in the park on her lunch break, larceny has been committed. If, however, the purse is violently snatched from the victim as she walks down the street, robbery has been committed.

8. Explain the difference between robbery and extortion (or blackmail).

The distinction between robbery and extortion (or blackmail) is that:

- Robbery is committed by a threat to do immediate bodily harm.
- Extortion (or blackmail) is committed by a threat to do harm in the future.

In other words, both crimes are accompanied by threats, but the threats in a robbery case are imminent and the victim has reasonable fear that they will be carried out immediately.

9. What is uttering, and how does it relate to the crime of forgery?

Uttering is the attempt, successful or otherwise, to unlawfully trick others with a forged document. Forgery is not actually committed until the element of uttering is fulfilled. For instance, if a person forges checks or wills, he is not guilty of forgery until he tries to fool other people with them and trick them, such as by trying to have them give him something of value in exchange for these forged documents.

10. What are the differences between forgery and fraudulent making?

Forgery is the application of a false signature–that is, a signature of a person that is written by someone other than that individual–to a legitimate piece of writing, such as a document transferring the title of real estate or an automobile. Fraudulent making is the creation of a fictitious document, such as a deed for property that does not exist or cannot be sold to private parties. The most famous anecdotal examples of this are the schemes in which unsuspecting people have been sold the Brooklyn Bridge.

Problem-Solving Exercises

1. SHOPLIFTING
   Answers could include the following:
   a. Since he was aware that she was preparing to leave the store without paying, he should have stopped her. See the case *People v. Lorenzo* (Application Case, page 381) for a similar situation in which a defendant was acquitted of charges of larceny by false pretenses.

   b. Many students will not want to arrest her, because it is not clear that she intended to steal it. Even if she did not have enough money to pay for it, she may not have been aware of that as she approached the cashier. Some students will feel that the lack of money is a clear indication of probable cause.

   c. Answers will vary, but should rely on the facts presented here and an understanding of the elements of whatever crime she is being charged with (or not charged with).

2. EMBEZZLEMENT
   Answers could include the following:
   a. Technically, yes, but many students will agree that no harm has been done. However, you can point out that suchß actions damage the integrity of the evidence. If he took the items unlawfully and broke or lost some of them, this could create problems.

   b. It minimizes the chance that he would lose or break anything, but his behavior is still risky.

   c. Most students would not want him to get into serious trouble because it could be seen as an innocent mistake, but he should be made aware of the need to leave evidence intact and untouched in order to prosecute criminals properly.

Workplace Applications

1. BURGLARY
   Answers could include the following:
   a. He has committed breaking and entering, as well as robbery. His attempted crime is burglary.

   b. This is a trick question: His crime is actually burglary since he is committing the crime in a person's habitation. He did not complete the crime, but he did satisfy the breaking and entering element and did show the intent required to be tried for attempted burglary.

   c. Many jurisdictions differentiate types of robbery by the value of the goods stolen.

2. SHOPLIFTING WITHOUT LARCENY
   Answers could include the following:
   a. Student answers will vary. This law could define shoplifting by the type of business in which it occurred, or by the types of items stolen.

   b. No, because both larceny and shoplifting are crimes in which the offender possesses intent to permanently deprive the owners of the property.

   c. This law does seem confusing. To make it easier to understand, many students will recommend covering all such crimes under the single crime of larceny. Some will feel comfortable with the distinction between the two crimes, and may choose to clarify it by defining the elements of shoplifting more clearly to distinguish it from larceny.

Internet Application

1. **FALSE PRETENSES**

   Answers could include the following:

   a. Foreign governments may pose as businesses to try to find out information about defense and technology companies in the United States. They may attempt to find out product information by requesting product information or bids for contracts, as though they are interested in purchasing the company's products.

   b. E-mails from other countries, companies that nobody has heard of, and people who seem to be interested in gathering lots of information with no real purpose are all clues that espionage may be taking place.

   c. Businesses should be wary of strangers asking for detailed information and know their clients well before engaging in detailed discussion with them.

2. **WORK A ROBBERY CASE**

   Answers could include the following:

   a. Investigators had very little evidence and leads at the beginning, so students should be able to list and name these accurately.

   b. After the preliminary investigation, investigators had some leads, but nothing conclusive.

   c. Main obstacles included the dearth of evidence at the beginning of the case and the length of time if took to solve the case. Students will likely be able to name others.

   d. First, they interviewed employees to determine how many suspects they needed to look for and what they looked like. Next, they questioned known criminals, people in the neighborhood, and residents of nearby tenements. Eventually, continued efforts to narrow down the suspects led to the correct men. Many students will agree that the FBI's work on this case was exhaustive and may be one of their finest efforts. Few will believe that they could have done more, but some suggestions may be useful.

Ethics Issues

CHEESEBURGER BRIBES?

Answers could include any of the following:

a. No, because she made no threats of future harm to the manager, which is an element of extortion. However, she may be guilty of accepting a bribe, albeit reluctantly.

b. In this case, yes, because it is clear that Janene holds no ill will toward the restaurant manager.

c. He should contact the chief of police to discuss the matter, and the police chief should investigate to ensure that, if this is true, it does not continue.

Advanced Web Research

1. INTERNET

CARJACKING

Tell students to read an actual Crime Alert flyer regarding a carjacking that took place at California State University, Los Angeles, at *http://www.calstatela.edu/univ/police/CrimeAlert_2.html*. Then have them write a report by answering the following questions:

- What elements make the crime of carjacking different from the crime of car theft?

- What further information on the suspects and the car would be helpful?

Students should be able to understand that carjacking is the robbery, not the theft, of a car because it is accomplished with the use of force or fear–the element that separates robbery from different types of theft, such as larceny.

The description of the suspects is extremely vague, but this may be due to the victim's surprise at the attack and also the time of night (11:00 p.m.). More helpful would be a description of their appearance, approximate ages, and any distinguishing clothing or marks. If the car is still missing, information on its license plate and color would be helpful too, as the car may possibly still be in their possession.

2. INTERNET

EXTORTION

Tell students to read "Student Charged with Online Extortion Attempt" at APBOnline.com, located at *http://www.apbnews.com/newscenter/internetcrime/2000/05/25/blackmail0525_01.html*. When

they are done, have them answer the following questions:

- How did the suspect allegedly try to commit extortion? How did the victim respond?

- How has the suspect been charged, and what bail restrictions does he face? Why is this?

The suspect sent ten e-mails threatening the online company that if they did not provide him with free books, cash, and a new car, he would break into their computer system and cause havoc. The victim at first agreed to provide everything but the cash, but then called the police after some negotiations with the suspect.

He is being charged with one count of using the Internet to send extortion threats, and could face up to two years in prison and a $100,000 fine. His bail restrictions are that "the judge barred Holcomb from any Internet access and from disseminating information about the company." This is obviously to prevent him from attempting to commit any further extortion or perhaps getting revenge against the company who turned him in.

3. INTERNET

FORGERY

Have students read the article "Man Says Net Forgery is Not a Crime" at *http://www.usatoday.com/life/cyber/tech/cti028.html*. Then assign students the following questions to discuss in class:

- What did the defendant do, and what charges were filed against him?

- Do you feel that forgery has been committed? Why or why not? Explain your reasons in detail.

The defendant allegedly hijacked a company's computer system to send millions of e-mails to America Online customers, using an address that did not belong to him (and thus was a false address) to send information about porn and various other schemes. He was charged with forgery and computer tampering, which could bring a sentence of up to seven years' imprisonment.

Most students will agree that forgery has been committed because he used an e-mail address that did not belong to him. Others may feel that, instead of or in addition to forgery charges, he could be charged with theft of company resources. Some may not be sure about whether or not forgery applies to e-mail cases, but you can explain to them that e-mail acts in lieu of traditional correspondence and the misuse of it carries the same restrictions.

Extended Workplace Applications

1. Debate

First, give students the following situation: It is the written policy of a local movie theater to let all law enforcement personnel, including police, dispatchers, secretaries, and volunteers, into the movies for free as long as they show their law enforcement identification. This policy is not extended to any other group or employer, and it is not known to the public. Next, lead the class in a discussion with the following questions:

- Is this theft or any other crime? Why?
- Is it wrong for the law enforcement personnel to go to the movies for free?

Students should be able to understand that it is not theft, but it is bribery because the law enforcement personnel are accepting gifts that are not their due while in their official positions.

Although it seems harmless, the ulterior motive behind giving law enforcement bribes is to ensure that the business owner gets preferential treatment when he or she is in need of police assistance. Anything that creates bias in the mind of police violates the Fourteenth Amendment provision that guarantees everyone equal protection under the law.

2. Role Play

Give students the following scenario: You work at a car dealership, and every Friday your supervisor leaves early at 2:00 p.m. When he leaves, he asks his favorite employee, Tim, to punch out his clock at 5:00 p.m. so that the owner thinks he has been around all day. When 5:00 p.m. comes, Tim punches out his clock and his supervisor's, then takes one of the cars that is on the lot home for the weekend. He uses it for his personal use, then has the dealership staff wash it and return it to the lot on Monday morning. One weekend, Tim crashes one of the cars, and the owner is shocked because he cannot believe that the supervisor let him leave with it. The police are questioning you to describe what has been going on.

- What do you tell them?
- With what crimes can Tim and the supervisor be charged?

Students should come clean and tell the police about the false timeclocks and the car "borrowing." Although they may have seen what Tim and the supervisor were doing, it is hard to blow the whistle on corrupt coworkers and keep one's job, and the police should not hold them liable. However, the ongoing misdeeds of Tim and his supervisor should be openly discussed.

Both Tim and the supervisor can be charged with embezzlement. Some students will also want to charge Tim with joyriding, and others will state that he should be forced to pay civil damages to his employer.

3. Analyze

Give students the following scenario: You are at the reading of your grandmother's will, and you are surprised when the lawyer produces a neatly typed document because your grandmother's wills were always handwritten on large stationery. Since this is legal in your state, she always stated that there was "no sense in wasting my time at a typewriter." Your two cousins insist that they were present when she had the latest version of her will typed up, and that she had a change of heart because she was worried about her shaky handwriting. They were indeed present because they both witnessed it, which presents a legal issue because heirs generally should not witness wills. In addition, there is a signature by a third witness who the cousins insist was a close friend of the family, but whom nobody else has heard of and whom the lawyer could not locate. As the lawyer reads the will, you and several others are shocked as it becomes clear that, according to this will, your grandmother left all of her real estate, cash holdings, and valuables to your two cousins. You complain to the lawyer that the will appears to be false. You also question the validity of the third witness and do not think that your grandmother's signature seems authentic because it lacks the pen pressure usually seen in her writing. Does this seem to be a case of forgery? Fraudulent making? Uttering? Or are all of the above occurring here? Why?

All of the above. It should be clear to students that this will appears to be a fraudulent document *with* a forged signature, trying to "pass" as an authentic will, which the cousins appear to be guilty of uttering. The fact that the cousins witnessed a will to which they were the chief heirs, the grandmother's tradition of using handwritten wills, the dubious origins of the third witness, and, obviously, the fact that the two cousins were willed nearly everything all point to fraud.

You could explain to students that a forgery expert could probably pinpoint the discrepancies that were seen in the grandmother's signature, and that circumstantial evidence could provide enough evidence for convictions on all three charges.

4. Role Play

Give students the following scenario: You have just arrested a young man who attempted to pickpocket a 62-year-old woman. The woman caught him and started to scream and hit him, forcing him to flee. She wants him charged with attempted robbery, since she was in great fear when she caught him and felt like he would have used force on her if she had not fought back. However, you think that his intent was not robbery, but larceny from the person. Which is correct?

Students should understand that the police officer is correct because pickpocketing, due to its secretive nature, inherently lacks the element of force or fear and is central to the crime of robbery. Although the victim felt fear and suspected force when she caught him attempting to pickpocket her, the pickpocket did not plan this because he did not expect to get caught.

White-Collar Crimes

KEY TERMS

white-collar crime	intangible rights theory	adulteration	tying arrangement
tax evasion	securities fraud	misbranding	monopolize
tax deficiency	insider trading	antitrust laws	attempt to monopolize
willfulness	parking	horizontal price-fixing	
mail fraud	churning	vertical price-fixing	

Lecture Outline

12.1 UNDERSTANDING WHITE-COLLAR CRIME

12.2 TAX EVASION
Existence and Proof of a Tax Deficiency
Affirmative Act
Willfulness
Defenses Against Tax Evasion

12.3 FALSE ADVERTISING
False Advertising Under Federal Law
False Advertising Under State Law

12.4 MAIL FRAUD
Scheme to Defraud
Intent to Defraud
Use of the Post Office or Private
   Interstate Carrier
Furtherance of the Scheme to Defraud

12.5 SECURITIES FRAUD
Substantive Fraud
Offer, Purchase, or Sale of a Security
Use of Interstate Commerce or Mails
Defenses

12.6 CRIMES AGAINST THE FOOD AND
DRUG ACT
Definitions
Defenses

12.7 ANTITRUST CRIMES AND MONOPOLY
Key Federal Acts
Other Issues

In-Chapter Questions

12.1 SelfCheck page 402

What issues arise when the government or consumers try to prosecute corporations for white-collar crimes?
   Laws have traditionally not provided for the criminal prosecution of corporations, only for individuals who work for corporations. However, this is changing.

Friedberg v. United States page 405

In what ways can a person defend him- or herself against tax evasion charges?

Typical defenses include pleading ignorance of the law, the cash-hoard defense, a lack of willfulness, and a third-party defense.

 Spies v. United States page 406

What is the difference between a willful omission and an affirmative act?

A willful omission can be viewed in the same way as an affirmative act because it reveals a deliberate lack of action that leads to criminal liability.

12.2 Self Check page 407

1. What is the difference between willfulness for a felony versus a misdeamenor tax evasion charge?

Proactive actions such as keeping a double set of books will lead to a felony tax evasion charge. Omissions such as neglecting to file an income tax return will lead to a misdemeanor charge. However, if a person commits a series of omissions that appear to create a willful pattern of tax evasion, that can count as a proactive action in some cases.

2. What are some common defenses against charges of tax evasion?

Common defenses are ignorance of the law, a defense that is valid for few other crimes but applies here because tax laws are so complex; third-party liability, such as when an inept or dishonest accountant creates incorrect or misleading documents; and the cash hoard defense, which justifies tax years in which the defendant's cash outflow is larger than his or her income because he or she had been hoarding cash savings.

 Truck Components Inc. v. K-II Corp. page 409

Do you think companies should be allowed to advertise products they are not "legally entitled" to sell?

Many students will agree that this is valid when they are making truthful comparisons, or if the item being sold is used simultaneously with the product that the company manufactures (such as water bottles that clip to bicycles).

 American Home Products Corporation v. Johnson & Johnson page 410

Should advertisers be required to include all the information available about their products?

Most, if not all, students will agree that this is necessary, and will be wary of companies that provide less information than others.

12.3 Self Check page 00

When bringing charges of false advertising, what legally constitutes a representation or advertisement?

A representation or advertisement can be in either words or pictures, and it must be about a product or service. For example, if a company advertises to sell shelves and displays a picture of a shelf on a brochure, a representation has been made about the shelves for sale. If the company then subsequently sells a shelf of inferior quality than the one pictured, the representation may be deemed to be false.

Criminal Law Online page 412

How can mail fraud affect you? How can you protect yourself from mail fraud?

Mail fraud can not just cause people to give away money to criminals, but it can also cause people to give away personal information such as social security numbers and driver's license information.

Photo caption page 412

What is the main difference in Congress' legal authority over the U.S. Postal Service and over private carriers?

Congress has complete authority over the dealings of the U.S. Post Office, as well as any illegal actions against it, due to a right provided by the U.S. Constitution. It has limited authority over private carriers, covering only interstate commerce.

 McNally v. United States page 414

Should mail fraud laws protect the intangible rights to honest government? Why or why not?

Most, if not all, students will agree that government officials should never be given preferential treatment in such matters, which appeared to be the case before this issue was resolved. They should be subject to the same laws and penalties as private citizens in such matters—and some students may suggest that they deserve harsher penalties if they misuse taxpayer revenues while committing mail fraud.

12.4 Self Check page 416

1. What are some schemes to defraud, and why has there been difficulty in defining a "scheme"?

Schemes involving traditional fraud deprive one of money or other tangible property through misrepresentations, including omissions, which are reasonably calculated to deceive. Some examples of traditional fraud cases involving mail fraud are false loan applications and fraudulent investment schemes.

Schemes are difficult to determine because they are not defined in the federal statute.

2. What is the intangible rights doctrine, and how has the debate surrounding it been resolved?

This doctrine covers a type of prosecution under mail fraud that was primarily used to protect citizens from dishonest public officials. The U.S. Supreme Court tried to deny this in *McNally v. United States*, but Congress responded by superceding the court and making such fraud a crime.

 ***Dirks v. SEC* page 418**

Do you think the defendant in this case had a duty to make information about the fraud public? Why or why not?

Most students would agree the defendant undoubtedly had such a duty, although others may find this requirement uncertain.

Criminal Law Online page 419

What types of fraud seem most common? What civil and criminal charges are being brought against defrauders?

Most students will state that credit card fraud, whether online or not, is the most common. Defrauders can face criminal charges and may also be sued in civil court for the financial damages caused by their actions.

12.5 Self Check page 420

1. What is insider trading, and who qualifies as an "insider"?

Insider trading is a type of substantive fraud that involves the purchase and sale of securities based on material, nonpublic information.

Insiders may be directors, officers, major shareholders, lower-level employees obtaining information because of their jobs, outside professionals and advisors (e.g., accountants and lawyers), press, companies and firms of the above-mentioned individuals, and even their families.

2. What are common defenses against charges of security fraud?

Common defenses that individuals faced with such charges are:

- No knowledge
- Good faith
- Reliance on counsel

Photo caption page 422

Does food need to come in direct contact with outside contaminants in order to be considered adulterated?

No. Food that is stored in an area where contamination is proven to have occurred can be legally defined as "adulterated."

 United States v. Dollerweich
***United States v. Park* page 423**

Does it seem that the president in the *Park* case had intent or was he negligent? Explain your answer.

Most students would agree that such behavior was too extreme to be a result of mere negligence, and that negligence is not a valid claim. Others may feel that it is valid, given the circumstances of this case.

 Food and Drug Inspector page 424

What qualities do you think make a good food and drug inspector?

Qualities such as honesty, integrity, meticulousness, and a background in a field such as biology would be helpful.

12.6 Self Check page 425

For a felony conviction under the FDCA, one of two requirements must be satisfied. Name these.

Along with the elements needed for a misdemeanor conviction under the FDCA, one of the following two requirements must be satisfied:

- Intent

- Evidence of a prior FDCA violation

12.7 Self-Check page 429

1. How does price-fixing harm competition? Do vertical price-fixing and horizontal price-fixing affect it differently?

    It can harm competition by forcing market prices to levels that other companies cannot sustain.

    The different types of price fixing can affect competitors in different ways.

2. Why is an attempt to monopolize a crime?

    Because, as with other attempted criminal charges, the defendant has reached a dangerous proximity to succeeding in the attempted crime. Criminal intent is present, as are the voluntary actions that would have made a monopoly occur if it had not been detected and stopped.

Review and Applications

Review Questions

1. Define tax deficiency and give an example.

    A tax deficiency occurs when the proper amount of tax to be paid is greater than the amount shown on a taxpayer's tax return.

    For example, if a taxpayer owes $5,000 in taxes but manipulates his or her tax return to state that he should pay only $4,000, a tax deficiency of $1,000 exists.

2. What are the various defenses for tax evasion?
    Some common valid defenses are:

- Ignorance of the law, a defense that is valid for few other crimes but applies here because tax laws are so complex

- Third-party liability, such as when an inept or dishonest accountant creates incorrect or misleading documents

- The cash hoard defense, which justifies tax years in which the defendant's cash outflow is larger than his or her income because he or she had been hoarding cash savings

- A defense against the element of willfulness, in which the individual shows that he or she acted in good faith

3. What are the different methods, direct and indirect, of proving a tax deficiency?

    Direct evidence can be used by the "specific items" method, which involves examining and searching through the defendant's records for all taxable income, then comparing it to the tax return filed.

    Indirect methods include:

- the *net worth method*, which requires the government to establish that during the year for which the defendant is accused of evading taxes, his or her net worth increased by more than what is reflected on his or her income tax return for that year.

- the *cash expenditures method*, which involves the prosecution establishing to a reasonable certainty that all the expenditures the defendant made within the fiscal year under examination exceed the amount of income reported on the taxpayer's return.

- the *bank deposits method*, in which the prosecution merely examines the deposits the defendant made into a bank account within the relevant year. If the total amount of the deposits exceeds the amount reported on the income tax return, the excess is presumed to be unreported income.

4. What is the difference between a misdemeanor violation and a felony violation for tax evasion?

    The presence of an affirmative act to evade tax payments is the critical element in determining whether an individual's tax evasion is a misdemeanor or felony crime. Performing an affirmative act toward the evasion of taxes constitutes a felony. Mere neglect to file a tax return or pay required taxes results in a misdemeanor conviction.

5. When is an act in furtherance of a scheme to defraud?

To support a conviction of fraud, the prosecution must prove that the "in furtherance," element has been satisfied. In general, this means that the actions for which the person is being prosecuted must contribute to the success of a fraud scheme. In mail fraud, using the mail must be part of at least one key element of the mail fraud scheme.

6. Explain the role of material omissions and misrepresentations according to the Securities Exchange Act of 1934.

To prove that a person has made a misleading statement or omission regarding a material fact, the government must prove four (sometimes five) of the following elements:

- The defendant made a false statement or omission
- that is material
- that is made with knowledge
- and that caused the injured party's damages
- (in the case of an omission only) and the defendant had a duty to disclose the information.

7. Why is the crime of "parking" committed?

Parking, which is the sale of securities that are purchased with the understanding that they will be repurchased by the seller at a later time, is generally part of larger illegal stock manipulation schemes. It is generally used to:

- manipulate the supply and demand of stock, which will affect its price.
- circumvent margin rules and minimum net capital requirements.
- avoid the reporting requirements ... of the 1934 Act.

8. List and explain the elements of "churning."

Churning is a type of broker-dealer fraud that occurs when a stockbroker excessively purchases and sells securities for a client without regard or concern for the client's investment objectives, but rather to advance his own interests, usually that of generating commis-

sions. For a conviction, the government (or investor) must establish that:

- The broker exercised control over the trading in the account.
- The trading was excessive in light of the character of the account.
- The broker showed an intent to defraud or showed willful and reckless disregard for the investor's interests.

9. Define the terms offer, purchase, and sale, as they relate to securities transaction.

The 1933 Securities Exchange Act defines them as follows:

- An offer for sale, or offer, is "every attempt of offer to dispose of, or solicitation of an offer to buy a security or an interest in a security, for value."
- A purchase is "any contract to buy, purchase or otherwise acquire" a security.
- A sale includes "any contracts to sell or otherwise dispose of" a security. These definitions include a corporation's purchase or sale of its own securities, mergers, and acquisitions.

10. What is the difference between horizontal and vertical price-fixing?

Horizontal price-fixing agreements are direct or indirect agreements made between market participants at the *same level* within a given market, regarding the prices they will charge for a similar product they both sell.

Vertical price-fixing agreements are direct or indirect agreements made between market participants at *different levels* within a given market, regarding the price at which their product will be resold.

Problem-Solving Exercises

1. MAIL FRAUD
Answers could include the following:
a. Any use of the U.S. Mail can be prosecuted, but only interstate shipping with the private courier companies can be prosecuted under federal law.

b. Any U.S. mail that has been sent intrastate or interstate may be used as evidence, but intrastate shipping by private couriers cannot. This is because Congress has limited power over prosecuting the use of private couriers for mail fraud and cannot regulate their intrastate commerce.

c. Most students will agree that it can be used, and you can explain that federal laws have jurisdiction over import and export issues, including the illegal use of the mails (this can also apply to drugs and obscenity).

2. DRUG INSPECTION

Answers could include the following:

a. They are guilty of facilitating false advertising through the misleading journal articles, and of violations of the Sherman Act by unlawfully restraining trade with competitors. Referring to crimes discussed in other chapters, they are also guilty of bribery to doctors.

b. Although a food and drug inspector is not directly involved, you should report the antitrust and bribery violations to the appropriate government agencies. In addition, your testimony would be valuable in any criminal prosecution against this company.

c. Obviously, this company is guilty of unnecessarily drugging children for its own profit, and your knowledge should be used to attempt to stop them from further unethical activities.

3. TAX DEFICIENCY

Answers could include the following:

a. Yes, because tax laws are extremely complex and change frequently. The Supreme Court has decided that it would be unreasonable to expect the average taxpayer to completely understand them.

b. Yes, because he misinformed her. His inefficiency gives her the opportunity to claim a third-party defense in addition to her other defense, because it helped create the situation.

4. FALSE ADVERTISING

Answers could include the following:

a. It could matter if no other purchases were involved, but since the CD giveaway influenced the purchasing decisions of people who visited the store to get the free CD, it is material in this case.

b. Since it baited people to come to the retail establishment through false advertising, it placed them in an environment where they were encouraged to purchase more music. In short, they probably would not have been there in such great numbers without the CD giveaway, which did increase sales.

Workplace Applications

1. FOOD INSPECTION

Answers could include the following:

a. The Federal Food, Drug, and Cosmetic Act (FDCA) is being violated because the presence of the rat constitutes the adulteration of the food in the storeroom. If you ask the class whether they think that this rat's presence indicates that there are more rats in the storeroom, most would agree that this is a reasonable assumption.

b. The Act prohibits "the adulteration or misbranding of any food, drug, device, or cosmetic in interstate commerce." Again, the rat's presence comprises the adulteration of food in the storeroom.

c. Since rodent contamination throughout the storeroom is a reasonable possibility, the entire area is affected. Refer students to *United States v. Park* (1975), which is covered in the Application Case on page 423.

2. TYING ARRANGEMENTS

Answers could include the following:

a. They are violating the Sherman Act, which criminalizes monopolizing, attempting to monopolize, or conspiring to monopolize a market through unfair practices.

b. They have committed monopoly "the willful acquisition or maintenance of such power through unlawful means, and not from fair competitive practices such as high quality products, business acumen, or historical accident."

c. It shows that some of their behavior contributes to customer preference, but since their unfair practices allow them greater distribution than their competitors, their ability to offer lower prices may be proven to be a result of these unfair practices.

Internet Applications

1. FDCA

Answers could include the following:

a. According to the Web site, "FDCA uses multiple routes for case referrals. First, certain cases are developed through FDCA's network of field offices, reviewed by FDCA headquarters, and then sent, pursuant to longstanding DOJ policy, to OCL. OCL reviews the referral and determines whether to pursue civil or criminal remedies. If the referral is accepted, OCL usually attempts to enlist the assistance of the USAO in the district in which the case will be brought." Student answers should essentially reflect this information.

b. Most students would agree that consumers should seek monetary damages on their own behalf, and that sometimes they can sue the FDCA for inaction. The government's best option is to use the OCL to prosecute fraudulent behavior.

c. Fraud against consumers generally involves monetary fraud under any definition and has traditionally satisfied the "intent to defraud" requirement for felony behavior. Fraud against the FDA are generally non-monetary and can fit one of two categories: black market operations in which defendants attempt to hide their entire business operation from FDA; and firms actively regulated by FDA, but which engage in fraudulent behavior by, for example, submitting fraudulent data to FDA.

2. ANTITRUST LAWS

Answers could include the following:

a. This union has allegedly, due to the greed of its leadership, engaged in unfair business practices that have actually harmed their members.

b. They base their complaints upon several years of alleged corrupt and abusive practices. Students should be able to name at least a couple of examples of these practices.

c. Since unions can control the commerce related to a particular industry, a corrupt union can unfairly restrain trade against businesses that do not provide them with bribes or other inducements.

Ethics Issues

1. INSIDER TRADING

Answers can include the following:

a. You can, because you do not have a fiduciary duty to this company and thus can report information about it without breaching any obligations to them.

b. You should only repeat information that sounds true and comes from a reliable source. In addition, you may wish to preface it with a statement that this information may not be completely correct. You want to do this to avoid slander charges.

c. No, because it does not appear that your advice would be the cause of the stock losing value.

2. Answers can include the following:

a. Although it is understandable that the interim supervisor was not aware of the visit, her management was and should have warned her to be prepared for it.

b. They should comply with the FDA regulations and not make a fuss, since they will probably lose the case and gain bad publicity otherwise.

Additional Activities

NOTE TO INSTRUCTOR: These additional activities are exclusive to this IRM. They are designed to meet the special needs of your students. If you or your students cannot access a Web site referred to here, go to *cl.glencoe.com* for the latest updated links.

Advanced Web Research

1. INTERNET

HEALTH CARE PROVIDERS

Have students visit the Health Administration Responsibility Project at *http://www.harp.org*. Ask them to read "About This Site," then scroll down to "Federal and Pending Legislation" and read about federal and state cases regarding patients' rights regarding HMOs. Be sure to tell students to visit all other parts of the site that interest them. Next, have students answer the following questions:

- Why does this site exist, and what resources does it offer consumers? Which did you find most helpful, and why?

- What current legislation is being debated or enacted?

- Do you feel that this current legislation is adequate to address current problems with health care providers, or that more needs to be done? Why or why not?

The Health Administration Responsibility Project is, in their own words, a "resource for patients, doctors, and attorneys seeking to establish the liability of HMOs, Managed Health Care Organizations, and Nursing Facilities for the consequences of their decisions." They offer information on their plans for political change, lawsuit information, links, and legal information. They are also planning to set up a Legal Aid Society. Student answers will vary regarding which of these

resources is most helpful, as all are quite helpful. If any join the listserv, they may find this to be the most helpful because it contains the most updated, real-world information.

A Patients' Rights Bill has been long debated by the federal government, and HARP also recommends strict application of tort (civil) laws to hold doctors responsible for their mismanagement of patients at the behest of managed care organizations. Most students will feel that this is a good start, but perhaps not enough to address all of the problems that Americans currently face with health care providers.

2. INTERNET

FRAUD

Have students visit the Web site for the Association of Certified Fraud Examiners at *http://www.cfenet.com*. Ask them to pick one of the headlines under "Today's Fraud Headlines" and read the article, then answer the following questions:

- What specific type of fraud is discussed in the article you chose, and how is it committed?

- Does the article contain any information about trends regarding this crime? What about tips to avoid becoming a victim to such a crime?

- Was there any other useful information that you learned?

Answers will vary, but the articles generally provide a fair amount of detail regarding the types of fraud committed and how it was done.

Again, answers will vary, but many of the articles will talk about the general problem of the type of fraud being discussed, and may include tips about fraud prevention in this area. Students will generally report that this site and its articles were very useful and helpful.

3. INTERNET

Fraud Tips

Have students learn about the Internet Fraud Complaint Center (IFCC), which is the result of a partnership between the Federal Bureau of Investigation (FBI) and the National White Collar Crime Center (NW3C). Their main page is at *https://www.ifccfbi.gov*. Ask students to read their main page and the entire section entitled "Fraud Tips'" and answer the following questions:

- What types of services does the IFCC provide?
- How does the Fraud Tips section help consumers?
- What are the six main areas covered under the Fraud Tips section?

To prevent Internet fraud, the IFCC offers services for both victims and law enforcement. In their own words, "For victims of Internet fraud, IFCC provides a convenient and easy-to-use reporting mechanism that alerts authorities of a suspected criminal or civil violation. For law enforcement and regulatory agencies at all levels, IFCC offers a central repository for complaints related to Internet fraud, works to quantify fraud patterns, and provides timely statistical data of current fraud trends."

The Fraud Tips section is a nearly exhaustive list covering a wide variety of Internet scams to avoid, and should be helpful to any reader.

The six main areas covered under Fraud Tips are Internet auction fraud, non-delivery of merchandise, credit card fraud, investment fraud, Nigerian letter scam, and business fraud.

Extended Workplace Applications

1. Analyze

Explain the following to students: The conduct of white-collar criminals is often subject to multiple criminal sanctions for the same scheme. For example, someone seeking to defraud an insurance company would be charged with one count of mail fraud for each letter mailed in furtherance of the scheme and might also be charged with a scheme to defraud and larceny connected with the underlying criminal plan.

Then ask students the following questions: Do you think that this is fair, since it could conceivably lead to dozens or even hundreds of criminal counts? Why or why not?

Some students will state that the application of this law could lead to excessive penalties, and may discuss cases in which people receive sentences that last far longer than any human life. Others will state that defrauders know what they are getting into and should be prepared to accept any penalties that they face, and that multiple attempts at fraud do constitute separate crimes.

2. Evaluate

Ask students to evaluate the following situation by answering the questions below: In Operation Blown Engine, the FBI arrested 12 people involved in an alleged highly organized fraud ring that staged auto accidents to cheat insurance companies out of millions of dollars annually. Their alleged ringleader, Sam "Nico" Lahooti, was believed to orchestrate potentially dangerous automobile accidents and recruit bogus victims to file insurance claims. The alleged defrauders also included two chiropractors who would "treat" the victims and file hugely inflated medical bills. The ringleader and doctors were alleged to have received millions of dollars through their fraud scheme, but those claiming to be accident victims received no more than $1,000 each.

- Which of the defendants is guilty of fraud?
- Can the ringleader also be liable for the reckless endangerment of human life?
- Can the chiropractors lose their licenses to practice?

All of the defendants appear to be guilty of fraud. The fact that they received very different amounts is irrelevant, although their level of involvement is: Lahooti should be charged with several counts of fraud, but people who posed as a victim only once should be charged with only one count of fraud.

Most students will agree that Lahooti's actions showed wanton recklessness toward human life and that he should be held criminally liable for that as well.

Yes, the chiropractors can and should lose their licenses to practice because of their willingness to participate in a fraudulent scheme.

3. Review

Ask students to review the following situation by answering the questions below: Four former executives have been indicted on federal charges for allegedly "cooking the books" at their former employer Aurora Foods, the manufacturer that creates the Duncan Hines and Mrs. Paul's food products. The U.S. Attorney's Office of New York City indicted them for conspiracy to commit securities fraud by manipulating company financial statements. The four defendants allegedly hid from investors at least $43 million in higher-than-expected trade promotion expenses. This was done because a company's financial statements contains crucial factors that potential investors consider when making investment decisions regarding a company.

- Why does it appear that Aurora Foods hid these expenses?

- What do you think investors did when the indictment was issued and the fraud was made public? Why?

Aurora Foods hid these expenses because the excessive $43 million made them look fiscally irresponsible and perhaps even corrupt.

Most students would state that investors lost confidence in the company. Indeed, you can share with them that Aurora Food's stocks plummeted from $8.50 a share to $3.38 a share when the indictment was announced.

Chapter 13

Crimes Against Public Order, Safety, and Morality

Chapter Resources

For the Instructor
Instructor's Resource Manual, pp. 127–135
Additional Activities, p. 133
PowerPoint Presentation and ExamView Pro Testbank
    CD-ROM for Chapter 13
cl.glencoe.com Web site

For the Student
Student Edition, Chapter 13, pp. 436–471
Review and Applications, p. 466
Tutorial with Simulation Applications
    CD-ROM for Chapter 13
cl.glencoe.com Web site

KEY TERMS

public order and
    safety offenses
mala prohibita
mala in se
unlawful assembly
rout
riot
disorderly conduct

vagrancy
nuisance
abatement
reckless driving
driving under the
    influence (DUI)
DUI manslaughter
vehicular manslaughter

firearm
assault weapon
obscenity
indecent exposure
exhibitionism
prostitution
Mann Act
solicitation

pimping
pandering
adultery
fornication
sodomy
gambling

Lecture Outline

13.1 PUBLIC ORDER AND SAFETY OFFENSES
Offenses that Create a Public Disturbance
Nuisances
Traffic Violations
Weapons Offenses

13.2 PUBLIC MORALITY OFFENSES
Obscenity
Indecent Exposure
Prostitution, Solicitation, and Pandering
Adultery, Fornication, and Illicit Cohabitation
Sodomy and Related Sexual Offenses
Gambling

In-Chapter Questions

 Papachristou v. City of Jacksonville **page 00**

What changes do you think could be made to this statute to make it constitutional?

If it were less vague and covered only activities that were clearly illegal, and if it used less outdated language, it could be made into a constitutional statute.

Criminal Law Online page 441

Is this law constitutional? Are parts of it constitutional, and other parts not? Why or why not?

Some students will feel that the law is unconstitutional because it does contain some vague areas, but others will feel that it is fine as it is. You can ask both groups what they think of vagrancy laws in general, then help them determine if their pre-existing views on vagrancy as a crime affect their objective understanding of the law.

Criminal Law Online page 444

What kind of information is provided? How will this help somebody understand his or her liability for driving drunk?

This guide provides information on the criteria for driving drunk, the penalties for being caught while driving drunk, and the harm to human life that is caused by drunk driving.

 Chemical Dependency Counselor page 00
What characteristics do you think a good chemical dependency counselor should possess?

A good counselor in this field should be perceptive, compassionate, and yet firm in handling the issues surrounding addiction recovery.

Photo caption page 446

What is another, more serious offense that may result from driving under the influence?

The most serious offense that can result from drunk driving is DUI manslaughter, which is the death of a human being caused by a vehicle that is being driven by a drunk driver.

13.1 Self Check page 450

Of the traffic offenses listed in the section above, which do you think is the most common and why?

The most common traffic offense is speeding because anyone who drives is easily capable of it and people frequently do not see it as a behavior that causes a social harm.

 Arcara v. Cloud Books, Inc. page 453
Should the owners and operators of a building be liable for crimes that, unknown to them, occur in their building?

If they are completely unknown to them, most students will agree that they should not be liable. On the other hand, if they practice willing ignorance of a public nuisance, they should be held liable.

 United States v. Thomas and United States v. Maxwell page 454
Considering the Bill of Rights grants defendants a trial "by impartial jury of the state and district wherein the crime shall have been committed," should a California couple be tried by a Tennessee jury?

Yes, if the crime has occurred in Tennessee because of the couple's physical presence there or because their Internet business created their virtual presence there.

 United States v. U.S. District Court page 455
Do you agree with the court's decision or should he producers have been liable despite their lack of knowledge?

It depends on what kind of proof the actress presented to "prove" that she was an adult at the time she made the movies. If she produced an authentic-looking driver's license or birth certificate, they may have been reasonably fooled. If not, the producers should be liable.

 People v. Garrison page 457
If the defendant did not have the "intent to arouse or to satisfy his or her sexual desire," should he have been found guilty? Why or why not?

Most students would agree that if the behavior were equally offensive, he probably would have been found guilty anyway. However, depending on the exact wording of the statute, this may not be the case.

 State v. Tookes page 460
Should the practice of allowing police and volunteers to engage in intercourse to obtain evidence be discontinued? Why or why not?

Most students will agree that it should, because police can obtain a conviction based on solicitation alone and to allow them to have intercourse encourages vice.

Photo caption page 465

How do you think illegal gambling can be tracked down and eradicated?

Students will probably have several good, creative suggestions for this. Undercover agents, informants, and investigative work in other vice crimes (such as prostitution or drug dealing) can all lead to uncovering and prosecuting illegal gambling activities.

13.2 Self Check page 465

Why do you think that adultery and fornication are no longer illegal in most jurisdictions?

Most students will answer that changing values, as well as the ongoing emphasis on an individual's right to privacy, have contributed to old adultery and fornication laws being removed from the books. Some will plainly state that such laws are "outdated."

Review and Applications

Questions For Review

1. Why do public order offenses exist, and how do they differ from more serious crimes?

   Public order and safety offenses are a modern outgrowth of common law crimes aimed at keeping peace. They are designed to protect the general public.

   They differ from more serious offenses because they deal with behavior that is not necessarily morally wrong, but nonetheless affects the peace and safety of the community.

2. What is the history of vagrancy laws, and why are they no longer in common use today?

   At common law in England and in the United States, vagrancy was vaguely defined as being idle, or wandering, without a visible means of support. At one time, all states had anti-vagrancy laws; however, many states today have repealed these laws because the U.S. Supreme Court has issued decisions that effectively rendered them unconstitutional.

3. Why is speeding a strict liability offense?

   Speeding is a strict liability offense because all drivers have received notice of the law and thus are held instantly liable if found guilty of the offense. For instance, drivers are provided with the speed laws by posted signs and by the local department of motor vehicles, to whom they must show an understanding of traffic laws before receiving a license to drive.

4. What are the characteristics that define firearms, and what commonly used weapons do not qualify as firearms?

   A firearm includes machine guns, along with certain other types of weaponry:
   - Any weapon, including a starter gun, that can, is designed to, or may readily be converted to expel a projectile by the action of an explosive
   - The frame or receiver of any such weapon
   - Any firearm muffler or firearm silencer
   - Any destructive device.

   More common types of guns, such as most ordinary rifles, shotguns, and handguns, are not considered firearms.

5. What is a DUI offense, and how is DUI manslaughter different from vehicular manslaughter?

   A DUI offense generally contains the two following elements in most jurisdictions:
   - The defendant operated a motor vehicle upon a roadway within the jurisdiction of the court.
   - The operation occurred while the defendant was either under the influence of an intoxicant, narcotic, or hallucinogenic to the extent that his or her normal faculties were impaired; OR the operation occurred while the defendant was driving with a blood or breath alcohol concentration above a prohibited level.

   DUI manslaughter occurs when an individual is driving under the influence and, by reason of the operation of a motor vehicle, causes the death of any human being. Vehicular manslaughter is the killing of a human being by the operation of a motor vehicle in a reckless manner likely to cause death or great bodily harm to another; it can also occur when one drives a vehicle in the commission of an unlawful act, not amounting to a felony, and with gross negligence.

6. What are the elements and required culpability for indecent exposure?

Under modern law, indecent exposure involves:

- The unlawful public exposure of the human body, particularly a person's genitals or the female breasts,

- where public exposure may occur on a street, building, beach, or even within a private location, provided that the exposure may be viewed from another public or private place,

- to protect the public sensibilities and prevent public lewdness.

Almost every jurisdiction recognizes indecent exposure as a criminal offense, and a general criminal intent is usually required to hold a person criminally liable for this offense.

7. What are the differences between prostitution, solicitation, and patronizing a prostitute?

Prostitution, which is often referred to as the world's oldest profession and is described in history's earliest written records, is committed when one person agrees to engage in sexual or deviate sexual intercourse in return for something of value, usually money.

Solicitation occurs when a customer offers to pay another, or a prostitute agrees to receive payment from another, for sex.

The crime of patronizing a prostitute is similar to solicitation on the customer's part. A typical statute for this crime provides that a person is guilty of patronizing a prostitute when pursuant to a prior understanding:

- The patron pays a fee to another person as compensation for such person or a third person having engaged in sexual conduct with him; or

- The patron pays or agrees to pay a fee to another person pursuant to an understanding that in return therefor such person or a third person will engage in sexual conduct with him; or

- The patron solicits or requests another person to engage in sexual conduct with him in return for a fee.

8. What is the difference between pimping and pandering?

Pimping is the promotion of prostitutes. Pimps live off of the earnings of prostitutes, and the prostitute works for the pimp. Because of the financial gains, pimps have a motive to encourage and coerce young persons into prostitution.

Pandering consists of either procuring a female for a place of prostitution or procuring a place for a prostitute in which she can ply her trade. If a person has engaged in either of these two activities, he or she is guilty of pandering even if no sexual activity has yet taken place.

The principal difference between pimping and pandering is that a pimp solicits patrons for the prostitute and lives off her earnings, while a panderer recruits prostitutes and sets them up in business.

9. For what reasons is sodomy still illegal in some jurisdictions?

Forcible sodomy is illegal because it is a serious felony comparable to rape. However, the true controversy surrounding sodomy laws does not pertain to forcible, but to consensual, sodomy. Most students will agree that consensual sexual acts between adults are a private matter, and that laws outlawing consensual sodomy are outdated and should be universally repealed. Some will state that such laws constitute a violation of the separation of church and state, since sodomy laws generally have religious origins. Regardless, sodomy is a controversial topic that may not be resolved for some time.

10. What forms of legal gambling exist today, and under what circumstances?

In most jurisdictions, the only forms of gambling that are lawful are state-operated lotteries, racing, and bingo or other contests sponsored on a nonprofit basis by social organizations. Statutes regulate gambling done through interstate transportation, wire communications, the U.S. Postal Service, or any other form where gambling is conducted between the states.

Problem-Solving Exercises

1. VAGRANCY STATUTES

Answers could include the following:

a. Yes, because it forbids behavior that may be committed by innocent, law-abiding people.

For instance, "persons wandering or strolling around from place to place without any lawful purpose or object" should not be criminalized because this unfairly impinges on their liberty.

b. The wisest move would probably be to acquit the defendants and overturn or update the law. The easiest move would be to simply acquit them and let the law stand until the next controversy arises.

c. Most students will agree that the law should be struck or updated so that innocent and law-abiding people are no longer arrested for no good reason.

2. CONSENSUAL SODOMY
Answers could include the following:
a. Most students will agree that their First Amendment rights are being violated because it affects their personal freedom of expression. If some students adamantly disagree, you may ask them if the same should apply to unmarried heterosexual couples engaging in sodomy.

b. Many students will agree that this is an unnecessary use of arrest warrants because it interferes with the couple's First Amendment rights.

c. Students will be divided about this. Just as judges sometimes apply their personal beliefs to their findings, the personal opinions of the students will affect their opinion of this issue. Regardless of their opinion, try to make sure that everyone gives an objective reason for their decisions.

3. TRAFFIC VIOLATIONS
Answers could include the following:
a. Yes, speeding and failure to stop. Although the officer who was stopped for speeding has a good reason for hurrying, technically the two actions are still considered criminal behavior because law enforcement officers are subject to the same laws as private citizens.

b. The fact that the officer is needed to testify at a trial is very relevant, and the state police officer's behavior seems negligent, unprofessional, and even possibly suspicious. Some

students will feel that the officer was morally justified in driving away, and that he could successfully fight the charge of failure to stop because of the circumstances that forced him to leave. A few might wonder about the motives of the state police officer, although no clear sign of wrongdoing appears in this vignette.

Workplace Applications

1. UNLAWFUL ASSEMBLY
Answers could include the following:
a. Students will be divided on this. If they allow it to continue, it may die out peacefully because the speakers are allowed to speak freely, but it may escalate into a riot or at least a rout because of the inflammatory nature of the speakers' comments. On the other hand, if they try to shut it down early, they may succeed or may face violent resistance by people who already feel wronged by the police and, inflamed by the speakers, may be seeking a fight.

b. At this point, it would be wise to contact your station and advise them of the situation, then request back-up to guarantee that the public assembly ends promptly when it is scheduled to end. (Public assemblies generally require city permits that place limitations on the location and time in which the assembly can be held, and it is legal to require an assembly to stop when it is scheduled to.)

c. It would be helpful to know past audience reactions to these speakers, as well if there are any recent trends of rioting or public disturbances that may encourage those present. Students will likely think of other types of information that would be helpful.

2. INDECENT EXPOSURE
Answers could include the following:
- Even though the sunbathers do not appear to mean any harm, they are guilty of indecent exposure because the backyard in which they sunbathe is visible to others, and as such is not entirely private.
- Since children have been involved and they possess intent to commit indecent exposure,

they can be found guilty of indecent exposure to a child. Some students may point out that they do not appear to have sexual intentions, and you may want to discuss whether this affects their level of criminal intent.

c. At this point, it would be wise to cite them for indecent exposure, explaining the law to them and also explaining that this is a particularly serious problem when children are involved. Some students would recommend arresting them, but most will feel that a court appearance to answer to misdemeanor charges is adequate. A few may feel that a warning will be adequate. Part of your students' decisions will be formed by the mores of your community, as well as their personal beliefs.

3. GANG NUISANCE

Answers could include the following:

a. Such orders are constitutional when they can clearly prove that they are necessary to abate a nuisance, because it is generally agreed that such nuisances affect community peace and safety and must be stopped. When such orders are vague, however, they can create constitutional problems because they can be misused to apply to innocent people as well as guilty ones.

b. Most students will agree that the good of the community is a higher priority, especially since the nuisance abatement does not significantly inhibit the liberty of known nuisances.

Internet Applications

1. INTERNET SEX OFFENDERS

Answers could include the following:

a. This site will help you by providing helpful demographic and behavior information about typical child sex offenders.

b. This site also has practical information for police regarding the procedures and evidence that will help them win cases against such suspects.

c. All of it can be useful. The Keene, NH, Police Department is a leader in the field of preventing child sexual abuse that is initiated via the Internet.

2. ONLINE GAMBLER'S ANONYMOUS

Answers could include the following:

a. Although this site provides much helpful information on the nature of gambling addiction, many students will answer this question according to their personal opinions of the subject. Some will believe that gambling is a social evil that is committed by willing individuals, and some will believe that gambling addiction is a disease.

b. Student answers will vary depending on their definition of "victimless." Some will feel that the only possible victim would be the gambler, who is making a decision to gamble. Others may feel that the gambler is victimized by those who facilitate his or her addiction. Still others may feel that the loved ones of gamblers may be victimized when gamblers lose their homes or cash holdings.

c. Most students, even those who enjoy and support gambling, feel that it should be regulated to ensure a high quality of life in communities and also to check the influence of organized crime in gambling.

Ethics Issues

PROSTITUTION AND PANDERING

Answers can include the following:

a. She is guilty of pandering because she knowingly provided a place for her roommate to continue her prostitution business. She can also be found guilty of providing an unsuitable home for her children, which can lead to having them removed and put into foster care.

b. Because the parolee did not just commit pandering, but also allowed prostitution to be conducted in the same home as her children, many students would recommend that her parole be revoked. Others may state that she was in a bind and could not replace the babysitter immediately, so she should be given leniency.

Additional Activities

Advanced Web Research

1. INTERNET
CHRONIC NUISANCES

Have students learn how the Kankakee (IL) Police Department handles chronic nuisances by going to *http://www.keynet.net/~patrol/nuisance. html*. Once they have read this page, ask them the following questions:

- Why was this ordinance created?

- How can the behavior of nuisances create liability for the person who permits his or her property to become public nuisance property?

- What is the procedure for dealing with nuisances?

Students should be able to understand that this ordinance was created "in order to stop problems with persons and/or properties that adversely effect the neighborhoods." Kankakee officials believe that the ordinance is "essential for the public safety, health and welfare of the residents of Kankakee."

People who permit their properties to become nuisance property, such as by neglecting to evict the tenants who create the nuisance, will be in violation of the ordinance and "subject to its remedies."

The City of Kankakee employs a five part process that includes: 1) The police document at least two nuisance incidents within a 60-day period, 2) the police contact the County Tax Assessors Office to find the registered property owner, 3) letters of notification are sent to the property owner by the police department, 4)

property owners are required to meet with the Chief /Deputy Chief within ten days, and 5) the landlord/owner comes to an agreement with the Chief or Deputy Chief on how the nuisance will be abated, usually by the eviction of the tenant.

2. INTERNET
GUN CONTROL

Have students check out the Brady Bill II, also known as the Gun Violence Prevention Act of 1994, at *http://www.shadeslanding.com/firearms/ brady2.html*. Ask them to read "Section 2. Findings and Declarations," then lead the class in a discussion by asking the following questions:

- Do you agree with the findings? Why or why not?

- Do you feel that a firearms bill provides the right solution to the findings discussed here? Why or why not?

Many students will agree with these findings because violent crime is rather pervasive in American culture. Others may feel that they are exaggerated, especially those who oppose the bill as an unconstitutional violation of the Second Amendment. A few may feel that this bill is too lenient.

Students will be divided on this issue. Although this does help to maintain the Second Amendment clause pertaining to a "well-regulated militia," it does not really help to address problems with illegally-owned firearms or problems with the American fascination with and glamorization of violent crime, which creates a permissive attitude toward crime.

3. INTERNET
OBSCENITY LAWS

Ask students to read about the 1973 U.S. Supreme Court case that helped determine today's obscenity laws. *Paris Adult Theatre I v. Slaton* can be found at *FindLaw.com*. The exact address is *http://caselaw.lp.findlaw.com/cgi-bin/ getcase.pl?navby=case&court=US&vol=413&invol=49*. (Students do not have to read the footnotes.)

Have students answer the following questions in a one- to two-page summary:

- What was the Georgia Supreme Court's original findings?
- How did the U.S. Supreme Court findings differ? Why?
- How did the U.S. Supreme Court's findings resemble their findings in *Roth v. United States* (1957)? How did they differ?

The Georgia Supreme Court found the Paris Adult Theatre guilty of obscenity, and the U.S. Supreme Court held that states have the right to regulate allegedly obscene material, provided that the Georgia Supreme Court maintains the standards set in this opinion and that of *Miller v. California*. They differ because the Supreme Court's opinion was based upon the case law relating to obscenity, while the Georgia court's opinion was simply that hardcore pornography was not constitutionally protected.

The Court reaffirmed the basic holding of *Roth v. United States*, which held that obscene material has no protection under the First Amendment.

> NOTE TO INSTRUCTOR: This is a fairly detailed analysis of a U.S. Supreme Court opinion. If you feel that some students will not be able to digest it, you can assign it as a group project or as an optional extra-credit project.

Extended Workplace Applications

1. Indict

Give students the following scenario: You are a juror hearing the case of a known compulsive gambler who has been arrested for starting and promoting high-stakes craps (dice) matches. Some of the people that he gambled against were under 21 (the legal age for gambling in your state, where gambling is allowed), and two were under 18. He is being charged with illegal gambling and one count of the corruption of minors for each of the people under 21 that

gambled with him (seven counts total). Based on these facts, of what crimes would you find him guilty, and why?

Most students would agree to all of the charges, although some may want to convict him for only two of the corruption of minor charges–the ones that applied to the youths under 18. He should be found guilty because, although he is a compulsive gambler, his behavior constituted affirmative acts toward promoting gambling among others, including minors; in short, his behavior was beyond that necessary to satisfy his addiction.

2. Analyze

Give students the following scenario: Two men are arrested in your county for pimping. They claim that they are not involved in prostitution, but in the movie business, because their customers are paying them "acting fees" for "models and actresses" who have sex with the clients on film for money. Therefore, they claim, they are running a pornography business (which is legal), not a prostitution business (which is not). Their clients take the only copy of the films that are made, and none of these films are used for commercial purposes. You are the local prosecutor and must decide whether to press charges against them. Do you charge them with pimping or not? Explain your reason.

Many students will contend that this is a flimsy attempt to portray a standard prostitution business as something different. Although pornography can be made for noncommercial reasons, this is not truly amateur pornography because of the "acting fees" involved. The fact remains that these clients are basically paying for sex, and the home movie is a bonus that happens to come with the sexual services.

Some students will state that, legally, they are making pornography. You may want to ask them how the acting fees figure into something that is being created for noncommercial use, and how it is essentially different from prostitution.

3. Role Play

Give students the following scenario: You are a local police officer. Your town has strict nuisance ordinances because of the large number of disorderly college students that rent homes and create disturbances, especially on weekends. Recently, a number of people have called to complain that one house appears to have ongoing drug dealing, and recently someone was severely beaten up on the front lawn. The local court has contacted the landlord, but he is afraid to evict the tenants because he thinks that they will physically harm him. What can you do to resolve this issue and restore the quality of life in the neighborhood in which this nuisance is occurring?

Students should be able to come up with the two basic options: Since the landlord is afraid to evict, your town may have an option of legally compelling him to evict them, thus removing for him the burden of responsibility (and, presumably, any possible revenge committed by the tenants) while at the same time forcing the tenants to leave. Another, perhaps better, option would be to investigate the tenants' vice activities and arrest all of them.

4. Evaluate

Give students the following scenario: You are patrolling a low-income neighborhood when you see two young teens throw two rifles over a fence. Since your partner and you saw the weapons in their hands, you take them into custody for possessing unregistered weapons and underaged possession of weapons. Both of them, although only 13 and 14 years old, have prior records involving gun-related offenses;

one of them had been adjudicated for armed robbery when he was only 12. You write up your reports for the prosecutor, then call the youths' mothers to come get them. When the mothers arrive, they yell at you for arresting their sons, who they say are "good boys" who "have to" carry guns for their safety. They are very belligerent and rude, and by speaking with them it is clear why their sons are so delinquent. You ask them a few questions and find out that they keep guns in their house for their children to carry and use at any time. Answer the following questions:

- After this conversation, what recommendations will you make to the prosecutor regarding the cases of these two boys?

- Can you charge the mothers with any offenses? Why or why not?

- Should these boys be removed from their homes? Why or why not?

Most students would recommend to the prosecutor to press charges against these boys, and to recommend a sanction that combines punishment with some rehabilitative aspect such as counseling. Some students would recommend leniency, but you may want to ask them what this would accomplish.

If the weapons that the mothers own are unregistered, the mothers could be charged with these offenses. In addition, students may state that they are providing unsuitable homes for their children.

Many students will feel that these youths come from dysfunctional, unsuitable homes and that they should be removed.

Drug- and Alcohol-Related Crimes

Chapter Resources

For the Instructor
Instructor's Resource Manual, pp. 137–147
Additional Activities, p. 145
PowerPoint Presentation and ExamView Pro Testbank
    CD-ROM for Chapter 14
cl.glencoe.com Web site

For the Student
Student Edition, Chapter 14, pp. 472–511
Review and Applications, p. 506
Tutorial with Simulation Applications
    CD-ROM for Chapter 14
cl.glencoe.com Web site

KEY TERMS

controlled substances
psychoactive drugs
actual possession
constructive possession
possession with intent to deliver

delivery of a controlled substance
simulated controlled substance
drug conspiracy
drug loitering
drug transportation

drug paraphernalia
dram shop laws
offense of drunk driving

Lecture Outline

14.1 TYPES OF PSYCHOACTIVE DRUGS

14.2 HISTORY OF DRUG LEGISLATION IN THE
UNITED STATES
Drug Use in Nineteenth-Century America
Drug Legislation from the 1800s to
    the Present
Current Drug Use
Current Drug Policy
Drugs and Religious Freedom

14.3 DRUG OFFENSES
Possession
Other Drug Offenses
Narcotics or Drug Addiction as a Defense

14.4 ALCOHOL LEGISLATION AND OFFENSES
Temperance and Prohibition
Changing Views on Alcohol Use and Abuse
Drunk Driving Offense (Driving Under
    the Influence)
Intoxication and Alcoholism as Defenses

In-Chapter Questions

14.1 Self Check page 475
Which categories of drugs seem the most dangerous?
The most addictive? Why?
    Although designer drugs, inhalants, marijuana,
and hallucinogens are supposed to be the most
dangerous and addictive, not many students will
pick these, perhaps because of the marijuana

category and because students are sometimes less familiar with the effects of hallucinogenic drugs. Some will feel that depressants and some stimulants, such as cocaine and Ritalin, seem to contain drugs that are far more dangerous and that are better known for their addictive qualities.

Photo caption page 481

What evidence separates the person guilty of possession from the person guilty of possession with intent to deliver?

People guilty of possession with intent to deliver often carry large amounts of drugs and cash, plus weighing devices and other items necessary for the sale of drugs. Small to moderate amounts of drugs, baggies, and paraphernalia, when not accompanied by other evidence, do not constitute possession with intent to deliver.

Criminal Law Online page 482

Should they be punished? If so, why and how? If not, why?

Many students will state that punishment is not an option that works because it is too harsh and excessive for such a minor crime. Others will state that punishment is a good idea because even non-violent drug offenders must learn to respect the law, but they may feel that incarceration with violent and predatory felons is not the answer.

14.2 Self Check page 484

1. For what reasons was the Uniform Controlled Substances Act created?

It was created to ensure that drug policies throughout the United States took a uniform approach to prosecuting and punishing drug crimes.

2. In general, have efforts to fight and criminalize the use of psychoactive substances been successful in the United States? Why or why not?

No, because many Americans favor drug use and because efforts to stop drug use have not addressed this issue, but have only unsuccessfully tried to suppress it.

 Wheeler v. United States page 485

Should the other inhabitants of the room be charged with constructive possession? Why or why not?

Many students would say yes because they were close enough to exercise control of the controlled substance. Many other students may say no because the substance was not actually the other inhabitants' responsibility.

 Jones v. State page 487

Should Jones have been convicted if he had only the cocaine, not the screen?

Many, if not all, students would agree that he should have been convicted if this were the case.

 State v. Brown page 488

What additional evidence do you think should change a crime from possession to possession with intent to deliver? Why?

Answers will vary, and students may name various types of evidence such as cash, weighing devices, packaging materials, the location at which the person is arrested (such as an area where drug loitering occurs), the presence of a pager and/or cellular phone, and the person's behavior toward undercover police or informants. More detailed evidence could include phone records, and conspicuous wealth but undeclared (to the IRS) income.

 State v. Davis page 489

Do you think the Court of Appeals should have reversed this conviction? Why or why not?

Answers will vary, and students may name various types of evidence such as packaging materials, the location at which the person is arrested (such as an area where drug loitering occurs), the presence of a pager and/or cellular phone, and the person's behavior toward undercover police or informants. More detailed evidence could include phone records, and conspicuous wealth but undeclared (to the IRS) income.

United States v. Civelli page 491

Do you agree with Civelli's conviction? Why or why not?

Some students will think that Civelli may have been innocent and not merely willfully blind to Bedoya's drug dealing. For instance, perhaps Civelli offered same-day local delivery of important business documents.

On the other hand, many students will feel that his behavior showed willful blindness, and that he used this as a ruse to avoid prosecution. Some of these students, however, may feel that although it was correct to let the conviction stand, the sentence was too long.

United States v. Eastman page 492

Should other members of a conspiracy be allowed to escape prosecution by testifying against a defendant? Why or why not?

Many students will agree that although this practice does provide protection for a small amount of criminals, it also can greatly help prosecutors obtain convictions for other members of a conspiracy.

This practice should be used sparingly so that only a very small amount of defendants escape prosecution. Ideally, prosecutors should target one higher-level member of a conspiracy and try to use him or her to obtain evidence on all of the others.

City of Tacoma v. Luvene page 493

Do you agree with this conviction? Why or why not?

Some students will believe that it is uncertain, but you may wish to remind them that these are only summaries of cases and that the evidence was examined in greater detail during the trial. Therefore, this may be enough evidence to sustain a conviction.

United States v. Jewell page 494

Do you think it is possible for a person to transport 110 pounds of marijuana and be unaware of its presence? Why or why not?

This is highly doubtful, especially in an ordinary passenger car, but perhaps a friend could store something in suitcases in the trunk. Also, it may be easy to transport this quantity in a commercial vehicle (such as a truck or a train) without telling anyone.

Chemical Dependency Manager page 495

What qualities do you think a person should possess to be a good chemical dependency manager?

Answers may vary and could include compassion, firmness, and dependability.

Photo caption page 495

Do police need to catch drug loiterers with drugs or paraphernalia in order to successfully prosecute them?

No. If the totality of circumstances indicates that drug loitering has occurred, drug loiterers can be arrested and successfully prosecuted.

Robinson v. California page 496

Do you think drug addicts should be allowed an addiction defense? Why or why not?

If they are merely showing signs of addiction and do not appear to be selling or otherwise trafficking drugs, many students will agree that this defense could be appropriate. Many will also feel that perhaps this should be a partial or mitigating defense that allows the defendant to escape fines or incarceration but does provide for drug treatment.

Criminal Law Online page 496

How do they operate differently from regular criminal courts? Do they seem to work? Why or why not?

These courts focus solely on low-level drug charges, and their focus is on treatment. They seem to work because they focus on rehabilitating drug abusers, rather than punishing them.

14.3 Self Check page 496

1. Why does possession with intent to deliver need more proof than mere possession?

Because police must prove not only that the person is in possession of controlled substances, but that he or she also has the means and intent to deliver them to other parties.

2. How can police officers determine if people are drug loitering, or just loitering?

The presence of known drug dealers, whether the location is a known drug-selling area, actual drug transactions, or other suspicious behavior can all point to drug loitering.

 ***Schmerber v. California* page 00**

Should a person have the right to refuse a blood or breath test without being presumed guilty? Why or why not?

Many students will believe that this is a definite sign of guilt, and that a person should agree to breath tests when they are requested to do so. Blood tests are somewhat more touchy because of the current use of blood samples to create DNA databases; an innocent defendant may feel that this is an unfair violation of his or her rights.

 ***Driver v. Hinnant* page 504**

Should alcoholism be allowed as a defense against certain crimes? Why or why not?

Many students will agree that it is an acceptable decision only for crimes that directly relate to intoxication. Many students will believe that this is a poor excuse for more serious crimes because many alcoholics engage in denial, which encourages them to avoid responsibility for more serious actions and this should not be encouraged.

 ***State ex rel. Harper v. Zegeer* page 505**

Do you agree with the decision of the *Harper* court? Why or why not?

Many students will agree that it is an acceptable decision because it extends this defense only to crimes that directly relate to intoxication, but not to other offenses. Students may hotly debate whether alcoholism is a disease.

14.4 Self Check page 505

1. What are some legal actions that can be taken against a drunk driver?

They can be fined, have their license suspended, be forced to pay restitution, and serve jail or prison time for their crimes.

2. When can alcohol be used as a defense? When is it not an acceptable defense?

It can be used as a defense when a person has an uncontrolled reaction to it. It is not acceptable when a person voluntarily drinks and then voluntarily chooses to engage in risky behavior, such as drinking and driving.

Review and Applications

Questions For Review

1. Explain the differences between marijuana and hallucinogens.

Marijuana is in its own category, although it has been classified as a hallucinogen, a stimulant, and a depressant. It actually fits all of these categories to a certain extent, but not to the same extent as drugs that are officially classified in these categories. For example, its hallucinogenic qualities are much weaker than those found in true hallucinogens.

Hallucinogens act on the central nervous system to cause visual or auditory hallucinations. They include LSD (lysergic acid diethylamide), PCP (phencyclidine), mescaline and peyote (derived from a small cactus, the mescal button), psilocybin (derived from a fungus), and numerous synthetic drugs.

2. Explain the Supreme Court's findings on the use of peyote in traditional Native American religious ceremonies.

After decades of inconsistent drug laws and application of drug laws regarding the Native American use of peyote, the U.S. Supreme Court found in *Department of Employment v. Smith* that Native Americans may legally use peyote for traditional religious ceremonies. This case provided lawmakers with a consistent guideline for how to handle such cases.

3. Outline the history and outcome of the "War on Drugs."

The War on Drugs was an effort initiated by President Ronald Reagan to fight American drug use through the use of law enforcement, intelligence activities, and strict punishments for all drug offenders, even nonviolent ones convicted of mere possession. The result has been nearly disastrous: After two decades and millions of dollars spent, drug use is still relatively common in American society, jails and prisons are overcrowded in part because of the lengthy incarceration of nonviolent drug offenders, and new drugs like crack and Ecstasy are being used in large quantities by young people. Because of this disappointing outcome, lawmakers are reexamining the War on Drugs and looking for new options in fighting drug abuse.

4. What does the Uniform Controlled Substances Act forbid? Give at least five examples.

Answers may include any of the following. The Uniform Controlled Substances Act forbids and makes it a crime to:

- manufacture or deliver a controlled (forbidden) substance.
- possess with the intent to manufacture or deliver a controlled substance.
- create, deliver, or possess with intent to deliver a counterfeit substance.
- offer or agree to deliver a controlled substance and deliver or dispense a controlled substance.
- possess a controlled substance.
- knowingly keep or maintain a store, dwelling, building, vehicle, boat, or aircraft, etc. resorted to by persons illegally using a controlled substance.
- acquire or obtain possession of a controlled substance by misrepresentation, fraud, forgery, deception, or subterfuge.

5. What is a simulated controlled substance? Is possession of this a crime?

A simulated controlled substance is any nondrug substance, such as baking soda, that resembles a known drug and could be packaged in such a way as to fool onlookers or potential drug purchasers. Possession of a simulated controlled substance is a crime.

6. What elements are required to convict a person of cultivating marijuana?

In most states, in order to prove the crime of cultivating, drying, or processing marijuana the prosecution must prove the following two elements:

- The defendant knew plants were growing on his or her property.
- He or she knew the plants were cannabis.

7. Define drug paraphernalia, and provide three examples.

Drug paraphernalia is defined as "any equipment, product or material of any kind that is primarily intended or designed for use with a controlled substance." Examples of drug paraphernalia include:

- Bongs
- Pipes
- Rolling papers
- Scales
- Hypodermic needles

8. What is narcotics addiction? Is it legal or illegal? What Amendment relevant to this discussion, and why?

Narcotics addiction is the repeated or uncontrolled use of controlled substances.

Being a drug addict is not a crime, although any other involvement with drugs, such as possession or use of controlled substances, is. Although narcotics addiction used to be illegal, the U.S. Supreme Court found this to be unconstitutional in the case *Robinson v. California*. You can refer students to the Application Case on page 496 for more information about this case.

The Eighth Amendment to the Constitution of the United States, applicable to the states through the due process clause of the Fourteenth Amendment, protects people from cruel and unusual punishment. The Court in *Robinson* held that making drug addiction illegal violated this protection.

9. What procedures does an officer use after pulling over a suspect whom he or she believes is driving drunk?

Generally, the process is as follows:

- The arresting officer observes the erratic operation of the vehicle or the behavior of a driver, which often leads to a stop for investigation of DUI/DWI.

- These observations serve as evidence of being under the influence.

- After the stop, the officer will take note of the physical appearance of the driver to determine whether he or she may be intoxicated.

- During the investigation, the officer will ask the driver questions and observe the driver's demeanor.

- If the officer is still suspicious, he or she will administer a series of field sobriety tests (FSTs).

- If the officer's observations may confirm his or her suspicion that the suspect is under the influence, this provides the constitutional foundation for a breath, blood, or urine test to determine the driver's BAC.

10. What are dram shop acts?

Dram shop laws hold alcohol servers responsible for harm that intoxicated or underage patrons cause to other people. You can explain to students that this is so alcohol servers will take more responsibility for their actions and not serve drunk people drinks to make money or because it is easier.

Problem-Solving Exercises

1. POSSESSION AND INTENT TO DELIVER

The fact that he is a suspected drug dealer may lend some circumstantial evidence, but may not be enough to guarantee that he possesses intent to deliver. This is because his drug dealing has not yet been confirmed; also, his small amount of cash makes it seem unlikely that he is dealing drugs.

2. DRUG LOITERING

This should be enough evidence, but the officer can also approach the youths and search them for drugs on their person, which would provide further evidence.

3. PROBATION AND DUI

Answers could include the following:

a. Most students will agree that he should be, because he has taken drugs and drove while on these drugs. It is up to the probation officer whether to handle this formally or informally, because other factors such as the probationer's overall conduct and attitude might be factors.

b. Most students agree that the fact that he drove while on drugs is a serious crime that should be prosecuted.

Workplace Applications

1. PEYOTE IN RELIGIOUS CEREMONIES

Answers could include the following:

a. This claim should be investigated because if not, Running Bull could bring suit against your department for an unlawful arrest. In addition, you need to be careful to follow the law in such instances.

b. This would be wise, since you already have the drug test results and do not want to exacerbate the situation. However, some students will support detaining him so that, should he be lying about the religious ceremony, he does not have the ability to ask people to create an alibi for him.

c. Although this may seem tempting, it is best to not ignore a valid excuse such as this. You may still be able to arrest him, but it is best to first hear his story and determine if it checks out.

d. If his assertions are correct, his actions have been legal and he should not be arrested.

2. **PREGNANCY AND ADDICTION**

Answers could include the following:

a. Most students would agree that drug use during pregnancy is a horrible crime and should be punished. If these charges can be brought without violating the mother's rights, many students will agree that this is wise. In addition, some may also wish to see child abuse charges brought against the mothers for knowingly causing health problems such as drug addiction to their newborn children.

b. Perhaps. Some students will state that the drug would be inevitably delivered to the fetus, and that there was a strong possibility in a full-term pregnancy that this fetus would have been born; therefore, the mother should bear responsibility for the results. Others may state that this is making drug addiction a crime, which is unconstitutional. You may want to ask them if drug addiction, not merely abuse, is always the issue, and if mothers who are addicted to drugs should not be held responsible for harming others.

c. Many students would charge the mother with drug delivery and child abuse charges. They may also express an interest in having the child removed from the home.

d. These crimes should be reported to the police and to Child Protective Services.

3. **DRUG TRANSPORTATION**

Answers could include the following:

a. Many students will think that the passenger should be held for further questioning. He could be asked more detailed questions about where he traveled and with whom he was in contact before boarding the plane.

b. In all airplane flights that originate in the United States, passengers are required to answer questions to confirm that they packed their bags themselves, have had their bags in their possession since they packed them, and are not carrying items for anyone else. Therefore, if the passenger had answered these questions truthfully, this issue would have been resolved at check-in. However, it is not guaranteed that such questions will be asked in airports in other countries, and it is possible that a friend's package was carried in the person's luggage. This person, however, was responsible for learning the contents of the package before attempting to bring it to the United States.

Internet Applications

1. **MEDICAL MARIJUANA**

Answers could include the following:

a. The Court found that marijuana had no medical value, and it determined this by expert testimony that backed these claims.

b. They were outraged, and many of them continue to use it regardless of the Court's finding.

c. Student answers will vary depending on their opinion of marijuana. Many will find that the Court's finding was incorrect, because marijuana has appeared to help many terminally ill patients. Others will feel that the Court was correct because they are opposed to any type of drug use.

2. **DUI/DWI**

Answers could include the following:

a. Yes, it plays a large role in assaults, particularly in family violence such as spouse and child abuse, because alcohol abusers choose to use their drunken state as a time to vent their emotions.

b. They have dropped considerably. Alcohol awareness through groups such as MADD have also played a role in this.

Ethics Issue

1. **PROBATION AND DRUG USE**

   Answers can include the following:

   a. He can be warned and let go, warned and given stricter probation restrictions, or have his probation revoked. Many students will either let him go with a warning or make his probation stricter in some way without actually revoking it.

   b. Perhaps making his probation stricter or revoking it altogether is the only answer. Many students will agree that a warning alone will not be serious enough.

   c. It does appear that this problem will not happen again because he has been a model probationer in all other respects, and the death of his mother is an unusual circumstance. Some students, however, will show concern that he chose to escape into drug use to deal with his depression.

2. **MEDICAL MARIJUANA**

   Answers can include the following:

   a. Student answers may depend on whether they live in a state that prescribes medical marijuana. Many students feel that marijuana is an acceptable treatment for terminally ill patients, especially in comparison to harder prescription drugs. Some will feel that it is an unacceptable crime and disagree.

   b. Since the U.S. Supreme Court has found medical marijuana to be illegal, there are no other legal alternatives until somebody brings another case to the Supreme Court. In the meantime, many doctors have responded by ignoring the Court's orders and continuing to prescribe it anyway.

Advanced Web Research

1. INTERNET

DRUG POSSESSION

Ask students to read a question-and-answer article on possession with intent to distribute at FindLaw.com. The exact address is *http://criminal-law.freeadvice.com/drug_crimes/VAlaw_charged.html*. Then, have them answer the following questions:

- Why is it sometimes difficult to determine whether a person possesses drugs for personal use or with an intent to sell them?

- Can the law be clarified in any way? Why or why not?

- How could this defendant convince a court that he or she is only using the drugs for personal use? Is it a problem that anyone could use such a claim? Explain.

Because people sometimes have large quantities for personal use, such as someone who has just bought a supply that is meant to last a long time. Sometimes your location at the time of arrest is important, but the law is very vague in this regard. It could be further clarified in terms of location and whether the defendant can be proven to be involved in drug sales. However, this will not be enough to resolve all cases.

He or she could repeat what has been said here, i.e., that he or she bought the drugs for personal use and has never been known to sell drugs or even contemplate selling them.

2. INTERNET

REHABILITATION PROGRAMS

Have students check out the world-famous Betty Ford Center at *http://www.bettyfordcenter.org*. Ask them to read the main page and the section entitled "Programs," and answer the following questions:

- What programs are available?

- Does this resemble your idea of a typical rehabilitation program? Why or why not?

- How can these programs be customized for individual patients?

Programs can be gender specific, specialized in other ways, and are based upon 12-step programs. Most students will state that this sounds fairly typical because many rehab centers focus on 12-step programs and most offer treatment options for special populations.

They can be customized based upon the patient's gender, special needs, desire to have their families involved in their treatment, and in other ways.

3. INTERNET

MADD

Ask students to visit the Mothers Against Drunk Drivers (MADD) Web site at *http://www.madd.org*. Have them read "About MADD" and "Under 21." Next, ask them to answer the following questions:

- Why was MADD formed, and what is the scope of their programs and services?

- What does MADD do to combat myths about drinking that are frequently believed by people under 21? Why do they focus on this?

MADD was formed in response to a drunk-driving accident that killed an 18-year-old girl. To date, they have greatly influenced legislation affecting drunk drivers, and they have also provided educational information to millions of people.

MADD provides a section on their Web site called "Under 21," which addresses and refutes common myths about alcohol that glamorize it to young people. It explains the cost of irresponsible drinking and the negative effect it can have on people's lives. They focus on this to help educate people at an early age about the dangers of alcoholism and drunk driving.

Extended Workplace Applications

1. Role Play

Give students the following scenario: As an off-duty parole officer, you are driving home from a nightclub with a friend who is also off-duty. Your friend, the driver, consumed two beers at the club. On the way home, the police stop your vehicle for a minor traffic infraction. Your friend asks you to tell the police that you were driving the car. You have not had anything to drink the entire evening. Do you tell the police that you were the driver?

Most students would refuse to lie for someone like this, especially since the police will likely see the two of you changing seats. Also, since the police could still cite you for the traffic infraction, which will affect your insurance and cost you money, you have no reason to put yourself in such a situation.

2. Evaluate

In 1998, voters in Washington, D.C., were presented with proposition 59, the "Legalization of Marijuana for Medical Treatment Initiative." Have students view the text of that legislation at the Act-Up DC Web site: **http://www.actupdc. org/text59pg.html**. Explain that the initiative allows the use of marijuana for medical purposes when a licensed physician found the use of marijuana to be medically necessary and

recommends its use for the treatment of various chronic or long-term illnesses. Also tell students that a report on the medical uses of marijuana identified by AMA(American Medical Association) certified doctors can be found at **http://www.mpp.org/nr092099.html**. Next, ask students the following question: Given the information in the two Web sites, do you think that marijuana should continue to be listed as a Schedule I controlled substance?

Many students will agree that it should be listed as a controlled substance, but that Schedule I is too harsh, especially since such a categorization places it in a more dangerous category than heroin or crack cocaine.

3. Role Play

Give students the following scenario: While off duty, you get into an accident. The other driver's eyes are red and he smells like marijuana. You personally believe that marijuana should be legalized. Do you arrest the driver, or exchange insurance information and leave the scene of the accident without reporting him?

Since the other driver is choosing to drive while under the influence, the issue goes beyond that of the recreational use of marijuana. His behavior is endangering others, much as is seen with alcohol abusers. Therefore, he should be arrested, and most students will agree that this is the correct response.

4. Discuss

Read the following to the class and lead a discussion with the question below:

The only Supreme Court decision on the issue of the legal use of peyote by Native Americans is, *Employment Division v. Smith*, which was immediately accepted as the controlling authority on this issue. This dismayed antidrug advocates who believe that all drugs should be outlawed, but also disappointed people who wanted Native Americans to have the right to use peyote for any reason, not just for religious ceremonies.

- Which opinion do you most agree with, and why?

Some students will feel that *Employment Division v. Smith* creates a double standard and that all drugs should be made illegal, regardless of a person's religious beliefs. This may be a good time to discuss the validity of psychoactive prescription drugs, which although legal may be equally addictive as certain illegal drugs. Some antidrug students will also feel that these should be more closely regulated, but others will feel that they serve a medical purpose and thus should be excepted from scrutiny.

Some students will feel that *Employment Division v. Smith* was a good compromise because it allowed Native Americans to use peyote for legitimate reasons, but did not allow unchecked drug use.

Some students, generally those who favor decriminalizing drugs, will feel that Native Americans should be allowed to use peyote whenever they wish because such use is also part of their tradition and does nobody any harm.

Crimes Against the Administration of Justice

KEY TERMS

obstruction of justice	false swearing	compounding a felony	constructive contempt
bribery	subornation of perjury	misprision of a felony	criminal contempt
quasi-bribery	witness tampering	escape	civil contempt
commercial bribery	suppressing evidence	contempt of court	
perjury	resisting arrest	direct contempt	

Lecture Outline

15.1 CRIMES AGAINST THE ADMINISTRATION OF JUSTICE

15.2 BRIBERY
  Modern Bribery
  Commercial Bribery

15.3 PERJURY
  Subornation of Perjury

15.4 OBSTRUCTION OF JUSTICE
  Witness Tampering Laws
  Suppressing Evidence

15.5 RESISTING ARREST
  Modern Statutes

15.6 COMPOUNDING AND MISPRISION OF A FELONY

15.7 ESCAPE

15.8 CONTEMPT OF COURT

In-Chapter Questions

15.1 Self Check page 515

Which do you think are more serious: crimes that are committed by citizens who try to disrupt the legal system or crimes that are committed by those in positions of authority? Why?

It depends on the crime being committed, and in what circumstances. If a private citizen has the same level and breadth of influence as a public official does, their crimes may be equally serious. However, many students will agree that corrupt public officials have a greater ability to create far-reaching harm to a community.

Florida v. Saad page 516

Do you agree with Saad's conviction for bribery? Why or why not?

Many students will agree that he should not have agreed to bribe officials, even if he felt it was for an ultimately legitimate reason. This is an excellent example to illustrate to students that a crime is a crime and that, as the case summary says, the end does not justify the means.

15.2 Self Check page 519

1. What are some ways in which bribery is different from quasi-bribery?

Bribery involves public officials whose influence can affect an entire community. Quasi-bribery involves people other than public officials whose influence may or may not be equally far-reaching.

2. Should commercial bribery carry different penalties than regular bribery or quasi-bribery? Why or why not?

Many students will believe that it should because corporate corruption can affect an entire industry and its consumers. In the case of industries in which people rely on manufacturers to consider their health and well being, such as food or automobiles, this is particularly important.

People v. Sharpe page 521

Do you think the defendants deserved consecutive or concurrent sentences? Why or why not?

Some students will feel that concurrent sentences would be adequate because their crimes are all interrelated and could be punished with a single sentence. Others will feel that their crimes were serious enough to warrant individual sentences, and may question the effectiveness of concurrent sentences.

15.3 Self Check page 522

1. Why do you think that the laws regarding false swearing have changed since common law?

They have changed because modern law wishes to recognize the significance of such actions and punish them more appropriately.

2. What are the elements that are required for subornation of perjury?

The three elements are:

- Perjury in fact

- The perjured statements were procured by the accused

- Proof that the suborner, who is the person who agrees to commit subornation of perjury, knew or should have known that such oaths or testimony would be false

Photo caption page 524

How can witness protection programs help prevent witness tampering?

If federal witnesses know that they will be protected after giving testimony, the threats of people who try to intimidate them into not testifying will be less effective.

United States v. Baldyga page 525

Do you agree with the defendant's conviction on witness tampering charges? Why or why not?

Many students will agree that he deserved to be convicted, especially since he tried to avoid creating incriminating evidence against himself by handing the witness a note and silently pulling a gun on him.

15.4 Self Check page 526

1. Should the federal witness tampering statute apply only to witnesses who are *not* involved in undercover operations? Should it apply only to classic cases of intimidating or threatening witnesses?

Most students will believe that it should apply to all witnesses, since all of them can be crucial to the criminal trial for which they are testifying. Most students will also believe that it should not be limited to overt threats or intimidation, but to any attempt to cause witnesses to deviate from the truth.

2. What are some ways that evidence can be suppressed? Among the participants in a trial, who seems most likely to suppress evidence?

Suppressing evidence occurs when a defendant, or a person working on behalf of the defendant, suppresses (hides), destroys, or refuses to produce evidence relevant to a grand jury investigation. Defendants and defense counsel are the most likely to suppress evidence.

Criminal Law Online page 527

What is their general advice about resisting arrest, and why?

Their general advice is to not resist arrest, even when you know it is unlawful, because it could create further legal problems for you and you have other forms of redress when unlawfully arrested.

 United States v. John Bad Elk page 528

Do you think this defendant should have been acquitted? Why or why not?

Many students will agree that he should not have been because, as they have learned in this and previous chapters, this situation did not justify the use of deadly force. The defendant was not reasonably provoked into taking such action, nor was he in a situation that required the use of deadly force as self-defense. All students will likely agree that the issue of the incorrect jury instructions could be resolved and that the defendant could receive an appropriate sentence.

15.5 Self Check page 530

1. Should individuals have the right to resist unlawful arrest? Why or why not?

   Some students will agree that resisting unlawful arrests should be allowed because people should not be unfairly deprived of their liberty and may have a legitimate reason to fear the police. Some feel that since it may be impossible to determine at the time of arrest whether it is lawful, people should not create extra legal problems and should agree to be arrested, then seek appropriate redress.

2. What factors make it difficult for jurisdictions to decide whether resisting unlawful arrest should be legal?

   Factors can include issues regarding violating the civil rights of arrested people, such as by taking their liberty unlawfully; concern about the use of unnecessary force against police or suspects when arrest is resisted, and possible harm or death caused by this; and public fears about police brutality or discriminatory treatment.

 Judge page 531

What qualities do you think a good judge should have?

Typical responses include objectivity, intelligence, thorough understanding of the law, firmness, compassion, reasoning skills, strong perception, and fairness.

15.6 Self Check page 532

1. Why is misprision of a felony considered a more serious crime than compounding a felony? Do you agree with this?

   Because misprision of a felony does not just involve accepting a bribe to not follow up on a felony, but it involves taking positive steps to conceal or destroy evidence. Many students will consider this more serious than compounding a felony because of the efforts taken to conceal or destroy evidence, but some may feel that accepting a bribe to not press charges is equally or more damaging to the justice process.

2. Should society be more concern about felonies and insist that all felonies be prosecuted, as opposed to prosecuting misdemeanors?

   Most students will agree that this is a good idea, especially since the justice system is overwhelmed and many jails are overcrowded.

 People v. Trujillo page 533

Do you think fear for one's safety should be an affirmative defense to escape charges? Why or why not?

Most, if not all, students will agree that this is a valid defense when serious physical injury or death seem imminent because prison officials are sometimes unable to detect and prevent such behavior in other inmates before any harm occurs.

Photo caption page 534

What is one affirmative defense that prison escapees can use?

One affirmative defense, which has been upheld by the courts, is escape out of fear for one's safety or life. Inmates who are escaping possible violence or death are generally excused from escaping prison.

15.7 Self Check page 534

Under what circumstances are escape statutes interpreted to exclude certain inmates? Do you agree with this? Why or why not?

Inmates who face a strong possibility of physical abuse, sexual abuse, or death are generally not punished for attempting to escape prison because the courts have held that their attempts at self-preservation are justified.

15.8 Self Check page 535

Can constructive contempt be as harmful as direct contempt in some circumstances? Why or why not?

Yes, because it can undermine the court's will with equal severity as direct contempt.

Review and Applications

Questions for Review

1. What are the elements of the offense of bribery?
   Under modern law, bribery forbids:
   - The results of influencing a public official.
   - The act of bribery itself, whether the attempt to bribe is successful or not.
   - In addition, the Model Penal Code forbids:
     - ➤ Law enforcement and public officials to receive gifts from individuals subject to their jurisdiction.
     - ➤ A public servant who has the authority and discretion over contracts or transactions to accept or solicit gifts from any person "known to be interested or likely to become interested" in such contract or transaction.
     - ➤ Any criminal justice professional to accept or agree to accept a gift from an individual in your custody as a prisoner.

2. What is quasi-bribery, and how does it differ from regular bribery? Give an example.
   Quasi-bribery is an extension of the crime of bribery that covers people other than public officials, whose functions are nonetheless considered important to the public welfare. Although it has the same essential effect as standard bribery, its recipients are private citizens. For example, the bribery of officers of political conventions, officers or employees of public institutions, and representatives of labor organizations are considered positions important to the public that could be unduly influenced by quasi-bribery.

3. What is subornation of perjury, and how are the defendant and the perjurer punished for it?
   Subornation of perjury is the influencing of another, either through payment or pressure, to commit perjury. It has three elements:
   - Perjury in fact
   - The perjured statements were procured by the accused
   - Proof that the suborner, who is the person who agrees to commit subornation of perjury, knew or should have known that such oaths or testimony would be false

   If the accused causes another to make false statements under oath, he or she can be guilty of a distinct and separate crime of subornation of perjury. In addition, an accused will be held liable for his or her knowingly false statement.

4. In what situations does the obstruction of governmental administration occur?
   When a statute addressing the obstruction of justice encompasses more than interference with police officers and other such administrative officials, it is sometimes called *obstruction of governmental administration* or *obstructing governmental operations*.

5. What is witness tampering, and what are two examples of it?
   Witness tampering is a type of obstruction of justice that involves illegal and misleading conduct with the intent to influence witness testimony. This can include threats or other types of manipulation of witnesses.

Two examples are:

- Typical witness tampering cases involve approaching a potential witness with threats or other means in an attempt to prevent the witness from testifying.

- A defendant who attempts to frustrate the government's plan to infiltrate his or her operation can also face witness tampering charges.

6. What are the ways in which evidence can be suppressed?

Suppressing evidence can occur when a defendant, or a person working on behalf of the defendant, commits any of the following actions regarding evidence relevant to a grand jury investigation:

- Suppresses (hides) evidence

- Destroys evidence

- Refuses to produce evidence

7. What are the laws regarding resisting lawful arrests? What about unlawful arrests?

Nobody is allowed to resist lawful arrest. In addition, the MPC and most states provide for criminal charges against those who resist even unlawful arrests. Since law enforcement personnel is rarely authorized to use deadly physical force to arrest a suspect, self-defense would prohibit an individual from the use of deadly physical force to resist an arrest.

8. In what situations may the crime of escape occur? In what situations, which are discussed in your text, is it deemed to have not occurred or is excused by the courts?

The elements of the crime of escape are when a person, without lawful authority, commits one of the following acts:

- Removes or attempts to leave official detention

- Fails to return to official detention following a temporarily granted leave

Escape is excused in certain circumstances, such as when inmates who escape custody as the result of reasonable fear for their safety while incarcerated.

9. When and where can direct contempt take place?

Direct contempt occurs in the presence of the court and occurs when a person openly resists the power of the court. One example of direct contempt is the use of profane language toward an officer of the court.

10. Identify and analyze the difference between the offenses of criminal contempt and civil contempt.

Criminal contempt is an act in disrespect of the court. One type of criminal contempt is direct contempt, which is discussed in the previous question.

Civil contempt consists of the failure to do something that is ordered by the court for the benefit of another party to the proceeding.

Problem-Solving Exercises

1. POLICE PERJURY
   Answers could include the following:
   a. Yes, because he did not actually see the assault.

   b. Although circumstantial evidence clearly indicated that the boyfriend did indeed commit the assault, the officer has still committed perjury because he has not told the exact truth.

   c. Most students will agree that this was an unnecessary risk, although they may sympathize with the officer because it is hard to find witnesses in domestic violence cases.

2. COMPOUNDING A FELONY
   Answers could include the following:
   a. Darrell has committed the crime of compounding a felony. Although reimbursing the neighbor is not automatically illegal, it became illegal when Darrell hinted to him that the neighbor should not go to the police.

   b. He still has because he has indicated that he does not want the neighbor to go to the police since he has been paid off.

   c. No, because he may prefer to settle it in this informal manner.

   d. This is extortion and should be treated as a crime.

3. WITNESS TAMPERING

Answers could include the following:

a. Yes, it definitely is because the defendant has expressed an interest in harming the defendant and has made subtle threats regarding the defendant's family.

a. The fact that the defendant expressed an interest in harming the defendant and has made subtle threats regarding the defendant's family surviving "the whole mess."

Workplace Applications

1. RESISTING ARREST

Answers could include the following:

a. Not technically, but most officers would find this behavior very irritating.

b. If she does this after the officer begins to arrest her, yes. If she does this ahead of time, perhaps not, but perhaps she could be charged with some other crime for attaching herself physically to someone else's private property.

c. He should identify himself before arresting her to avoid problems.

2. PERJURY

Answers could include the following:

a. Since his statement is factually correct, he has not committed perjury. Although his statement is truthful, it does also conceal the truth regarding his payment to Steve.

b. In this case, yes, since the prosecutor is asking about a specific date.

c. Most students will agree that he should, but more will feel that the prosecutor should not have limited himself by including an incorrect date in his questioning. Most prosecutors tend to ask questions like, "At any time, did you give $1,000 to Steve?"

3. RESISTING ARREST VERSUS ESCAPE

Answers could include the following:

a. He should be charged with escape because he was arrested without incident, but tried to illegally escape while under your lawful custody.

b. No, because he was under legal custody and this does not change regardless of the suspect's exact location.

Internet Applications

1. MOST WANTED

Answers could include the following:

a. Their crime, photograph, and other information on their appearance is provided. It might be helpful to have more information on where they might be hiding and what their personal interests are.

b. People with information on their whereabouts can call a phone number that is provided.

c. Absolutely not, because these suspects are dangerous and could possibly be armed.

2. PERJURY

Answers could include the following:

a. Most students will feel that the cries of perjury by politicians during both the Clinton and Ashcroft scandals were politically motivated and selectively made, because both parties had an interest in bringing disgrace to their opponents.

b. Most students would agree that it should, because such an inconsistency is a violation of the Fourteenth Amendment's provision for equal protection under the law and should be corrected.

c. Nearly every student will agree that this is true, because it tends to make people take the government and justice system less seriously.

Ethics Issues

1. BRIBERY

   Answers can include the following:

   a. It is against the law to accept any kind of gift from any inmate because this constitutes a bribe.

   b. Since inmates cannot carry currency, this is a questionable idea at best. It can still constitute a bribe because even the act of selling someone sports tickets can be construed as a favor, especially if these tickets are considered valuable and hard to find.

   c. This is better, but again, remember that inmates cannot carry currency and he may still expect preferential treatment anyway.

2. WITNESS TAMPERING

   Answers can include the following:

   a. This is unethical because the subpoenaed witness is required to appear at the trial and provide testimony. The defense attorney is encouraging her to defy the subpoena, which is illegal, and also is undermining the prosecution's evidence in the process.

   b. Witness tampering. In addition, on a non-legal level, he could also face discipline or find himself disbarred from his state bar association.

Additional Activities

Advanced Web Research

1. INTERNET

WITNESS TAMPERING

Ask students to read "Teen Murder Suspect Charged with Attempted Witness-Tampering" at *http://www.cnn.com/2001/US/03/01/teacher.shot*. Once they are done, ask them the following questions:

- What are the alleged crimes of 14-year-old Nathaniel Brazill?

- Why do you think he wrote these letters?

- Does a defendant's contact with witnesses have to be hostile or threatening to constitute witness tampering? Why or why not?

Apart from the original murder charges, he has also been charged with attempted witness tampering. He wrote letters to witnesses telling them, "You know how to lie. My life is on the line," in an apparent effort to get them to lie for him while testifying in court.

No; it can be an appeal for help that attempts to manipulate the witness's emotions, as these letters appear to be. The issue is not whether or not the witness was intimidated, but whether or not the witness was influenced by the defendant to commit acts that constitute an obstruction of justice, such as perjury.

2. INTERNET

PERJURY

Have students read "Perjury: The Ashcroft Exemption" at About.com. The exact address is *http://uspolitics.about.com/newsissues/uspolitics/library/weekly/aa013001a.html*. When they are done reading all four pages, have students answer the following questions:

- In what instances had Ashcroft allegedly committed perjury? Why did this create a controversy when he was nominated Attorney General?

- Why are the numerous quotes regarding perjury, which were made by Republican U.S. Senators during President Clinton's impeachment trial, relevant to the Ashcroft case?

- Do you believe that this is a valid comparison? Why or why not?

Ashcroft contradicted himself repeatedly on issues such as desegregation, the nominations of Judge Ronnie White and Ambassador James Hormel, job discrimination against gays and lesbians, abortion, and a host of other issues. The key issue here is that "a significant question arises as to whether our next Attorney General might be a man who broke the law in his zeal to get the job."

These quotes are egregious examples of hypocrisy because they indicate that although these senators were concerned enough to criticize perjury by a Democrat, they were silent or engaged in rationalizing to justify the appointment of Ashcroft. Most students will believe that this is a valid comparison, even if they personally dislike either Clinton or Ashcroft, because both issues pertain to key leaders of the American federal government.

3. INTERNET

SUBORNATION OF PERJURY

Ask students to read the brief definition of subornation of perjury at the 'Lectric Law Library. The exact address is **http://www.lectlaw.com/def2/s191.html**. Next, assign them the following questions:

- What are the two ways in which subornation of perjury can be committed?

- Does this crime have to be completed in order to constitute a crime? Why or why not?

The two definitions are, "When someone persuades another to testify falsely before a tribunal and the other person does so knowing the testimony was false," and, "The procuring of another to commit legal perjury, who in consequence of the persuasion takes the oath to which he has been incited."

Yes, because attempts to solicit the crime will not complete it.

Extended Workplace Applications

1. Review

Give students the following situation: Misprision of a felony refers to the act of failing to report, or prosecute, a known felony and taking positive steps to conceal the felony. It differs from the offense of compounding a felony because the person failing to report or prosecute the felony is not necessarily the person who was injured by the felony. It also does not require the exchange of consideration. You are a state lawmaker who has been asked to review the statutes pertaining to these laws. Currently, compounding a felony is punished with the same severity as misprision of a felony, and both charges are considered Class D felonies, which are the lowest level of felonies. Would you change the class of these felonies, and would you provide for different levels of severity for each crime? Why or why not?

Many students will state that they wish to provide for a stricter sentence and higher grade of criminal charges for those guilty of misprision of a felony, since taking positive steps to conceal evidence is a serious crime and should be punished accordingly. Some may feel that the laws are adequate, especially in regard to keeping the charge of compounding as a Class D felony, but most will want to make some changes.

2. Prosecute

Give students the following situation: You are a prosecutor in the case of a man who is being tried for raping five different women over a three-year period. During the trial, his girlfriend testifies as a character witness that he has always treated her well and has never caused her to think that he was a criminal. However, his criminal record reveals that a neighbor once called the police when the defendant was beating his girlfriend. Although she refused to press charges, she was treated for a broken nose and he was fined for assault.

- Can you use this evidence to bring charges of perjury against his girlfriend? Why or why not?

- How is her alleged perjury material to the case?

Yes, you can bring charges, because his abusive behavior contradicts her unequivocal statement that he has "always treated her well." In addition, the fact that he was found guilty of a crime contradicts her statement that he has "never caused her to think that he was a criminal."

Her false statements are relevant to the case because they show a past record of violence toward women, and also because they indicate that the girlfriend is misrepresenting the defendant to the court in order to make him seem like a peaceful, law-abiding citizen.

3. Debate

Give students the following situation: You are a juror who is hearing a case in which a man is being tried for murder. His wife and three-year-old son are present everyday, although lately the son has had a case of the flu. His constant coughing and whining are disrupting the courtroom and making it hard for you and the other jurors to concentrate. The judge politely asks the defendant's wife to take the child home so that he can get some rest and recuperate. The wife stands up and shouts at the judge, "Since you're gonna put my husband away, it's my right to sit here and be with him! You can't make me leave—it's my right!" The judge orders that the woman is in direct contempt of court and has her removed from the courtroom and booked for the charge against her. Do you agree with this charge? Why or why not?

Most students will agree that the woman's behavior is unreasonable and contemptuous, especially since the judge was polite and expressed concern for her child. In addition, many students will question whether her loyalty to her husband is justified, since she seems unconcerned about caring for the child in her care. Some will state that she may be under great stress and that this may be causing her reaction. You can ask if anyone who has a relative that is on trial should be given special allowances, especially if such behavior is making it hard for the jury to concentrate on the case at hand.

4. Role Play

Give students the following scenario: You are a judge who is hearing a bench trial case of an escaped prisoner who is claiming that his escape was justified because he was subject to threats from other inmates. He states that three different inmates were threatening to rape him, and that his two formal complaints to prison staff were ignored. You ask for the record of these complaints, but prison officials tell you that none exist. The inmate swears that he is being framed because the prison staff does not want to get in trouble for failing to protect him. Regarding the threats, the only evidence is his words against that of the other inmates; however, all three of the other inmates have violent crime records, and two are convicted sex offenders. How will you decide, and why?

Although the issue regarding the missing inmate complaints is a tricky one, the judge may be able to decide the case based on the testimony and character of the inmate and the three other inmates who allegedly threatened to rape them. If the inmate who escaped seems genuine, the judge may wish to consider the crime records of the other inmates and acquit the escapee of the escape charges. After all, his guilt cannot be proven beyond a reasonable doubt.

Organized Crime, Gangs, and Terrorism

KEY TERMS

organized crime	protectors	money laundering	cholo/chola
boss	shakedown	Racketeer Influenced	terrorism
underboss	racketeering	and Corrupt	international terrorism
captains and	loan sharking	Organizations Act	
soldiers	bookmaking	(RICO)	
crews	dirty money	criminal street gang	

Lecture Outline

16.1 ORGANIZED CRIME
    Historical Development
    Elements and Participants of
        Organized Crime
    Typical Organized Crime Activities
    Laws that Target Organized Crime

16.2 STREET GANGS
    Structure of a Modern Street Gang
    Crimes Committed by Gangs
    Identifying Gang Organizations
    Laws that Target Gangs

16.3 TERRORISM
    Terrorism Distinguished from Other Crimes
    Laws that Target Terrorism

In-Chapter Questions

Criminal Law Online page 544

What obstacles did the FBI have to overcome in bringing him to trial? How did they succeed in having him convicted?

For a long time, the FBI had an extremely difficult time finding witnesses who held high-ranking positions in Gotti's crime family; these were the only types of witnesses who would be able to provide valuable testimony.

Finally, the FBI was able to convince Gotti's underboss, Sammy "The Bull" Gravano, to provide evidence against Gotti in exchange for prosecutor leniency toward his crimes.

Photo Caption page 544

What is wrong with this portrayal?

It is incorrect because organized criminals are actually very diverse and hard to categorize in a single way. Although most organized criminals in the United States are male, they can be of any national origin. As the text states, "There is a Russian Mafia, a Chinese Mafia, a Jewish Mafia, and countless other ethnically distinct criminal organizations."

 United States v. Gotti page 554

Do you think the government would have succeeded in convicting Gotti without Gravano's help? Why or why not?

It is unlikely because Gravano provided a large amount of extremely useful evidence that could not have been obtained elsewhere.

 United States v. Andrews page 557

What implications does this case have for gangs and the prosesution of gang-related crime?

It shows that gangs cannot escape RICO prosecution, even under appeal, simply because they do not fit the older stereotype of a typical organized crime family. The broad language of RICO was written precisely to ensure that such gangs are also prosecuted.

Criminal Law Online page 558

What information did you find on international efforts against organized crime, white-collar crime, and terrorism?

Students will likely be surprised at the extent to which organized crime, white-collar crime, and terrorism occur around the world. They will find that many of these crimes do operate on an international level for a variety of reasons, including profit and the desire to avoid getting caught.

16.1 Self Check page 560

1. Why did the criminalization of drugs and, for a time, alcohol benefit criminals? Can this be undone? Why or why not?

Because it creates the need for underground and illegal drug and alcohol distribution systems, which organized criminals provide in exchange for great profit. Although drug decriminalization may undo some of the damage, the fact remains that these druglords currently control the growth and distribution of these substances, and this may remain the case if drugs were made legal.

2. Why do organized criminals need to launder money, and how is this done?

Organized criminals launder the money they earn from illegal sources in order to justify their high incomes to the government. Money laundering is accomplished by processing illegally earned money through legitimate channels until its illegal origins are untraceable.

 Mexican Mafia Crackdown page 564

Would you categorize the Mexican Mafia as a gang or as organized crime? Explain your answer.

Many students will state that they are both: that their organization and structure is typical of a gang, but that their criminal activities are those of an organized crime association.

 Federal Prosecutor page 567

What qualities do you think a federal prosecutor should have?

Many students will cite traits such as aggressiveness, integrity, intelligence, meticulousness, and perceptiveness.

Ethics in Criminal Law page 568

1. Will it benefit you in any way to inform the media of this crime?

Many students believe that the media, although unpredictable, should be made aware of this crime because publicity will shed unwanted focus on the street gang and also show that the judge is not afraid of them.

2. What will you do to ensure that jury members or witnesses are not being harassed in a similar way?

It might be wise to meet with all of the jurors to discuss what to do if they face any kind of witness tampering. In addition, if the judge shows a steadfast character in the face of such crime, the jurors will be encouraged to do the same.

3. Assume that the defendant is found guilty of all charges. What sentence will you impose?

Most, if not all, students will say that they will "throw the book at him." As students read in Chapter 5, members of a criminal conspiracy can be held responsible for the crimes of others, regardless of whether they ordered or had any knowledge of the crimes. If it can be proven that members of this street gang shot through the judge's window, the ringleader who is on trial can face charges of criminal conspiracy to attempt to kill a federal judge and his family.

 City of Chicago v. Morales page 570

Do you think the benefits of anti-gang laws like this outweigh their constitutional vagueness?

Many students will agree that they do outweigh the negatives most of the time, but that it should not be difficult for lawmakers to create more specific statutes and thus preclude the possibility of net-widening.

16.2 Self Check page 571

1. Why, in your opinion, have gang activities changed so much over the years? Are drugs solely to blame?

Many students will agree that drugs are a large part of it, but many will also feel that poor family structures, increasing drug and alcohol awareness, and societal indifference to violence are also contributing factors.

2. Why do you think that girls and women are more involved in gang activities?

As society changes and girls and women gain more rights, their life options increase. Although this almost always has positive results, it can also result in some high-risk activity such as crime.

How has this event changed America's ideas and U.S. policy toward terrorism?

Americans are now more aware of the dangers of terrorism and U.S. policy has provided for the strict punishment of such offenders.

 United States v. McVeigh page 573

Do you agree with the court's decision to deny McVeigh an appeal? Why or why not?

Perhaps every student will agree, since the evidence against him was so overwhelming and the small amount that was uncovered at the end would not have changed a reasonable person's opinion regarding his guilt.

16.3 Self Check page 573

1. How have American perceptions regarding terrorism changed since the Oklahoma City bombing?

Since the Oklahoma City bombing, many Americans realized that terrorism is not a crime that is committed solely by other people in other countries. This crime made people realize that domestic terrorism can be committed by Americans with extreme, anti-government political agendas.

2. Which do you feel is a bigger threat to the United States: international or domestic terrorism?

Despite the terrorist attack in Oklahoma City and the presence of several extremist groups in the United States, some students still feel that international terrorism is more serious; they may point to the embassy bombings in Africa, and the terrorist attacks on tourists in Luxor, Egypt, as examples. Some feel that domestic terrorism is more important because it attacks people at home, where they should feel less at risk. You can ask the class if they consider the World Trade Center bombing by a foreign national to be domestic, international, or both.

Review and Applications

Questions For Review

1. How did the prohibition of drugs and alcohol help in the development of organized crime?

The effect of early narcotics legislation was disastrous because opium and morphine use and addiction continued as always, and criminals found an easy market in which to ply their trade. The prohibition of alcohol, however, had much worse results. When alcohol was outlawed in 1919, the demand for it continued as before, and those willing to break the law in order to provide the public with drugs and alcohol prospered. Rather than curbing the American desire for alcohol, the era of Prohibition allowed organized crime to create hugely profitable enterprises in bootlegging, which was the manufacture and sale of illegal alcohol.

The need to drink and use drugs in secret locations known as speakeasies also led to the growth of gambling and prostitution businesses in these locations. Although the era of Prohibition ended in 1933, organized crime did not. It merely found other criminal ventures to pursue, and continued to grow and prosper throughout the country.

2. What role have lotteries played in organized crime, and how has the role of lotteries changed over the years?

When lotteries started to be made illegal in the late nineteenth century, a syndicate of New York gamblers kept alive the Louisiana lottery by selling its lottery tickets by mail. This led to many legal battles over the role of the lottery, which culminated in *Champion v. Ames* (1903), which was also known at the *Lottery Case*. In *Champion*, the U.S. Supreme Court upheld Congress's power to ban lotteries under the commerce clause. This case attempted to disable the organized criminals that were keeping lotteries alive illegally.

During the eighteenth and nineteenth centuries, lotteries were quite popular. States used lotteries to raise revenue for public expenditures, including funding for events as important as the Revolutionary War. Over the next century,

though, lotteries were seen as a dangerous form of gambling, and by 1878 they were illegal in most places. Today, most states have lotteries again and they are extremely popular.

3. What is loan sharking?

Loan sharking, also known as *criminal usury*, is the practice of lending money at excessive interest rates, with the use of threats or extortion to force people to repay. These interest rates are much higher than if the person went though a bank or credit union. Unfortunately, the people who are usually the most in need of loan sharking services are people with poor or no credit, so the possibility of them getting a legitimate loan is unlikely and they generally feel compelled to work with a loanshark.

4. What is bookmaking, and how does a bookie make a profit?

Bookmaking is a form of illegal gambling in which customers use bookmakers, or bookies, to place bets on horse and dog races, professional sporting competitions, and other events.

A bookmaker makes a profit by charging or accepting a percentage, fee, or "vig" on the wager.

5. Describe money laundering and the two main ways in which this crime is committed.

Money laundering is the crime of transferring illegally obtained money through legitimate persons or accounts so that its original source can not be traced. Criminals launder money that they have received through illegal means (such as drug dealing or gambling) by placing it into legitimate sources so that the government cannot trace the criminal activity.

There are two main ways to commit this crime:

- An organization can take dirty money and give it to a legitimate business, so that it looks as if the money was actually received through the business.

- Another way to cleanse the money is for an organization to pay someone else to do it. For example, the Colombian-based Cali Cartel, one of the largest drug organizations in the world, launders their money this way.

Once a large-scale drug operation is complete, the Cartel holds an auction for professional money launderers who bid on the job.

6. What is RICO? How do CCE and state versions of RICO differ from RICO?

The landmark Racketeer Influenced and Corrupt Organizations (RICO) was enacted in 1970 by Congress as a federal law that criminalizes illegal activities committed by organized crime members. It was enacted to eradicate sophisticated organized crime syndicates, but in recent years has also been used to prosecute the crimes of street gangs.

The Continuing Criminal Enterprise statute (CCE) is similar to RICO, but applies only to organized criminal activity involving drugs. It provides that a criminal enterprise exists when a continuing series of federal drug-related felonies are committed in concert with other crimes 1) in which the defendant occupies a managerial role and 2) from which he or she obtains a substantial income.

Because RICO must involve some evidence of interstate commerce, many states have enacted their own legislation to combat intrastate organized crimes in their jurisdiction.

7. Summarize the various laws aimed at combating money laundering.

Several federal laws make it illegal to knowingly launder money, spend money that one knows is laundered, or assist in the money laundering process. For example:

- The Money Laundering Control Act of 1986 (MLCA) was enacted in response to money laundering problems that were facing significant growth.

- The Bank Fraud Act requires mandatory reporting provisions for financial institutions with regard to large sums of money.

- The Bank Secrecy Act also requires mandatory reporting provisions for financial institutions with regard to large sums of money.

8. How have the activities of gangs changed over the last century?

In the past, street gang behavior was fairly innocent and was usually lawful, despite occasional instances of rival gang fistfights and small-scale criminal activity.

Today, however, many modern street gangs are now involved in all kinds of criminal activity, including:

- Drug dealing and distribution
- Gambling operations
- Murder
- Bank robberies
- Financial crimes
- Extortion
- Bribery
- Racketeering
- Kidnapping
- Terrorism

9. What is the main difference between organized crime and terrorism?

Organized crime is committed for financial motives, and organized criminals focus primarily on making money through crime, power, and intimidation.

Terrorism is committed for political motives, such as when a terrorist has an agenda and chooses to resort to force to get his or her message heard.

10. What are some reasons why individuals resort to terrorism?

Individuals resort to terrorist behavior for all types of reasons, such as:

- Demanding territory for their ethnic or religious group
- Objecting to government authority
- Protesting that they are not getting the political rights they deserve

Problem-Solving Exercises

1. ORGANIZED CRIME
Answers could include the following:

a. You could press charges against Lonnie, but it may be more sensible to give Lonnie freedom and witness protection in exchange for his help in arresting the key figures of this crime family.

b. You need to know exactly where the crime family members, especially the leader, will be at the time the arrests are planned. You will also need to know how to implicate the crime leader in this sting.

c. It sounds like many of the high-ranking members can be arrested, but not the gang leader, Tracy Williams, because there is insufficient evidence to connect him with the crimes that were discussed during Lonnie's wiretapped conversations.

2. TERRORISM
Answers could include the following:

a. Terrorism and attempted murder are the two key charges. Students may also suggest aggravated assault and treason.

b. The defendant(s) could be charged with terrorism and first-degree murder.

c. This could mean several things. One possibility is that this organization has attracted some foreign followers. Another possibility is that the organization has hired foreign followers to help implement their terrorist acts. Yet another possibility is that another, foreign organization is trying to pin the blame on the Montana group. Students will likely have several other interesting theories.

3. EXTREMISM
Answers could include the following:

a. Since the group's threats could be construed as "fighting words," they may not be protected under the First Amendment and they could be liable for that. In addition, they could be found liable as accomplices to the actions of others if it can be proven that they provided "words of encouragement" that set the crime in motion.

b. This crime had a political motive because the criminal said he did it to help further the goals of the group.

Workplace Applications

1. KIDS AND GANGS
Answers could include the following:

a. An officer can and should get involved, especially when it is clear that the child's parent is concerned and will back his actions.

b. There are several options for helping to protect Jacob. For example, the officer could give Jacob some extra attention and guidance, and could place Jacob in a mentoring or after-school program that will keep him out of gangs.

c. She can talk more frequently with Jacob about the importance of staying in school and not joining a gang, plus keep in touch with the officer and reinforce the officer's words to Jacob.

2. ORGANIZED CRIME AND EXTORTION
Answers could include the following:

a. He could wear a wiretap during conversations with the extortionists, but in general law enforcement should strenuously avoid using innocent civilians in surveillance activities where they could be hurt.

b. Since corruption generally trickles upward, it may be wise to go directly to your chief of police to voice your concerns. If you find yourself receiving threats or losing your job after this, you can voice your concerns to the press and initiate a civil suit for unfair treatment.

c. You can address your concerns to the chief of police or, if that fails, to federal crime investigators and to the news media.

3. RICO AND GANGS
Answers could include the following:

a. No, because RICO was written to be flexible toward any type of organized criminal activity, whether it is committed by traditional crime families or by street gangs.

b. Yes, because their crime activities are sometimes very large-scale and they can pose an enormous threat to society.

Internet Applications

1. VICTIMS OF TERRORISM
   Answers could include the following:
   a. Student answers will vary: Some will have expected the figures to be higher, some lower.

   b. Many students think it will increase due to growing domestic discontent and the rise of extremist groups over the last decade.

   c. You may want more information about active local extremists that present a possible threat to your jurisdiction.

2. ANTI-GANG LEGISLATION
   Answers could include the following:
   a. This legislation covers several types of violent and/or gang-related crimes.

   b. Defendants who have violated this law can receive much longer sentences than they would receive for non-gang-related crimes.

   c. Most students would agree that this legislation is fairly comprehensive, but some may have additional suggestions. You may ask the class if they have any suggestions large enough to warrant a rewrite of the law.

   d. Most students will feel that it covers everything that needs to be covered, but, again, some may have additional suggestions.

Ethics Issues

1. TERRORISM AND THE MEDIA
   Answers could include the following:
   a. Some students will recognize this as an adaptation of the relationship between the *New York Times* and the Unabomber, Theodore Kaczynski. In this case, the *Times* agreed to publish the Unabomber's manifesto. This drew some criticism from people who stated that the *Times* was negotiating with terrorists, but it also led to Kaczynski's arrest when his brother read and recognized Ted's writing. Therefore, although it may seem like an unethical move, it could solve the case. However, each case is different, and this may not be a wise move. Students will probably have very different opinions of this.

   b. No, because although the terrorist's crimes are illegal, he still has the right to freedom of legal expression.

Additional Activities

NOTE TO INSTRUCTOR: These additional activities are exclusive to this IRM. They are designed to meet the special needs of your students. If you or your students cannot access a Web site referred to here, go to *cl.glencoe.com* for the latest updated links.

Advanced Web Research

1. INTERNET

UNION CORRUPTION

Have students check out "Union Corruption: Why It Happens, How to Combat It" at *http://www.nilrr.org/corruption.html*. Ask them to read "Chapter Three: The Peculiar Case of the Teamsters," and answer the following questions:

- Why is the Teamsters Union considered "the mother of American labor union corruption"?

- How has the Teamsters Union been linked to organized crime over the years, and for what motives?

- What actions have been taken over the years to stop Teamsters corruption, and what have been the results? Does this appear to be changing? Explain.

The Teamsters Union is considered corrupt ecause of its ongoing illegal partnerships with organized crime and their "long tradition of corruption on a grand scale [and] of making life unpleasant – and often short-lived – for whistle-blowers."

Students will be able to name several examples from this article. For example, they have allegedly been involved in extortion and in Mob-related terrorism against supermarkets that refused to bow under their pressure. They have allegedly terrorized and murdered supermarket employees and employers.

2. INTERNET

RACKETEERING

Have students read "LAPD Can Be Sued for Racketeering" at APBNews.com. The exact address is *http://apbnews.com/newscenter/breakingnews/2000/08/29/lapd0829_01.html*. Next, ask students the following questions:

- What incident(s) prompted the charges of racketeering?

- What are the pros and cons given for charging the LAPD with racketeering? What is your opinion? Why?

Corrupt officers allegedly violated the civil rights of private citizens in such a way that the LAPD can be sued under federal racketeering laws.

The pros are that they are held to a reasonable level of responsibility for their actions and will understand that they are not above the law; in addition, private citizens can seek satisfactory redress against their abuses. The cons are that people with no legitimate cause may start to sue police departments under the RICO statute, thus wasting the government's resources.

3. INTERNET

GANG CRIME

Ask students to visit the Gang Crime Prevention Center at *http://www.gcpc.state.il.us*. Have them read "What's New" and "About the GCPC," and answer the following questions:

- What are the goals of the GCPC, and how do they accomplish them?

- What other social problems are linked to, and contribute to, gang membership? Why?

Essentially, their goals are: involving private citizens in fighting street gangs and fighting the social conditions that contribute to street gangs; promoting prevention, intervention and suppression; and raising public awareness. They accomplish these goals by offering programs, experience-based knowledge, research, and technical support. Their programs "work to develop, implement, and evaluate specific organization- and neighborhood-based programs."

As the programs in the "What's New" section indicate, several other social problems are linked to gang membership. Among these are truancy, drug-related crimes, and drug and alcohol abuse. (If students have a hard time finding answers to this question, refer them to the "What's New" page for ideas.)

Extended Workplace Applications

1. Role Play

Give students the following scenario: You are a juror who is hearing the trial of a gang member who has allegedly committed drug crimes, violent crimes, and extortion for over four years. He is being tried for violating the RICO law. His attorney is, understandably, very critical of RICO and argues that this law, although intended to target high-ranking organized crime figures, could apply to almost anyone as long as the elements have been established. He also argues that this law has "federalized" virtually all criminal activities, even those normally within the jurisdiction of states' criminal statutes. The prosecutor then explains that RICO is to be used for certain types of criminal enterprises, and the gang to which the defendant belonged fit the qualifications. The defendant is clearly guilty of the crimes for which he is charged.

Next, ask students the following questions:

- Do you feel that he should be charged with violating the RICO law? Why or why not?

Most students will disagree with the defense counsel and doubt the sincerity of his claims, and most will agree that he should be tried under RICO because of his ongoing gang involvement,

and because of the variety of serious crimes that he committed to help further the gang's large-scale criminal activities.

2. Analyze

Have students analyze the following situation: Recently, an unknown intruder accessed some of Microsoft's closely guarded secrets over a three-month period. Company officials believe that the hacker may have been able to study Whistler, the company's new generation of Windows products. In addition, the hacker may have been able to view an enormous number of e-mail messages and internal company documents. Four months previously, Microsoft competitor Oracle admitted that it paid a private detective to sift through Microsoft garbage bins looking for evidence to assist its civil suit against Microsoft. Ask students what they think happened.

Many students will believe that competitors, some of which are tired of Microsoft's apparent monopoly over their industry, hacked into Microsoft's system. Experts believe that the hacker could have been a curious person or a major business. For their part, Microsoft believes that this was a case of corporate espionage–in which businesspeople use illegal means to learn about the operations of another business.

3. Debate

Have students debate the following issue in class: Executives from Citibank, J.P. Morgan, and Chase & Company were subpoenaed to testify for a Senate Committee that is investigating allegations that some banks knowingly have laundered drug money. A report by Democratic staff of the Senate Subcommittee on Investigations found that huge amounts of dirty money have flowed through so-called correspondent accounts held by high risk offshore and "shell" banks, including the three listed above, which are the nation's largest.

Citibank received special focus because investigators found that the bank opened more than 100 accounts for a Russian businessman, through which $725 million in questionable funds were moved from 1991 to 2000. The bank was also implicated during the impeachment trial of former Philippines President Joseph Estrada, who is accused of maintaining illegal money in Citibank accounts. Finally, Citibank has also been probed for its involvement with an Argentine bank. Should Citibank be tried under any of the money laundering acts described in this chapter? Why or why not?

Many students will feel that all three acts–The Bank Secrecy Act, the Bank Fraud Act, and the Money Laundering Control Act–could be used in this case. Some will feel that this is excessive. You may wish to ask the class who they would charge and who would be liable.

4. Discuss

Have students discuss the following issue in class: In recent years, terrorists bombed two American embassies in Africa. The defendants in both cases have been indicted and extradited, and have been sentenced to American prisons as a result of their trials in American criminal courts.

- How can defendants who commit crimes in other countries be charged in the United States?

Under American law, the United States may assert extraterritorial jurisdiction in certain cases, including terrorist attacks that result in the deaths of American citizens. You may want to explain to students that this is not always as easy as it sounds: The country in which the defendants are being held must first surrender them to American authorities, and American authorities sometimes face resistance in certain cases.

PowerPoint® Appendix

ExamView® Pro Testbank Generator Appendix

Appendix 1

CD-ROM Contents

Powerpoint® User's Guide

USING POWERPOINT PRESENTATIONS

INTRODUCTION | The enclosed CD-ROM contains 16 PowerPoint Presentations, one presentation for every chapter of *Criminal Law for the Criminal Justice Professional*. Each presentation lists the objectives for the chapter and includes important headings and figures that students will encounter while learning criminal law. In a sense, these presentations replace the transparency masters that were often provided to teachers in the past.

USING PRESENTATIONS IN THE CLASSROOM

Many teachers have not yet used PowerPoint Presentations in the classroom. The following suggestions may help you if this is your first time using them.

- PowerPoint Presentations are intended to supplement your presentation of the material in the textbook. They are not a substitute for the text or for your standup classroom teaching.

- If your school has a wireless mouse for your computer (or another means of advancing slides in PowerPoint Presentations), you can circulate around the classroom as you teach. This will allow you to focus on an individual student's work and deal with problems before a student falls too far behind.

- Even if your class does not have a wireless mouse, you will only need to return to your computer to advance the presentation one slide at a time with one keystroke. You will not be tied to the computer as you go through a procedure in front of the class.

- Using PowerPoint Presentations, you will never lose track of transparencies in front of the class and spend valuable minutes getting them back in order.

Ultimately, these PowerPoint Presentations can make your job easier, accelerate learning, and allow for more individualized teaching.

RUNNING POWERPOINT PRESENTATIONS

SETTING UP YOUR EQUIPMENT | Before you begin using PowerPoint Presentations, check your equipment connections. To use PowerPoint Presentations, you will need a computer (see System Requirements) and a projector or large screen monitor capable of displaying high-color images.

LOADING THE EQUIPMENT | The PowerPoint Presentations files have not been compressed; therefore, they can be run directly from the CD-ROM. In most cases, the PowerPoint Presentations will run faster if loaded on your hard drive. If you load the presentations on your hard drive, you may which to organize them in a separate folder.

RUNNING A PRESENTATION WITH POWERPOINT

The best way to run a PowerPoint Presentation is with PowerPoint software. The following instructions assume that PowerPoint is located on your hard disk, and that the extension ".ppt" is recognized by your computer as a PowerPoint Presentation.

1. In the Explorer, open the folder containing the PowerPoint Presentations.

2. Double-click the PowerPoint Presentation you wish to view.

3. Run the presentation as a slide show. You could either click the *Slide Show* button or choose the *Slide Show* from the *View* menu.

4. The following table lists the ways to move to the Next and Previous slides.

Running a Presentation	
NEXT SLIDE	**PREVIOUS SLIDE**
→ right arrow button	← left arrow button
↓ down arrow button	↑ up arrow button
N button	P button
ENTER button	BACKSPACE button
SPACE bar	
Click left mouse	

RUNNING A PRESENTATION WITH POWERPOINT VIEWER

If you do not have PowerPoint 97, you can go to Microsoft's home page (*www.microsoft.com*) to download a free PowerPoint viewer. Once this viewer has been installed, follow these directions.

1. Make sure your monitor is set to high-color mode. If your screen is not set properly, right click on the *Desktop*, choose *Properties*, and change the monitor settings.

2. Click the Start menu button and choose the *Programs* option.

3. Select *Microsoft PowerPoint Viewer* to start the Viewer program.

4. Click the *Look in*: pop-up menu and select your CD-ROM drive.

5. Choose the PowerPoint Presentation you wish to view.

6. When you start a presentation you will see an opening slide. Click the *Forward* button to proceed to the next slide.

7. From the *Contents* (or Main menu) slide you can access almost all of the PowerPoint Presentations resources. While viewing a presentation, click the navigation button to view the slide. Click the *Help* button for step-by-step instructions.

8. To end the presentation, click the *Exit* button or press the *Esc* (escape) key.

CUSTOMIZING A PRESENTATION

The PowerPoint Presentations were created using Microsoft PowerPoint 97 (Windows). Although you do not need PowerPoint to view the slides, you can customize any of the presentations if you have PowerPoint 97 (or a later version). Follow the steps provided in the *Help* system.

TROUBLESHOOTING TIPS

If you experience problems using PowerPoint Presentations, refer to the troubleshooting tips in the *Help* system. A comprehensive list of potential problems is provided along with suggested solutions. To access this information, start a presentation and click on the *Help* button. Select *Microsoft PowerPoint Help* and type in your question.

SYSTEM REQUIREMENTS

Verify that your computer meets the hardware and software requirements listed below:

Hardware:
- IBM PC or 100% compatible computer
- 386 or higher microprocessor
- 4× CD-ROM
- 8 MB of hard disk for "Typical" installation; "Custom" or "Complete" installation can require up to 35 MB
- VGA or higher-resolution video monitor (SVGA 256-color recommended)
- Mouse
- Printer (optional, but recommended)

Software:
- PowerPoint 7 for Windows 95, PowerPoint 97 or higher, or PowerPoint Viewer
- Windows 95 or later

EXAMVIEW PRO® TESTBANK GENERATOR USER'S GUIDE

TO THE TEACHER

The Examview Pro 3.5 Testbank Generator for Glencoe's *Criminal Law for the Criminal Justice Professional* allows you to generate readymade and customized objective tests using multiple choice, true or false, and essay questions. Grouped by cognitive type within each chapter, the questions cover all 16 chapters and 6 units in the *Criminal Law for the Criminal Justice Professional* text.

LEARNING OBJCTIVES

Learning objectives are suggested outcomes of what your students may be capable of achieving during or after your teaching. The objectives for each chapter are the same ones found in the Student Edition.

COMPONENTS

Components of the ExamView Pro 3.5 Testbank Generator for *Criminal Law for the Criminal Justice Professional* include:

- ExamView Pro 3.5 Testbank Generator *User's Guide* (Windows/Macintosh)
- ExamView Pro 3.5 Testbank Generator CD-ROM Software (Windows/Macintosh)

The following User's Guide contains instructions for the setup and use of the testbank generator. Be sure to use the correct guide for your system (Windows or Macintosh). The CD-ROM Software contains the testbank generator program that lets you retrieve the questions you want and print tests. It also lets you edit and add questions as needed.

STATE LICENSE

Your adoption of Glencoe's *Criminal Law for the Criminal Justice Professional* entitles you to site-license duplication rights for all components of the ExamView Pro 3.5 Testbank Generator with the restriction that all copies must be used within the adopting schools. This license shall run for the life of the adoption of the accompanying text.

USING THE TESTBANK

Before you begin, follow the directions in the *User's Guide* to make backup copies of the software. Then, set up your computer and printer and configure the software, following the instructions. The **User's Guide** contains all the instructions on how to use the software. Refer to this manual as needed to preview and select questions for your tests.

SOFTWARE SUPPORT HOTLINE

Should you encounter any difficulty when setting up or running the programs, contact the Software Support Center at Glencoe Publishing between 8:30 a.m. and 6:00 p.m. Eastern Time. The toll-free number is 1-800-437-3715. Customers with specific questions can contact us via the Internet at the following E-mail address: **epgtech@mcgraw-hill.com**.

INTRODUCTION

This user's guide accompanies a test generator program called *ExamView® Pro 3.5*–an application that enables you to quickly create printed tests, Internet tests, and computer (LAN-based) tests. You can enter your own questions and customize the appearance of the tests you create. The *ExamView Pro* test generator program offers many unique features. Using the QuickTest wizard, for example, you are guided step-by-step through the process of building a test. Numerous options are included that allow you to customize the content and appearance of the tests you create.

As you work with the *ExamView* test generator, you may use the following features:

- **an interview mode or "wizard" to guide you through the steps to create a test in less than five minutes**

- **five methods to select test questions**
    - random selection
    - from a list
    - while viewing questions
    - by criteria (difficulty code, objective, topic, etc.–if available)
    - all questions

- **the capability to edit questions or to add an unlimited number of questions**

- **online (*Internet-based*) testing**
    - create a test that students can take on the Internet using a browser
    - receive instant feedback via email
    - create online study guides with student feedback for incorrect responses
    - include any of the twelve (12) question types

- **Internet test-hosting ***
    - instantly publish a test to the *ExamView* Web site
    - manage tests online
    - allow students to access tests from one convenient location
    - receive detailed reports
    - download results to your gradebook or spreadsheet

- **online (*LAN-based*) testing**
    - allow anyone or selected students to take a test on your local area network
    - schedule tests
    - create online study guides with student feedback for incorrect responses
    - incorporate multimedia links (movies and audio)
    - export student results to a gradebook or spreadsheet

- **a sophisticated word processor**
    - streamlined question entry with spell checker
    - tabs, fonts, symbols, foreign characters, and text styles
    - tables with borders and shading
    - full-featured equation editor
    - pictures or other graphics within a question, answer, or narrative

- **numerous test layout and printing options**
    - scramble the choices in multiple choice questions
    - print multiple versions of the same test with corresponding answer keys
    - print an answer key strip for easier test grading

- **link groups of questions to common narratives**

* The Internet test-hosting service must be purchased separately. Visit **www.examview.com** to learn more.

INSTALLATION AND STARTUP INSTRUCTIONS

The *ExamView Pro 3.5* test generator software is provided on a CD-ROM or floppy disks. The disc includes the program and all of the questions for the corresponding textbook. The *ExamView Player,* which can be used by your students to take online (computerized or LAN-based) tests, is also included.

Before you can use the test generator, you must install it on your hard drive. The system requirements, installation instructions, and startup procedures are provided below.

SYSTEM REQUIREMENTS

To use the *ExamView Pro 3.5* test generator or the online test player, your computer must meet or exceed the following minimum hardware requirements:

Windows

- Pentium computer
- Windows 95, Windows 98, Windows 2000 (or a more recent version)
- color monitor (VGA-compatible)
- CD-ROM and/or high-density floppy disk drive
- hard drive with at least 7 MB space available
- 8 MB available memory *(16 MB memory recommended)*
- an Internet connection to access the Internet test-hosting features

Macintosh

- PowerPC processor, 100 MHz computer
- System 7.5 (or a more recent version)
- color monitor (VGA-compatible)
- CD-ROM and/or high-density floppy disk drive
- hard drive with at least 7 MB space available
- 8 MB available memory *(16 MB memory recommended)*
- an Internet connection with System 8.6 (or more recent version) to access the Internet test-hosting features

INSTALLATION INSTRUCTIONS

Follow these steps to install the *ExamView* test generator software. The setup program will automatically install everything you need to use *ExamView*. **Note:** A separate test player setup program is also included for your convenience. [See *Online (LAN-based) Testing* on page 149 for more information.]

Windows

Step 1	Turn on your computer.
Step 2	Insert the *ExamView* disc into the CD-ROM drive. If the program is provided on floppy disks, insert Disk 1 into Drive A.
Step 3	Click the Start button on the *Taskbar* and choose the *Run* option.
Step 4	If the *ExamView* software is provided on a CD-ROM, use the drive letter that corresponds to the CD-ROM drive on your computer (e.g., **d:\setup.exe**). The setup program, however, may be located in a subfolder on the CD-ROM if the *ExamView* software is included on the disc with other resources. In which case, click the Browse button in the Run dialog box to locate the setup program (e.g., **d:\evpro\setup.exe**).
	If you are installing the software from floppy disks, type **a:\setup** and press **Enter** to run the installation program.
Step 5	Follow the prompts on the screen to complete the installation process.
	If the software and question banks are provided on more than one floppy disk, you will be prompted to insert the appropriate disk when it is needed.
Step 6	Remove the installation disc when you finish.

Macintosh

Step 1	Turn on your computer.
Step 2	Insert the *ExamView* installation disc into your CD-ROM drive. If the program is provided on floppy disks, insert Disk 1 into a disk drive.
Step 3	Open the installer window, if necessary.
Step 4	Double-click the installation icon to start the program.
Step 5	Follow the prompts on the screen to complete the installation process.
	If the software and question banks are provided on more than one floppy disk, you will be prompted to insert the appropriate disk when it is needed.
Step 6	Remove the installation disc when you finish.

GETTING STARTED

After you complete the installation process, follow these instructions to start the *ExamView* test generator software. This section also explains the options used to create a test and edit a question bank.

Startup Instructions

Step 1   Turn on the computer.

Step 2   WINDOWS: Click the **Start** button on the *Taskbar*. Highlight the **Programs** menu and locate the *ExamView Test Generator* folder. Select the *ExamView Pro* option to start the software.

MACINTOSH: Locate and open the *ExamView* folder. Double-click the *ExamView* Pro program icon.

Step 3   The first time you run the software you will be prompted to enter your name, school/institution name, and city/state. You are now ready to begin using the *ExamView* software.

Step 4   Each time you start *ExamView*, the **Startup** menu appears. Choose one of the options shown in Figure 1.
Note: All of the figures shown in this user's guide are taken from the Windows software. Except for a few minor differences, the Macintosh screens are identical.

Step 5   Use *ExamView* to create a test or edit questions in a question bank.

ExamView includes three components: Test Builder, Question Bank Editor, and Test Player. The **Test Builder** includes options to create, edit, print, and save tests. The **Question Bank Editor** lets you create or edit question banks. The **Test Player** is a separate program that your students can use to take online (LAN-based) tests/study guides.

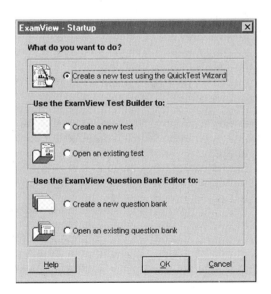

Using The Help System

Whenever you need assistance using *ExamView*, access the extensive help system. Click the **Help** button or choose the **Help Topics** option from the *Help* menu to access step-by-step instructions from more than 150 help topics. If you experience any difficulties while you are working with the software, you may want to review the troubleshooting tips in the user-friendly help system.

Test Builder

The Test Builder allows you to create tests using the QuickTest Wizard or you can create a new test on your own. (See the sample test in Figure 2.) Use the Test Builder to prepare both printed and on-line tests/study guides.

- *If you want ExamView to select questions randomly from one or more question banks,* choose the *QuickTest Wizard* option to create a new test. (Refer to Figure 1 on page 200.) Then, follow the step-by-step instructions to (1) enter a test title, (2) choose one or more question banks from which to select questions, and (3) identify how many questions you want on the test. The QuickTest Wizard will automatically create a new test and use the Test Builder to display the test on screen. You can print the test as is, remove questions, add new questions, or edit any question.

- *If you want to create a new test on your own,* choose the option to create a new test. (Refer to Figure 1 on page 200.) Then identify a question bank from which to choose questions by using the *Question Bank* option in the **Select** menu. You may then add questions to the test by using one or more of the following selection options: *Randomly, From a List, While Viewing, By Criteria,* or *All Questions.*

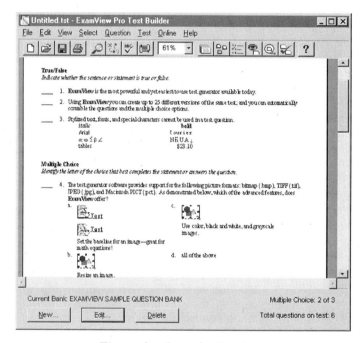

Figure 2 – Sample Test

IMPORTANT: The Test Builder and the Question Bank Editor systems are integrated in one program. As you work with *ExamView,* you can easily switch between the Test Builder and Question Bank Editor components using the *Switch to...* option in the **File** menu.

To create a new test:

Step 1   Start the *ExamView* software.

Step 2   At the Startup window, choose the *Create a new test* option.

Step 3   Enter a title for the new test.

                          After you enter the title, the program will automatically display the option for you to select a question bank.

Step 4   Choose a question bank.

Step 5   Select the questions you want to include on the test.

                          Use the question selection options that appear in the **Select** menu. Or, click the corresponding buttons on the toolbar. A description for each of the question selection toolbar buttons appears below.

Click the **Question Bank** toolbar button to select a question bank.

You can create a test using questions from one question bank or from multiple banks. Choose a bank, select the questions you want, and then choose another bank to select more questions.

Click the **Select Randomly** toolbar button when you want the program to randomly select questions for you.

Use the **Select from a List** command to choose questions if you know which ones you want to select. Identify the questions you want by reviewing a question bank printout.

Click the **Select while Viewing** button to display a window that shows all of the questions in the current question bank. Click the check boxes to select the questions you want.

You can use the **Select by Criteria** option to choose questions based on question type, difficulty, and objective (if available).

Click the **Select All** button to choose all of the questions in the current question bank.

Step 6   Save the test.

Step 7   Print the test.

You can use the options in the **Test** menu to customize the appearance of a test, edit test instructions, and choose to leave space for students to write their answers. When you print a test, you may choose how many variations of the test you want, whether you want all the versions to be the same, and whether you want to scramble the questions and the multiple choice options. If you choose to scramble the questions, *ExamView* will print a custom answer sheet for each variation of the test.

If you want your students to take a test online, first create the test. Then, publish the test as an Internet test/study guide (page 211) or use the Online Test Wizard (page 206) to create a test for delivery over a LAN (local area network). The software will walk you through the steps to turn any test into an online (Internet or LAN-based) test.

IMPORTANT: You may edit questions or create new questions as you build your test. However, those questions can be used only as part of the current test. If you plan to create several new questions that you would like to use on other tests, switch to the Question Bank Editor to add the new questions.

Question Bank Editor

The Question Bank Editor allows you to edit questions in an existing publisher-supplied question bank or to create your own new question banks. Always use the Question Bank Editor if you want to change a question permanently in an existing question bank. If you want to make a change that applies only to a particular test, create a new question or edit that question in the Test Builder.

A question bank may include up to 250 questions in a variety of formats including multiple choice, true/false, modified true/false, completion, yes/no, matching, problem, essay, short answer, case, and numeric response. You can include the following information for each question: difficulty code, reference, text objective, state objectives, topic, and notes.

Step 1	Start the *ExamView* software.
Step 2	At the Startup window as illustrated in Figure 1 on page 200, choose to *Create a new question bank* or *Open an existing question bank*.
	If you are working in the Test Builder, click the **File** menu and choose *Switch to Question Bank Editor* to edit or create a new question bank.
Step 3	Click the **New** button to create a new question or click the **Edit** button to modify an existing question. Both of these buttons appear at the bottom of the Question Bank Editor window. (See Figure 3.)
	You may add new questions or edit questions in a question bank by using the built-in word processor. The word processor includes many features commonly found in commercially available word processing applications. These features include the following: fonts, styles, tables, paragraph formatting, ruler controls, tabs, indents, and justification.
Step 4	Save your work. Then, exit the program or switch back to the Test Builder.

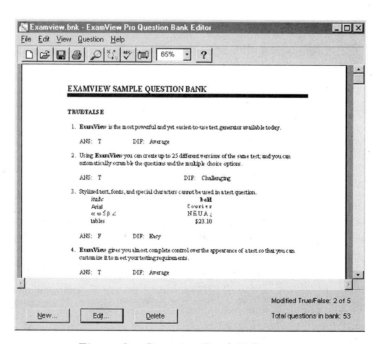

Figure 3 – Question Bank Editor

Online Testing (LAN-based vs. Internet)

The *ExamView* software allows you to create paper tests and online tests. The program provides two distinct online testing options: **LAN-based** testing and **Internet** testing. The option you choose depends on your particular testing needs. You can choose either option to administer online tests and study guides.

The **LAN-based** testing option is designed to work on a local area network server. That is, you can copy the test/study guide along with the Test Player software onto your local area network. Then students can take the test at computers connected to your server.

To take a LAN-based test you must provide access for your students to the Test Player program included with the *ExamView* software. The Test Player is a separate program that lets your students take a test/study guide at a computer. You can store the Test Player program and the test on a local area network for easy access by your students.

The **Internet** testing option provides a computerized testing solution for delivering tests via the Internet or an Intranet. This option is great for distance learning environments or simply to make a sample test/study guide available to students at home. Students do not need any other program (unlike the LAN-based option). When your students take a test, the results are automatically sent to you via email.

You can publish an Internet test to your own Web site, or you can use the *ExamView* Internet test-hosting service. If you subscribe to the *ExamView* test-hosting service, you can publish a test directly to the Internet with just a few simple steps. Students will have immediate access to the tests that you publish and you can get detailed reports. For more information on the Internet test-hosting service, visit our Web site at *www.examview.com.*

Section 3

ONLINE (LAN-BASED) TESTING

Online testing features are seamlessly integrated into the *ExamView* software. If you want to take advantage of these capabilities, simply create a test and then use the Online Test Wizard to setup the testing parameters. Students can then take the test at the computer using the Test Player program. IMPORTANT: If you want to prepare a test/study guide for delivery via the Internet, use the *Publish Internet Test* option as described on page 156.

ExamView includes many features that let you customize an online (LAN-based) test. You can create a test for a specific class, or you can prepare a study guide for anyone to take. Using the Online Test Wizard, you can schedule a test or allow it to be taken anytime. As your students work on a test, *ExamView* will scramble the question order, provide feedback for incorrect responses, and display a timer if you selected any of these options.

ONLINE (LAN-BASED) TESTING OVERVIEW

Refer to the steps below for an overview of the online (LAN-based) testing process. Specific instructions for creating a test, taking a test, and viewing results are provided on the following pages.

Step 1 — Talk with your network administrator to help you setup a location (folder) on your local area network where you can install the Test Player software and copy your tests/study guides.

Make sure that the administrator gives you and your students full access to the designated folders on the server. You may also want your network administrator to install the Test Player software.

Step 2 — Create a test/study guide, and then use the Online Test Wizard to setup the online (LAN-based) test. Save your work and exit the *ExamView* software.

Step 3 — Transfer the test/study guide file [e.g., chapter1.tst (Windows) or Chapter 1 (Macintosh)] and any accompanying multimedia files from your computer to the local area network server.

Copy the files from your hard drive to the folder setup by your network administrator. You need only copy the test file unless you linked an audio or video segment to one or more questions.

Step 4 — Instruct your students to complete the test/study guide.

Students must have access to a computer connected to the local area network on which the Test Player and test/study guide are stored.

Step 5 — After all students finish taking the test, copy the test/study guide file back to your hard drive. It is recommended that you copy the test to a different location from the original test file. The test file, itself, contains all of the students' results.

Note: If you set up a class roster, the test file will contain item analysis information and the results for each student. If you did not setup a roster, no results are recorded so you do not have to complete this step or the next.

Step 6 — Start the *ExamView* software and open the test file to view your students' results.

CREATING AN ONLINE (LAN-BASED) TEST

Follow the steps shown below to create an online (LAN-based) test or study guide. Depending on the options you set, you can create a test or study guide. Before you begin, make sure that you installed the ExamView test generator and test player software. Note: See the next section (page 208) for instructions to setup the test player. (See page 211 for Internet testing features.)

Step 1   Start the *ExamView* software.

Step 2   Create or open a test/study guide.

Select the questions you want to include on the test. You can include any of the following types: True/False, Multiple Choice, Yes/No, Numeric Response, Completion, and Matching.

Step 3   Select the *Online Test Wizard* option from the Online menu.

ExamView presents step-by-step instructions to help you prepare the online test/study guide. (See Figure 4.) Read the instructions provided and complete each step. **Note:** Click the **Help** button if you need more assistance.

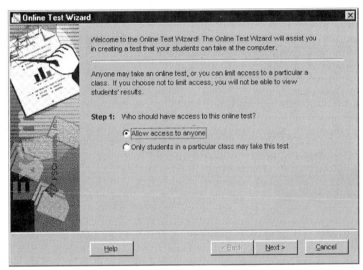

Figure 4 – Online Test Wizard (Step 1)

Step 4   Click the **Finish** button after you complete the last step using the Online Test Wizard. As you can see in Figure 5 on page 207, *ExamView* shows a summary that describes the settings for the online test.

Step 5   Save the test/study guide to a location where your students can easily access it. For example, save it in the same location where you installed the Test Player program.

It is recommended that you save the test/study guide to a location on a network server where students have read/write access. The Test Player will store all of your students' results (if you entered a class roster) in the test file itself. You can copy the test to individual computers, but this configuration takes more time to gather the results.

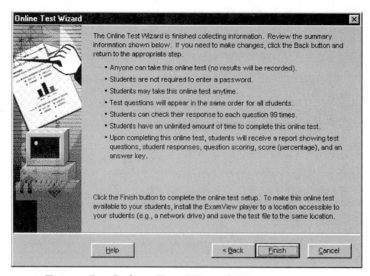

Figure 5 – Online Test Wizard (Summary)

Step 6 If you included multimedia links in any of the questions, copy those files to the same location where you saved the test/study guide.

If the multimedia files are on a CD-ROM or DVD disc, you may leave them on the disc, but provide this information to your students. To play one of these links, they will have to specify the location of the multimedia file.

NOTES:

- Use the *Test Preferences* and *Class Roster* options in the **Online** menu if you want to make any changes to the test parameters. These two options let you change any of the settings you selected using the Online Test Wizard.

- You must close the test before your students can access it with the Test Player.

- If you setup a class roster for a test/study guide, you cannot modify the test (e.g., edit a question, change the order, etc.) once any student has taken it unless you clear the results first.

- Provide your students with the Test Player setup program and a copy of the test/study guide if you want them to take it at home.

INSTALLING THE TEST PLAYER

Follow the instructions provided here to install the Test Player program for your students. You may copy the Test Player to a network (recommended), install it on individual computers, or provide it on floppy disk for your students to take home.

Even if you have a network, you can install the Test Player on individual computers. Students will still be able to access tests/study guides you store on a local area network.

ExamView Player Installation

Windows

Step 1	Turn on your computer.
Step 2	Insert the *ExamView* disc into your CD-ROM drive. If the software was provided on floppy disks, insert the *ExamView–Test Player* installation disk into Drive A.
Step 3	Click the Start button on the *Taskbar* and choose the Run option.
Step 4	If the *ExamView* software is provided on a CD-ROM, use the drive letter that corresponds to the CD-ROM drive on your computer (e.g., **d:\evplayer\setup** or **d:\evpro\evplayer\setup**).
	If you are installing the software from a floppy disk, type **a:\setup** and press **Enter** to run the installation program.
Step 5	When prompted for a location to install the program, select a folder (e.g., x:\programs\evplayer **for network installations** or **c:\evplayer** on your local hard drive).
Step 6	For local area network (**LAN**) installations, complete the following steps at each workstation:
	Click the **Start** button and choose Taskbar from the Settings menu.
	Click the **Start Menu Programs** tab and click **Add**.
	Type the location and program name for the Test Player software, or use the **Browse** button to enter this information (e.g., x:\programs\evplayer\evplayer.exe).
	Proceed to the next screen and add a new folder (e.g., ExamView Test Player).
	Enter ExamView Test Player as the shortcut name and then click the **Finish** button.

Repeat Steps 1–5 if you plan to install the software at each computer instead of installing the program once on your network.

| Step 1 | Turn on your computer. |

Step 2 Insert the *ExamView* installation disc into your CD-ROM drive. If the program is provided on floppy disks, insert the *ExamView–Test Player* installation disk into a disk drive.

Step 3 Open the installer window, if necessary.

Step 4 Double-click the installation icon to start the program.

Note: The installation program is configured to copy the test player to a new folder on your hard drive. You can, however, change this location. For example, you can select a location on your network server.

Step 5 When prompted for a location to install the program, select a folder on your local area network that is accessible to all students. If you are installing the software on a stand-alone computer, choose a location on the hard drive.

Step 6 At each workstation, enable file sharing and program linking if you installed the application on your network server.

For stand-alone computers, repeats Steps 1–5.

Installing the Test Player at Home

You can give your students the Test Player software to take home. If the *ExamView* software was sent to you on floppy disks, give your students the separate Test Player setup disk. If you received the software on CD-ROM, copy all of the setup files in the *evplayer* folder onto a floppy disk. Students should follow Steps 1–5 to install the software on their computer. When students take a test home, they should copy it into the same folder as the Test Player program.

TAKING AN ONLINE (LAN-BASED) TEST

Make sure that you have properly installed the *ExamView* Test Player software and copied the test/study guide to a location easily accessible to your students. If you linked multimedia files to any of the questions, it is recommended that you copy those files to the same folder as the test/study guide.

If you created a test with a class roster, students must correctly enter their ID's to be able to take the test/study guide. Provide this information to your students, if necessary. **Note:** If you do not want to track student scores, you should set up a test to allow anyone to take it.

Step 1 Start the *ExamView* Test Player software.

Step 2 Enter your name and ID. (See Figure 6.)

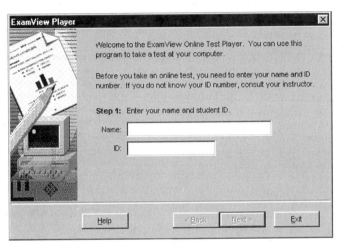

Figure 6 – Online Test/Study Guide Registration

Step 3 Select a test/study guide. (See Figure 7.)

If no tests (or study guides) appear in the list, click the **Folder** button to identify where the tests are located.

Step 4 *(Optional)* Enter a password, if prompted.

Step 5 Review the summary information and click **Start** when you are ready to begin.

| Step 6 | Answer all of the questions and click the **End** button when you finish. |
| | Verify that you want to end the test. If you do not answer all of the questions in one session, you will not be able to resume the test at a later time. |

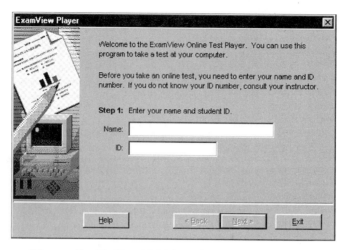

Figure 7 – Online Test/Study Guide Selection

| Step 7 | Review the test report. |
| Step 8 | Click **New Test** to take another test or click **Exit** to quit the program. |

VIEWING ONLINE (LAN-BASED) RESULTS

If you set up a test with a class roster (instead of allowing anyone to access a test/study guide), the *ExamView* Test Player will automatically collect the results for each student. The program saves this information in the test/study guide file itself.

Step 1	Start the *ExamView* software and open the online test/study guide that your students have already taken.
Step 2	Choose *View Test Results* from the Online menu.
Step 3	Review the results, item-by-item analysis, and statistics reports.
Step 4	Choose *Export Test Results* if you want to export the scores to your favorite gradebook program or spreadsheet application.

INTERNET TESTING

ExamView lets you easily create Internet tests and study guides. Build a test and then simply choose the *Publish Internet Test* option. You can choose to post tests to your own Web site, or publish tests directly to the ExamView Web site. (Visit us at **www.examview.com** to learn more about subscribing to the Internet test-hosting service.)

With the Internet test-hosting feature, you can publish a test or study guide directly to the ExamView website. Simply create a test and then follow the easy step-by-step instructions to publish it to the Internet. It's that simple! You can manage tests online, view reports, and download results. Students access your tests from one convenient location.

If you do not use the ExamView test-hosting service, you can manually post tests/study guides to your own Web site. If you create a test, your students' results are sent to you via email automatically. Or, you can create a study guide that your students can use to review various topics at their own pace.

INTERNET TESTING FAQs

Review the FAQs (frequently asked questions) below for more information on the Internet testing hosting features available to *ExamView Pro 3.5* users.

What are the advantages to using the Internet test-hosting feature? (1) Publishing an Internet test to your own Web site and setting up links can be quite challenging. With the Internet test-hosting feature, the process is completely automated. In minutes, you can post a test to the Internet. (2) When you post tests/study guides to your own Web site, only a few options are available. Using the *ExamView* test-hosting service, you have many more options available such as setting up a class roster and viewing detailed item analysis reports.

How do you register for the test-hosting service? Visit our Web site at **www.examview.com** to learn how to register. Before you can post tests/study guides, you must sign up to obtain a valid instructor ID and a password.

Is there an additional charge for the Internet test-hosting service? Yes, there is an additional yearly subscription charge to use this service. If you received the *ExamView* software from a publisher, you may be eligible for a discount or a free trial membership. (See our Web site for current prices and special promotions.)

Do you have to use the Internet test-hosting service? No, using the test-hosting service is not required. *The Publish Internet Test* feature includes an option to save an Internet test/study guide to a local hard drive. Then, you can manually post it to your own Web site.

Why aren't the same features available for tests posted to my own Web site? To offer the numerous Internet test-hosting features, we have developed many programs and databases that are stored on our servers. If you post to your own server or Web site, these programs are not available.

IMPORTANT: Your students must use a browser such as Netscape 4.0/Internet Explorer 4.0 (or a more recent version) that supports cascading style sheets (CSS1) and JavaScript. To post tests or study guides for delivery via the Internet, you must have your own access to an Internet server.

USING THE INTERNET TEST-HOSTING SERVICE

Using the *ExamView* test generator software you can publish tests directly to the ExamView Web site if you have signed up for the test-hosting service. With a few simple steps, you can publish tests and study guides directly to the Internet. Refer to the following instructions to: register for the Internet test-hosting service, create a test, publish a test to the Internet, take tests online, manage tests, and view student results.

Register for the Internet Test-Hosting Service

Step 1   Launch your Web browser and go to ***www.examview.com***.

Step 2   Go to the **Instructor Center** to register for the test-hosting service. Follow the instructions provided at the Web site to sign up.

                Record the instructor ID and password assigned to you. You will need this information to publish a test or study guide to the *ExamView* Web site. When you choose to publish a test, you will be prompted to enter this information.

Step 3   Quit the browser.

Publish a Test/Study Guide to the ExamView Web Site

Step 1   Start the *ExamView* software.

Step 2   Create a new test or open an existing test.

                Select the questions you want to include on the test. You can include any of the twelve (12) question types on a test, but only the objective questions are scored.

Step 3   Select the *Publish Internet Test* option from the **File** menu.

                ExamView presents a window with various Internet testing options to help you prepare the online test. (See Figure 8.) **Note:** Click the **Help** button if you need more assistance.

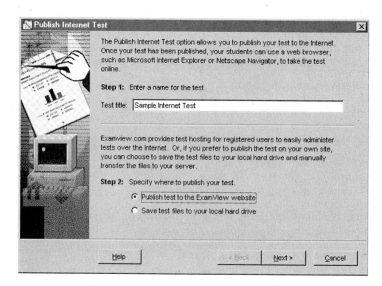

Figure 8 – Publish Internet Test Window

Step 4	Name the test.
Step 5	Select the option to publish your test to the *ExamView* Web site, and then click the **Next** button.
Step 6	Enter your instructor ID and password. If you do not already have an instructor ID and password, click the *Register Now* button to launch your Web browser and go to the **www.examview.com** Web site. You cannot proceed until you have a valid instructor ID and password.
Step 7	Choose whether you want to publish a test or a study guide.
Step 8	Specify when students may access the test/study guide.
Step 9	Enter the expiration date.
Step 10	Specify who should have access to this test/study guide. Anyone may take it, or you may limit access to a particular group of students. If you specify a roster, students must enter an ID and password.
Step 11	Enter a student password, and click **Next.**
Step 12	Review the summary information. Click the **Back** button if you need to make changes. (See Figure 9.)

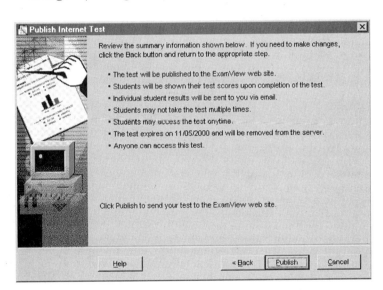

Figure 9 – Publish Internet Test Window (Summary)

Step 13	Click the **Publish** button when you are ready to post the test/study guide to the *ExamView* Web site.

The program automatically connects to the Internet and posts the test/study guide to the ExamView server. Access the instructor options on the *ExamView* Web site (**www.examview.com**) to preview a test, change selected parameters, or view results. If you need to edit or delete questions, you must change the test locally and then publish a new version. **Note:** An Internet connection is required to publish a test/study guide.

Step 14	Print a copy of the test/study guide for your records, create another test, or exit the software if you are finished.

Take a Test/Study Guide Online at www.evtestcenter.com

Once you publish a test/study guide to the ExamView server, anyone in the world can access it if you provide him or her with your instructor ID and the appropriate password. (IMPORTANT: *Do not give students your password, just your ID.*) Provide the instructions below to your students so that they can take the test or study guide.

Note: You must use a browser such as Netscape 4.0/Internet Explorer 4.0 (or a more recent version) that supports cascading style sheets level 1 (CSS1) and JavaScript. An active Internet connection is also required.

To take a test:

Step 1   Start your Web browser.

Step 2   Go to the URL: **www.evtestcenter.com**.

Step 3   Enter your instructor's ID code. (See Figure 10.)

                       Upon entering a valid instructor code, you will see a list of tests your instructor has published.

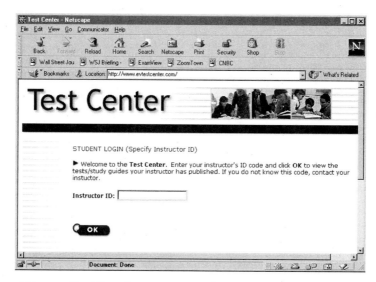

Figure 10 – Test Center Login (www.evtestcenter.com)

Step 4   Select a test.

Step 5   Enter your name (if requested), student ID, and password.

                       Contact your instructor if you have not been assigned a student ID or you do not have a password.

Step 6

Review the test and respond to all of the questions. (See the sample test in Figure 11.)

If you need help while working with a test, click the **Help** button shown at the bottom of the test. Click the browser's **Back** button to return to the test.

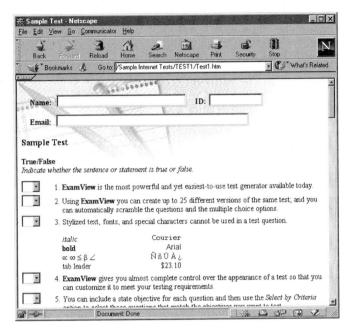

Figure 11 – Sample Internet Test

Step 7

When you complete the test, review the entire test and then click the **Grade & Submit** button located at the bottom of the test.

Your results will be emailed to your instructor. Depending on the test settings, you may be notified of your results immediately.

To complete a study guide:

Step 1

Start your Web browser.

Step 2

Go to the URL: *www.evtestcenter.com*.

Step 3

Enter your instructor's ID.

You will see a list of study guides and tests your instructor has published.

Step 4

Select a study guide.

Step 5

Enter your name (if requested), student ID, and password.

Contact your instructor if you have not been assigned a student ID or you do not have a password.

Step 6

Review the study guide and answer all of the questions.

If you need help while working with a study guide, click the **Help** button shown at the bottom of the screen. Click the browser's **Back** button to return to the study guide.

Step 7	When you complete the study guide, review your responses and then click the **Check Your Work** button located at the bottom of the study guide.
	Your work is scored and you will see whether you answered each question correctly or incorrectly. No results are sent to your instructor.
Step 8	Click the **Reset** button to erase all of your responses if you want to start over.

Review Student Results and Manage Tests

When your students complete an Internet test, their results are automatically stored on the server so that you can easily access this information. If you chose to receive results via email, you will also receive the following information for each student: (1) student name and ID, (2) raw score and percentage score for objective-based questions, and (3) responses for each question (objective and open-ended questions).

At the *ExamView* Web site, you may also change test-setup options, preview tests, download student results, and view your account information.

Step 1	Start your Web browser.
Step 2	Go to the URL: ***www.examview.com*** and access the Instructor Center.
Step 3	Log in using your instructor ID and password to view the main menu options. (See Figure 12.)

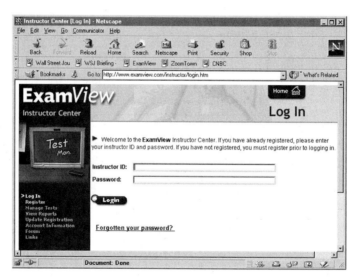

Figure 12 – ExamView Web Site (Instructor Center)

PUBLISHING TESTS TO YOUR OWN WEB SITE

If you choose not to sign up for the *ExamView* test-hosting service, you can still publish tests/study guides to your own Web site. You must save the test/study guide to your hard drive, upload the files to your Web site, and then provide access to your students. Refer to the following sections for step-by-step instructions.

Save an Internet Test/Study Guide to Your Hard Drive

Follow the steps shown below to create an Internet test/study guide and save it your hard drive. Before you begin, make sure that you installed the *ExamView* test generator software.

Step 1		Start the *ExamView* software.
Step 2		Create a new test or open an existing test.
		Select the questions you want to include on the test. You can include any of the twelve (12) question types on a test, but only the objective questions will be graded.
Step 3		Select the *Publish Internet Test* option from the **File** menu.
		ExamView presents a window with various Internet testing options to help you prepare the online test. (See Figure 13.) **Note:** Click the **Help** button if you need more assistance.
Step 4		Name the test.
Step 5		Select the option to save the test files to your local hard drive, and then click the **Next** button.
Step 6		Choose whether you want to publish a test or a study guide.
Step 7		Review the summary information. Make changes, if necessary.

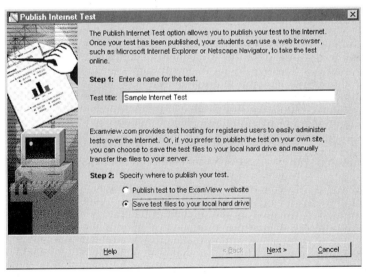

Figure 13 – Publish Internet Test Window

Step 8	Click the **Save** button to save the test/study guide files.
	When you choose to save an Internet test to your local hard drive, *ExamView* creates an HTML file and an accompanying folder with all of the necessary image files. This makes it easier for you to post the files to a Web server. If, for example, you enter a path such as **c:\examview\tests\chapter1** (Windows) or **HD:ExamView:Tests:Chapter1** (Macintosh), the software will create a file called chapter1.htm and a new folder called **chapter1_files** with all of the required picture files. (See the illustration below.)

Step 9	Post the test/study guide to a server to make it available to your students. (See the next section for instructions for posting a test to a server.)
Step 10	Once you post a test, you should verify that students can access it. You may also want to try the "Grade & Submit" feature for tests to make sure that the results are emailed to the correct address.

Note: When you create a test, *ExamView* encrypts the answer information so that a student cannot see the answers in the HTML page source. While this does help to prevent cheating, there is no foolproof method in an unsupervised environment.

Post a Test to your own Internet/Intranet Server

Once you save a test/study guide formatted for the Internet, you must post all of the related files to a location on a server that your students can access. You can post the files to a local area network, Intranet server, or an Internet server. You **must** have an Internet connection for students to be able to submit test results. (This is not required for a study guide.)

Note: Posting to a server can be a complex process. The specific steps will vary depending on the hardware and software configuration of your server. If you are not familiar with the required steps, contact your network administrator for assistance.

Step 1	Start an FTP program or other utility that allows you to copy files from your hard drive to an Internet/Intranet server.
Step 2	Log in to your server.
Step 3	Create a new folder on your server to hold the test/study guide files.

Step 4	Copy the **HTML** file and the accompanying folder to a location on your server that your students can access.
	When you choose to save an Internet test to your hard drive, *ExamView* creates an HTML file and an accompanying folder with all of the necessary image files. This makes it easier for you to post the files to a Web server.

IMPORTANT: By default, all of the file names are lowercase. Do not change the case since these files are referenced in the HTML document. You *must* copy the HTML file and the accompanying folder as is. Do not copy the HTML file into the corresponding folder. (See the illustration below.)

Step 5	Log off the server, if necessary.
Step 6	Record the URL for the test/study guide HTML document or set up a link to the test.

Take a Test or Study Guide Using the Internet

Once you post a test on a server, anyone in the world can access the test if you provide him or her with the Web (URL) address. Follow the instructions provided below to take a test or study guide.

Note: You must use a browser such as Netscape 4.0/Internet Explorer 4.0 (or a more recent version) that supports cascading style sheets level 1 (CSS1) and JavaScript. An active Internet connection is required to submit test results.

To take a test via the Internet:

Step 1	Start your Web browser.
Step 2	Type the Web address (URL) and test name (e.g., ***www.school.edu\economics\ test1.htm***), or enter an address for a page with a link to the test. (See the sample test in Figure 14 on page 220.)
	If the test is located on a local area network, use the open page command in the browser to open the test.
Step 3	Enter your name, student ID, and email address (optional).
Step 4	Answer all of the questions.
	If you need help while working with a test, click the Help button shown at the bottom of the test. Click the browser's Back button to return to the test.

Step 5   When you complete the test, review your responses and then click the Grade & Submit button located at the bottom of the screen.

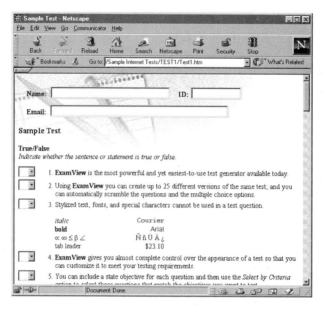

Figure 14 – Sample Internet Test

To complete a study guide via the Internet:

Step 1   Start your Web browser.

Step 2   Type the Web address (URL) and study guide name (e.g., *www.school.edu\history\study.htm*), or enter an address for a page with a link to the study guide.

Step 3   Enter your name.

Step 4   Answer all of the questions.

Step 5   When you complete the study guide, review the entire test and then click the Check Your Work button located at the bottom of the study guide.

Your work is scored and you will see whether you answered each question correctly or incorrectly. No results are sent to your instructor.

Step 6   Click the **Reset** button to erase all of your responses if you want to start over.

Receive Student Results via E-mail

When your students complete an Internet test, the browser sends the students' test results and all of their responses directly to you via e mail. The e mail will include the following information:

- student name and ID
- raw score and percentage score for objective-based questions
- responses for each question (objective and open-ended questions)

Note: You will not receive any student results for Internet study guides.

Notes

Notes

Notes

Notes